THE FLIGHT OF THE VIKINGS

To
the late Ragnar Ulstein
war hero, writer and indefatigable chronicler of North Sea escapes,

Siri Holm Lawson
dedicated creator the Norwegian Warsailors website,
including the escape boats

and
Antonia
for her constant loving support.

THE FLIGHT OF THE VIKINGS

DARING ESCAPES IN SMALL BOATS FROM NAZI-OCCUPIED NORWAY, 1940-45

ANDREW ORR

Pen & Sword
MILITARY
AN IMPRINT OF PEN & SWORD BOOKS LTD.
YORKSHIRE – PHILADELPHIA

First published in Great Britain in 2024 by
Pen & Sword Military
An imprint of
Pen & Sword Books Ltd
Yorkshire - Philadelphia

ISBN 978 1 03610 368 2

Typeset in INDIA by IMPEC eSolutions
Printed and bound in the UK by CPI Group (UK) Ltd, Croydon, CRO 4YY

Pen & Sword Books Limited incorporates the imprints of Archaeology, Atlas, Aviation,
Battleground, Digital, Discovery, Family History, Fiction, History, Local, Local History,
Maritime, Military, Military Classics, Politics, Select, Transport, True Crime, After the
Battle, Air World, Claymore Press, Frontline Publishing, Leo Cooper, Remember When,
Seaforth Publishing, The Praetorian Press, Wharncliffe Books, Wharncliffe Local History,
Wharncliffe Transport, Wharncliffe True Crime and White Owl.

For a complete list of Pen & Sword titles please contact

PEN & SWORD BOOKS LIMITED
George House, Units 12 & 13, Beevor Street, Off Pontefract Road,
Barnsley, S71 1HN, UK
E-mail: enquiries@pen-and-sword.co.uk
Website: www.pen-and-sword.co.uk

or

PEN AND SWORD BOOKS
1950 Lawrence Rd, Havertown, PA 19083, USA
E-mail: Uspen-and-sword@casematepublishers.com
Website: www.penandswordbooks.com

Contents

Maps

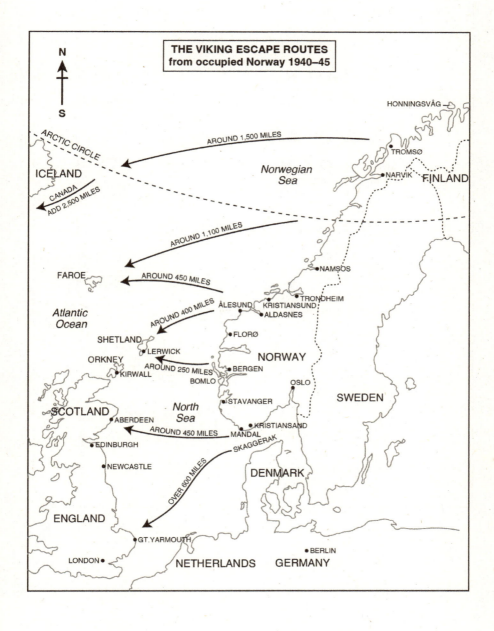

THE VIKING ESCAPE ROUTES
from occupied Norway 1940–45

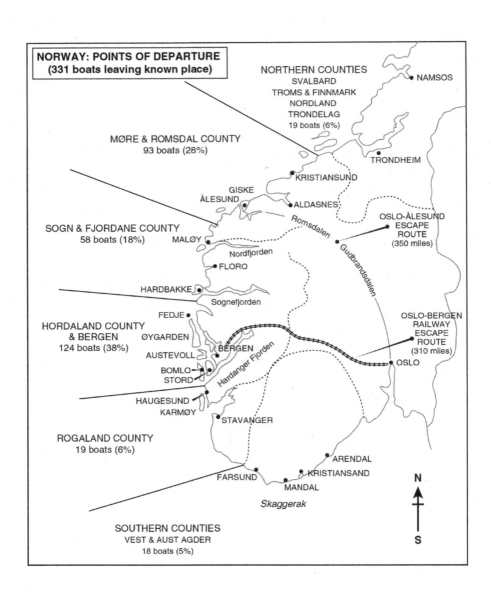

NORWAY: POINTS OF DEPARTURE
(331 boats leaving known place)

NORTHERN COUNTIES
SVALBARD
TROMS & FINNMARK
NORDLAND
TRONDELAG
19 boats (6%)

NAMSOS

MØRE & ROMSDAL COUNTY
93 boats (28%)

TRONDHEIM

KRISTIANSUND

GISKE
ÅLESUND

ALDASNES

Romsdalen

OSLO-ÅLESUND
ESCAPE
ROUTE
(350 miles)

SOGN & FJORDANE COUNTY
58 boats (18%)

MALØY

Nordfjorden

Gudbrandsdalen

FLORO

HARDBAKKE

Sognefjorden

FEDJE

HORDALAND COUNTY
& BERGEN
124 boats (38%)

ØYGARDEN

AUSTEVOLL

BOMLO
STORD

BERGEN

Hardanger Fjorden

OSLO-BERGEN
RAILWAY
ESCAPE
ROUTE
(310 miles)

OSLO

HAUGESUND
KARMØY

STAVANGER

ROGALAND COUNTY
19 boats (6%)

ARENDAL

KRISTIANSAND

FARSUND

MANDAL

Skaggerak

N

S

SOUTHERN COUNTIES
VEST & AUST AGDER
18 boats (5%)

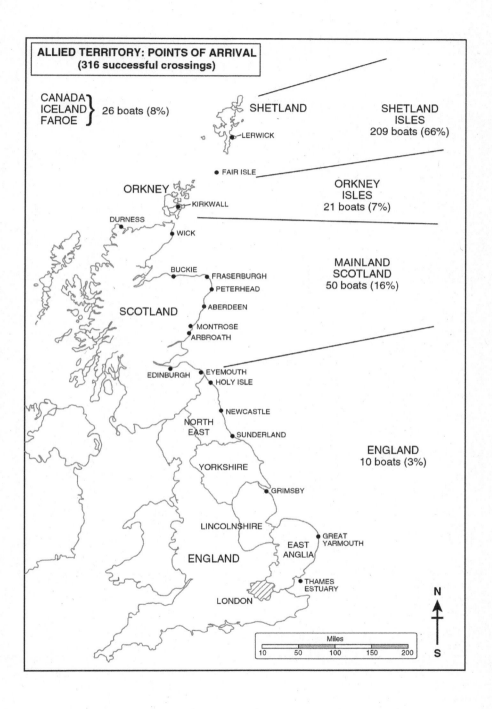

ALLIED TERRITORY: POINTS OF ARRIVAL
(316 successful crossings)

CANADA
ICELAND } 26 boats (8%)
FAROE

SHETLAND

SHETLAND
ISLES
209 boats (66%)

LERWICK

FAIR ISLE

ORKNEY

ORKNEY
ISLES
21 boats (7%)

KIRKWALL

DURNESS

WICK

MAINLAND
SCOTLAND
50 boats (16%)

BUCKIE FRASERBURGH

PETERHEAD

SCOTLAND

ABERDEEN

MONTROSE
ARBROATH

EDINBURGH EYEMOUTH
HOLY ISLE

NEWCASTLE

NORTH
EAST

SUNDERLAND

YORKSHIRE

ENGLAND
10 boats (3%)

GRIMSBY

LINCOLNSHIRE

GREAT
YARMOUTH

EAST
ANGLIA

ENGLAND

THAMES
ESTUARY

LONDON

N

Miles

| 10 | 50 | 100 | 150 | 200 |

S

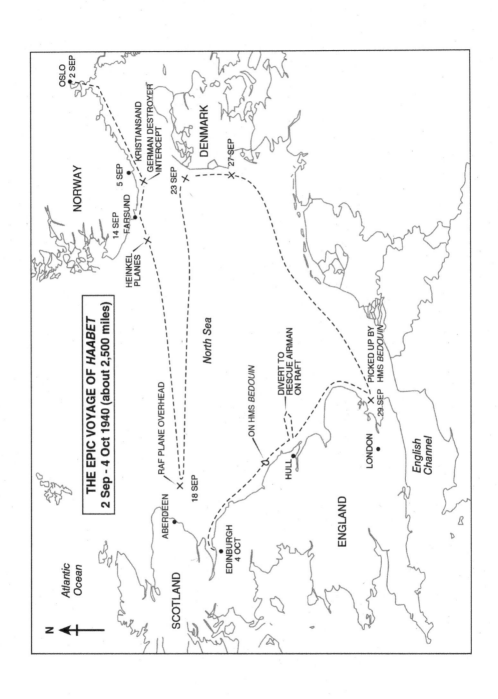

THE EPIC VOYAGE OF *HAABET*
2 Sep - 4 Oct 1940 (about 2,500 miles)

N

Atlantic
Ocean

SCOTLAND

ABERDEEN

EDINBURGH
4 OCT

ENGLAND

HULL

ON HMS *BEDOUIN*

LONDON

English
Channel

RAF PLANE OVERHEAD

18 SEP

North Sea

DIVERT TO
RESCUE AIRMAN
ON RAFT

PICKED UP BY
HMS *BEDOUIN*
29 SEP

NORWAY

OSLO
2 SEP

5 SEP

KRISTIANSAND

GERMAN DESTROYER
INTERCEPT

14 SEP
FARSUND

HEINKEL
PLANES

23 SEP

DENMARK

27 SEP

Epigraph
Look to Norway

If there is anyone who still wonders why this war is being fought, let him look to Norway. If there is anyone who has any delusions that this war could have been averted, let him look to Norway; and if there is anyone who doubts the democratic will to win, again I say, let him look to Norway.

He will find in Norway, at once conquered and unconquerable the answer to his question.

We all know how this most peaceful and innocent of countries was ruthlessly violated. The combination of treachery and brute force which conquered Norway will live in history as the blackest deed of a black era.

Franklin D. Roosevelt
16 September 1942

This address, which became known as the Look to Norway Speech, was delivered on the occasion of the handing over of the US-built warship *HNoMS King Haakon VII* (an escort vessel) at Washington Navy Yard, in the presence of Crown Princess Märtha and the Norwegian Ambassador.

Acknowledgements

O ver the twenty-year gestation of this book there have been many people who have helped me in diverse ways. I am grateful to everyone I have come into contact with: each one has helped to sustain my efforts. Additionally it has brought me great pleasure in meeting so many differing and interesting people. Some who have died or who have moved to other spheres are included in this list because their testimony and contribution live on. To those who I have missed out I offer my apologies and the excuse of advancing years.

Thanks for encouragement, advice and realisation
My family - Antonia Orr, Alasdair Orr, Hugh Orr, Jessica Grieve, George Grieve, Sarah Orr, Lisa Stevenson, Gill Kelly and Judy Bailey; Angus Whitson: Paul Bangay; Guy Puzey; Iain Dalzell-Job; Major-General Murray Naylor, Professor Sir Hew Strachan, Trevor Royle, John Griffith (computer charts); Captain John Campbell; Mona Rohne (Norwegian Consulate Edinburgh); Hans Petter Øset (Marinemuseet Horten); Michael McFarlane (Phoenix Photo Services); Charles Hewitt, Managing Director, Heather Williams, Commissioning Editor and all staff at Pen & Sword Books for giving me the chance to tell the story; last, and most particularly, Carol Trow, my editor, for patiently making sense of my offerings, dealing with my erroneous punctuation and (with her husband M.J. Trow) grappling with the gruelling index and the challenging Norwegian spellings.

Thanks to Norway:
Siri Holm Lawson; Konrad Lawson; Robin Vidnes; Jon Vidnes; Ole John Berthelsen; Steinar Hafto Myre, Vigdis Hafto and Kirsten Hafto;

Herman Eilertsen; Reidar and Eleanor Pedersen; Peter Sperre; Knut Olsen; Jakob Strandheim; Nicolai Løken and Henning Pedersen (Caledonian Society of Norway); Margrethe Kallestad and staff (Nordsjorfartsmuseet); Bjørn Tore Rosendahl and colleagues (Arkivet Foundation); Tony Teigland; Inge Eikeland (Vestagdermuseet) and those at Lista Kystkultursenter; Commander Hans Petter Øset and Thor S. Kristiansen (Marinemuseet Horten); Erling Eikli (formerly of Forsvaretsforum); Major-General Johan Brun (Veterans' Affairs); Steinar Engeset and Dana Briand (Convoy Cup Foundation); staff at Hjemmefrontmuseum Oslo.

Thanks to Scotland:
Bill Black (and his family); Gordon Ritchie and Graham Mitchell (Stonehaven Historical Society); Stuart Usher; Douglas Allen; staff at Signal Tower Museum Arbroath; Wing Commander George Swapp OBE; George Craig; Sam Jolly; George Leiper; John Ross; Leon Dundas; Donald Marr (Johnshaven Heritage Society); Richard McBay; Ivar McBay; Murray McBay; Ian Kenn (Portal to Portlethen); George Craig; John Røre (his father Kristian Røre); Commander Struan Robertson; Commander Hilary Foxworthy; Garry Irvine (Norwegian-Scottish Society); Dr Robert Martin; Robert Galey; Professor Peter Reid (Little Norway Buckie); volunteers at Buckie and District Fishing Heritage Centre and Burghead Visitors' Centre; Dr Stuart Allen (National Museums Scotland); Blair Bruce and Angus Johnson (Shetland Archives); Adam Civicio (The Shetland Times); Bill Moore (Scalloway Museum); Minnie Mouat (her family's story); Staff at Unst Boat Haven.

Preface
The Flight of the Vikings

In my retirement I treated myself to a 21ft modern fibreglass motor fishing boat, bristling with technology, VHF radio, distress beacon, global positioning system, depth finder and the like. The boat bobbed about at a mooring in a tiny harbour in north east Scotland. Johnshaven lies about 30 miles to the south of Aberdeen on a coast more suited to occupational boating than leisure craft. I soon became wary of the open expanse of grey North Sea, rarely calm and often menacing. A powerful tidal race up and down the coast, occasional deep seismic swells, unpredictable squally changes in the weather and walls of impenetrable sea fog (known in Scotland as haar) engendered a healthy caution for sea-going in those waters. I acquired a huge respect for the local fishermen who ran in and out of the narrow harbour entrance to make a living – and who were so kind to me with guidance when I first moored up.

The late Leon Dundas was the village elder fisherman, a lifelong resident living right on the waterfront. In his retirement he used to patrol the harbour every day with a keen eye for any occurrences. One day, whilst messing about with my new toy, lying in the inner harbour, I looked up and saw him quietly studying my efforts.

'Ye're the man who knows about they Norwegians that were in Montrose during the war?' he called out. Following an affirmative he continued 'Come ashore and let me show you some'at that might interest you'.

I climbed across several boats and up the ladder onto the quay and followed him to the other side of the harbour. There, tucked away at the side of the disused lifeboat station shed, lay a boat partially covered by a tattered old tarpaulin. After tugging away the cover, the rotting remains of an ancient fishing boat emerged. The boat was about 21 ft in length, the same as my own boat, but there the similarity ended. This was a heavy clinker built wooden open workboat, canoe-ended at both ends in Norwegian style, as opposed to a Scottish traditional cut-off transom construction. Possibly 100 years old, it had been held together by iron rivets, many of which had rusted to oblivion allowing the planks to spring apart, letting the sunlight filter through to the ground.

'In the war days we young lads were always on the lookout for action up and down the coast' began Leon, continuing, 'So we were really excited to hear of the arrival of this wee boat up the coast. They said that it had crossed all the way from south Norway with a few young boys escaping from the Nazis. That must be all of 400 miles, and all they had was a compass to help them.' Expanding his story, he went on, 'They had this really dangerous crossing, and they washed up on the rocks in a thick haar at Old Portlethen. It caused quite a stir when they were taken to Stonehaven and were locked up in the jail! But the bobbies let them out and gave them money for the pub!' Conspiratorially, and with a chuckle, he added 'Of course we weren't supposed to know about any of it. It was all supposed to be "hush-hush".' He put a forefinger to his lips in emphasis and continued, 'but word soon spread amongst the fisher folk.' With a sigh he added, 'she was such a lovely boat once'.

The little boat, renamed *Thistle*, had spent the rest of the war and the next 50 years working out of Stonehaven (south of Aberdeen), where she was much admired. Brought to Johnshaven, she never went to sea again and slowly disintegrated on the quayside. The villagers had made a number of serious attempts to save her – but to no avail.

'Now', said Leon, fixing me with a direct look, 'you seem to know all about those Norskies in that book of yours. You have the contacts. Surely you can get someone to take her back home.' With emphasis he added, 'You *must* do something'.

Therein lay the start of this book. Later I did indeed get *Thistle* home.

It's true that I already knew something about escapes from Norway across the North Sea on small boats. My earlier book, *Sea Dog Bamse World War II Canine Hero*, written with my friend Angus Whitson, featured some stories of Norwegians who had escaped from Norway determined to rejoin the fight against the occupiers of their country. The first seeds of an interest were already there – and here was something right on the doorstep, a story reaching out to be told. A very engaging story it turned out to be, as I peeled away the intervening years and investigated. Here was a boat that encapsulated the full excitement of four men defying the Gestapo, risking their lives in a hazardous 400-mile North Sea crossing, training to be tough commandos and then returning to Norway to wage war against the Nazis occupying their country.

My contacts in Norway helped me to find a museum keen to take the boat – to preserve and exhibit it in recognition of its vital wartime role. The museum at Lista in south Norway was very close to where the boat had set out from. Then, exactly on the seventieth anniversary of the arrival of the escapers, 29 July 2011, something magical happened. John and Martin Berthelsen, the two sons of one of the escapers, turned up on the quayside at Johnshaven. They had an emotional meeting with the little boat that had safely delivered their father to Scotland in 1941. Clearly the escape had great and enduring significance for the Berthelsen family. Meeting them gave me fresh impetus to complete the project to repatriate *Thistle* (originally just plain VA 92 L). In the process I was helped by media interest – newspapers, and then radio and television features.

By the time of the departure of *Thistle* on 7 Feb 2012, it had become a national news item on both sides of the North Sea. The village of Johnshaven turned out in force to wave goodbye, dignitaries gave speeches, the school children sang and a pipe band marched. John Berthelsen took over his father's story and produced an excellent booklet, and my version is told in Chapter 7 of this book. Was that to be the end of it?

As I waved little *Thistle* away from Johnshaven, I was aware that her story was but one of hundreds that happened in the years of Nazi occupation of Norway. Where was I to go next? If I didn't know how to move forward, the answer came just a few weeks later through the local newspaper, which put me in touch with Bill Black, a delightful 86-year-old pensioner. He had a story to tell about events in 1941 when he was a teenager in Stonehaven, and he requested my help in finding out more. Over his long life he had tried repeatedly to find out for himself, and I was soon drawn in to a remarkable adventure involving a float plane stolen from the Germans. My researches revealed a significant story that was unknown on both sides of the North Sea. Bill with his pin-sharp recollections showed me how such incidents can have a life-long impact. His account is also told in Chapter 7. In the aftermath Bill's story, I felt that to tackle the full panoply of escape stories was a task beyond my capabilities. Later, a chance introduction from Norway led to a meeting in Aberdeen that turned my reluctance into a determination to get to grips with the challenge.

In May 2015, I sat down in the Station Hotel in Aberdeen with Robin and Jon Vidnes who had just got off the ferry from Lerwick. They were making a pilgrimage in the footsteps of their father, Knut Vidnes, who had made his escape in September 1940. They had planned and undertaken their journey based on a meticulous journal written by their father, a journalist, during an escape that lasted for six weeks. A year later, the journal had been translated into English by Jon, and what a story it was – a truly extraordinary, dangerous and exciting adventure. My version of Knut's story appears in Chapter 4 of this book. Inspired and re-invigorated, I returned to the task of sorting everything out with the intention of telling the full saga of all these escapes.

I decided at the outset to concentrate only on escapes westward by boat (and the one float plane). Many Norwegians did escape eastwards on foot or skis across the border to neutral Sweden, but the circumstances and outcomes were very different – that is a gauntlet for someone else to pick up. Some also crossed to Sweden in small boats across the Oslofjorden, a less hazardous option, and these have recently been revealed in a new book, (*Smugglers for Norway's Freedom*, Jon Harald Holm, private publication, 2021). When I started, I understood that around 300 boats had set out westwards from Norway, carrying about 3,300 people. These were figures generally accepted following the painstaking work of Ragnar Ulstein, an escaper himself, a war hero and journalist who pursued the subject over many years. He compiled and published the lists upon which everything else was based. He wrote newspaper articles, he broadcast, he lectured and he wrote several books on the subject (*Englandsfarten*, two volumes, Nova Forlag 2011). He continued to write and give interviews into an advanced old age at Ålesund.

Thousands of miles away in Bartlesville Oklahoma in very different circumstances, another Norwegian consolidated Ulstein's work into a web-based digital form. Siri Holm started a home website at her kitchen table in 2001, describing herself as 'just a little old housewife who needed a hobby'. Over the next decade, she created a huge Second World War maritime archive, a section of which was dedicated to those boats which escaped.

These escapes would have been long forgotten if it wasn't for the work of these remarkable people. The importance of the work done by Ulstein and Holm is reflected in the high honours bestowed on them by the Norwegian government.

There was a problem, if that's an appropriate word, with these archives. They were exactly that – archives, lengthy lists, albeit with detail and isolated snippets of stories relating to individual escapes. There was no context, no continuity. I wanted to get a wide picture of these escapes as an entity, and to set them in the framework of what was happening in occupied Norway as the war progressed. I wanted to turn an archive into a narrative account – a saga worthy of Vikings.

By the time I finished this book I had found an additional 60 boats and 700 escapers, making over 360 boats and over 4,000 persons. Even so, it is certain that the figures should be higher as the circumstances of war obscured what really happened. I gathered all of these boats and figures onto a 'Master List of Boats Escaping', with the blessing of a modern spread sheet. This allowed me to sort by date order and make other analyses which provided clarity and context to the mass of data. These figures and others relating to Norway may seem at first glance to be small, but it's important to note that Norway had a really small population, around 2.9 million in 1940. By comparison, France had 41 million, and Great Britain 47 million, so in terms of scale Norway's statistics are proportionately much greater than first meets the eye.

The additional boats, numbers of people and extended stories were found by conventional hard graft at research. They cropped up in newspaper articles, books, field and museum visits, and internet searches. Three aspects about the internet deserve mention. First, the growth during this century of social media exchanges, personal websites and associated blogs. Discoveries here have added narrative detail to many of the escapes. They are very useful in cross-referencing and validating other information. Second, web-based translation has allowed access to material in Norwegian which has been a great help. Third, the digitalisation of newspapers revealing new escapes and their stories with a surprising amount of narrative, considering wartime censorship.

I have set parameters for inclusion of boats in the Master List that have to be explained. They have to be civilian boats, skippered and crewed by civilians, leaving Norway after the invasion of 9 April 1940. In the early days of fighting, boats carried civilian and military refugees mixed together. These have been included, but only if the escape boat was organised and conducted by Norwegian civilians. This therefore excludes all military boats (or civilian boats under naval command). It also excludes evacuations by the famous and much written about the 'Shetland Bus' organisation.

Boats to be included in the list also have to be small coastal craft. Up to half of them were really small boats, around 25ft and under. Mostly these were inshore fishing boats which could carry up to around seven or eight people, but some were as small as a rowboat of 15ft in length. There were even five kayaks. There were four solo attempts at crossing. Larger boats were the typical wooden two-masted Norwegian boats with a rear deckhouse (Hardanger or Møre cutters) of 35–70ft. A few larger non-fishing boats have been included because they were specifically engaged in carrying refugees across the North Sea. The average number of refugees per boat was eleven. Boats often came with their skipper-owners, some were purchased for their secret purpose and not a few were 'borrowed without consent' for the duration of the war.

In response to a frequently asked question, I have always said that this book is not 'yet another book about the Shetland Bus' (my quotes). The 'Bus' did not commence operations until 30 August 1941, by which time 227 escape boats had preceded it. However, for those interested in the Shetland Bus (and there are many) I did discover the seeds of the idea as early as May 1940, in raids organised and executed by Norwegians who had just escaped, who turned their boats around and went straight back to make mischief with the Nazis. These are discussed in Chapter 2.

These escape attempts quite often did not succeed (in around twelve percent) because of losses and attacks at sea, betrayals and arrests and being driven back by storms and engine failures. All these statistics can be found in Appendix A. Ninety percent of the crossings that did succeed arrived in Shetland, Orkney and mainland Scotland. Others arrived in England, the Faroe Islands, Iceland and even as far away as Canada. In Norway, 90 percent of all the boats leaving set out from the west where crossing distances were shortest. There were several sectors that were especially busy; these can be seen in the maps. Although the bulk of people escaping were men, there were also wives with families, and young women crossing of their own volition. In the data they cannot be identified separately, nonetheless, it is possible to estimate that 8.5 per cent were women and 1.5 per cent children.

Norwegian nomenclature used around these escapes is very confusing and needs to be explained. Ragnar Ulstein himself used the word *Englandsfarere* (English voyagers) in the title of his books. Also used in the nomenclature are the words *Englandsfarten* (English shipping) and *Englandsfeber* (English fever, or fever for England). In all of these expressions the word *Englands* is of course a misnomer, used in place of Britain. Apparently, this was a common misattribution amongst Norwegians in the war, as London, where their beloved King Haakon and their government were located, was the focus of their attention and the destination of their escape journeys. Later, when this was realised, the term *Nordsjøfarten* ('North Sea Traffic') became more commonly used.

In the course of researching and writing I accumulated a collection of truly extraordinary and exciting stories to go with many of the escapes. There were more than I expected and certainly more than I could hope to include in the book. Of the 361 escape attempts, I have only been able to include mention of around 160, of which about half have significantly exciting stories. That is not to say that the ones I have left out are less deserving. They were all risky undertakings, but perhaps lacking enough detail or dramatic impact.

In defiance of Nazi death warnings, with constant threat of betrayal and with the prospect of one of the cruellest seas in the world, these Norwegians did what their Viking ancestors did before them – they took to their boats. They were self-selected by their courageous decision to risk everything, and consequently they contributed much to the Allied war effort. Of the bravest, many went on to join the embryonic Special Operations Executive (SOE) – ordered by Winston Churchill to 'set Europe ablaze'.

This, then, is the story of these truly brave Norwegians who attempted, succeeded or died in escaping across the North Sea in 'The Flight of the Vikings'.

Chapter 1

Gulf Stream, Maelstrom, Flotsam and Jetsam

A book intending to be about the history of Norwegian Vikings might begin reasonably somewhere between the eighth and eleventh centuries when these extraordinary Scandinavian seafarers of that age took to their long boats and explored the seas and rivers of the known and unknown world. In retrospect, it was their flexible long boats and their seamanship that most impress us today, and their pursuits of raiding, pillage and plunder are less savoured. Their full achievements are only now being recognised as a result of modern study and academic archaeology. It seems that in addition to their more warlike conduct, they were also enthusiastic traders wherever they went. Their routes are marked by discoveries of coins and artefacts all over Europe to as far away as China. To the west they reached as far as Newfoundland where they settled for a while, also settling on the way in Greenland, Iceland and the Faroe islands. Closer to home, they frequently visited, raided and eventually settled in Ireland, Scotland and England. The islands of Shetland and Orkney were colonised by Vikings from the ninth century until they were ceded to King James III of Scots in 1472, in settlement of a dowry for his wife Margaret of Denmark. Further south they reached as far as Normandy where they took control of those lands, creating the Duchy. William the Conqueror was in effect a Viking who stole England through the back door. They enjoyed summer cruising, trading and raiding across the Mediterranean as far as the Black Sea. To the east, wherever there was a sizeable river in central Europe they would go with incredible perseverance, even as far as the Caspian Sea. Modern DNA genealogy shows us that few of us in Europe have escaped inheriting some Viking DNA. On mainland

Scotland the average the prevalence of Viking DNA is around 6 per cent but it is much nearer 50 per cent in Shetland and Orkney.

By the twentieth century Norwegians had put all their unpleasant traits behind them. They were no longer a warlike people; indeed, they were trying to maintain a neutral stance in a turbulent century of two world wars. But they never abandoned their love of boats and the water. The country has one of the highest ratios of boat ownerships to population in the world, and almost half the population owns or has regular access to a boat. Norway is a country with around 65,000 miles of coastline, with nearly 240,000 islands. Boats are not just for pleasure, they are essential, a way of life. A Norwegian would step into a boat in the same way that others might step into a taxi or catch a bus. Some Norwegians even came into the world in the bottom of a boat as their mother was being rowed, sailed or motored to the midwife! This enduring relationship between Norwegians, boats and the sea was to provide the means of escape for many of them when their neutral country was invaded and occupied by Nazi Germany in April 1940. To understand why the Vikings needed to escape you need to understand a little of why and how that violation happened.

A quirk of geography lay behind the events that brought neutral Norway into the Second World War. Far away, from the other side of the Atlantic, the warm waters of the Gulf Stream keep the mainland coast of the country free from icing up. This phenomenon keeps Norway's ports and its fertile coastal fishing grounds open in all seasons, a considerable boon to a country large in land mass (150,000 square miles) but small in population. Norway was politically a young country, having separated from a union with Sweden in 1905, and it was not a wealthy or industrialised nation, depending on its natural resources of timber, agriculture and fishing. It had remained neutral in the Great War and it had no wish to be dragged into the war that seemed to be becoming inevitable with the rise of Adolf Hitler. That ice free coast, however, had caught the strategic attention of the planners of German High Command.

The infamous Panzer tank weighed in at around 25 tons of steel, and that steel required at least 40 tons of iron ore to produce. Tank warfare had been identified by Germany as being central to its territorial ambitions and as the 1930s began to close, hundreds and then thousands of them rolled off the production lines. At least half of the high grade iron ore required to make a Panzer came from Sweden, from the far north mining centres of Kiruna and Malmberget which were supplying around 10million tons a year. The appetite for iron ore to supply the industrial Ruhr heartlands was insatiable. For six months of the year, the export route heading east via the port of Lulea on the Baltic coast was ice bound. The route to the west, however, crossed the Norwegian border and territory to the port of Narvik which was open all year round. In its simplicity the control of Narvik became essential to the production of the Panzer tank and of course Germany's entire armoury. Well before the war, the head of the German Navy, Grand Admiral Raeder, declared that it would be 'utterly impossible to make war should the Navy not be able to secure the supplies of iron ore from Sweden'. Thus, Narvik had become a key to the Nazi war machine.

Obviously the Narvik route was not the only consideration made by German planners whilst looking to Norway as a prize for the taking. The German Admiralty was well aware that the long Norwegian coast, convoluted by thousands of deep-water fjords and islands was ideal for naval bases and operations to attack and control the North Atlantic. If Germany gained this, they could stop the supply of food and war materiel to Europe and starve their enemies into submission. The Luftwaffe was also aware that aircraft based in Norway would have greatly extended range for operations over the Atlantic and over Scotland and northern England. The Luftwaffe also had designs on aluminium for its planes. Aluminium production requires huge quantities of electricity which Norway had in abundance from its hydroelectric schemes. There was even planning well in advance that Norway would make an excellent launch pad for an invasion of Scotland, as a second front to the main one planned for the south coast of England. The acquisition of Norway would, in political terms, complete the encirclement of Sweden, exerting pressure on that neutral country to comply with Germany's agenda. Beyond these military assessments were more prosaic ones, fish and food, as the expanding German Reich would require to be fed, and Norway had abundant supplies of fish. Not to be ignored was the sinister Nazi ambition that Norwegians with their Viking blood were particularly desirable bloodstock to add to their eugenics programme for the Aryan Master Race. Called euphemistically *Lebensborn* ('fount of life') this envisaged the procreation of pure 'Aryan' children by chosen Nazis with women selected for their genetic suitability. In its eventuality somewhere between 8,000 and 12,000 children were born in this scheme in Norway 1940–45, the highest number outside Germany. Most of these children were seized shortly after birth and sent to be raised in Germany. Germany's shopping list in Norway was a long one.

On 14 December 1939, barely three months into the war and with Norway still a neutral country, Adolf Hitler received a Norwegian visitor at the *Reichskanzlei* (Reich Chancellery) in Berlin. He was Vidkun Quisling, the founder and leader of the Fascist party in Norway and he was there to persuade the Führer that Norway was ready to be taken over by the Nazis. Not reticent, he envisaged that he would of course become *Statsminister* of the Norwegian government. He probably failed to mention that his party had very little support and had not a single seat in the parliament. That same day, Hitler ordered his long-time friend and ally General Alfred Jodl, Chief of Operations at High Command, to start planning the invasion of Norway.

Operation *Weserübung* descended on Norway at 0515 on 9 April 1940. It was a thunderclap – simultaneous landings at five spearheads between Oslo and Narvik from a fleet of around sixty Kriegsmarine warships. There was massive naval shore bombardment and overhead around 1,000 Luftwaffe planes bombed and strafed every prominent city and town, military and civilian targets alike. Airborne paratroops, used for the first time in history, dropped on Oslo's airports and took them with ease. Artillery and mountain troops were followed by nine infantry divisions. In total, Norway was to receive around 120,000 unwelcome visitors. It was the first land sea and air invasion 'combined ops' and also the largest simultaneous invasion mounted on a single day so far in the history of warfare.

Weserübung also included Denmark which, not without a fight, surrendered in six hours; it was the shortest military campaign in Hitler's progress. If High Command had anticipated the same with Norway, it was very much mistaken. Quisling was also mistaken when he forced his way into the radio studios of NRK (the national broadcaster), seized the microphone and claimed to be the new Prime Minister, ordering people to lay down their arms. This is said to be the first ever attempted coup d'état by radio, and it got short shrift from the listeners. The Norwegians were not there to be taken easily, fighting on for 62 days, the longest resistance to any of Hitler's incursions in Europe. The focus of their defiance was their king, Haakon VII, who the Germans wanted to capture as soon as possible to use a hostage. He had other ideas and took to the woods and the mountains, using the geography of his country to avoid capture, sometimes by a hair's breadth. By mid–May the west and the south was effectively under German control, and the King and his government had to head for the far north.

Moskenstraumen (maelstrom) is a word used to describe a patch of sea beset by violent undercurrents and eddies, interspersed with deceptive patches of slack water that give way to sudden deep sucking whirlpools. They are dreaded and avoided by all seafarers. It is also a useful description to apply to military campaigns following the German invasion. Because of the tortuous coastline, the deep fjords, fast rivers and high mountains, the Norwegians were able to suck the invaders in, resulting in some military successes. There was constant turbulent movement of forces, surprise, ambush and, ultimately, retreat northwards. At sea, the Royal Navy enjoyed some significant successes in engagements in the two major sea battles of Narvik. The Kreigsmarine was given a bloody nose, with 50 per cent of its entire destroyer fleet sunk. Such was the damage to the German fleet that it has been argued that this was responsible for keeping it away from the English Channel for the rest of that summer. The reluctance of the Kreigsmarine to engage further with the Royal Navy helped with the Dunkirk evacuations (26 May to 4 June 1940) and then delayed and ultimately led to the cancellation of *Unternehmen Seelöwe* (Operation Sea Lion), Hitler's master plan to invade Britain.

For land operations, a British, French and Polish expeditionary force of 38,000 was hastily assembled and despatched in three prongs aimed at Åndalsnes on the central west coast, Namsos further north towards Trondheim, and Harstad near Narvik. They arrived between 14 and 19 April. It was a commendably quick response, but it was not matched by proper preparation and planning. It was faulty in terms of strategy as in April Germany was poised to launch itself at the Allied forces in the Low Countries. There was a very real possibility of invasion across the channel. All military resources would be required to counter this threat and the priority of Norway should have been assessed in the context of the wider picture. This lack of focus led to the momentous Norway Debate in the House of Commons on 7-9 May, which led to the resignation of Chamberlain on 10 May.

It was deficient in tactics because a lack of consideration for the mountainous geography of Norway, the severe conditions and an inability to provide armour, artillery, anti-aircraft guns and air cover. Historians have not been kind to those responsible.

The southern Allied landings at Åndalsnes (Sickleforce) took place on 17-19 April. Their task was to thrust inland and then down the great Gudbrandsdalen valley towards Lillehammer to intercept German forces advancing northwards from Oslo. But, very poorly equipped for snow conditions, and with no transport vehicles, armour or artillery they were too late and had to fall back as soon as they made contact with the enemy. The first significant defensive stand at Tretten turned into a rout, at the end of which there was an order of 'every man for himself'. The second tranche of British troops was more successful with actions at Kvam and Otta where they held off far greater numbers of the enemy who had Panzers, artillery and trained mountain troops. In each case the battles ended with orders to retreat and to continue to do so. The ebb and flow of troop movements in difficult terrain washed away any meaningful gains. By the end of the month, they were on their way back to the coast, leaving men separated from their units and lost in the mountains. The main body was evacuated on 1–2 May. By this time the whole of the south, the central and west coastal areas of Norway were effectively under German control.

In the north, the Allies landed at Namsos (Mauriceforce) and Harstad (Rupertforce) joined up with Norwegian forces and had more success. The Royal Navy was able to provide a lot more support and acquitted itself well. However, on 10 May Germany had launched the Battle of France and with great pace was driving the Allied armies back to the English Channel. The Allied forces in Norway were needed to counter the threat of an invasion of the British mainland. This led to an order to evacuate which was given on 25 May, just as there was a major success, the re- capture of Narvik. The Germans could scarcely believe their luck as the Allies turned around and left the city they had just taken. The last of them were evacuated on 8 June, and a formal capitulation was signed at Narvik on 10 June. King Haakon and his government (with the country's gold reserves) had been rescued by HMS *Devonshire* three days before and were safely delivered to London. Unbowed, Haakon established a government-in-exile, and continued to be a potent figurehead for Norwegian free forces for the rest of the war. The Norwegian fight back was just about to begin.

The words *Flotsam og Jetsam* need no translation, describing the debris and the wreckage that comes in the aftermath of an encounter with a maelstrom. When the Norwegians signed the capitulation on 10 June, there was wholesale devastation of ports, towns, buildings and infrastructure. Seaways were blocked by sunken ships. Roads, bridges and airports were destroyed. Worse, there were the dead, many of them civilians, women and children. And there were the living, Norwegians driven from their homes, their lives shattered and harbouring a deep hatred for the Nazis who had snatched their country from them. Also amongst the living were others displaced by the chaos. There were British and other nationals, consular staff, Norwegian diplomats, government officials and despairing Jewish refugees. To this mix can be added servicemen (Allied and Norwegian) who had become cut off from their units during the fighting, or who had been rescued from sinking boats. They too had become refugees. Everyone had a desperate need to get out of the clutches of Nazi Germany. Many headed east and crossed into Sweden – but that's another story. This story covers those Norwegians who did what came naturally, they looked to the sea and to their small boats. They were heading for the coast. The Vikings were in flight.

Chapter 2

From Fight to Flight
(9 April to 10 June 1940)

J ust three weeks after the invasion, by early May, the whole of southern and western Norway had been over-run, and was under tight German control. Fighting was still raging in the North around Tromsø and Narvik. No one can be sure if there were any escape attempts during this phase as the Luftwaffe is known to have been indiscriminately attacking boats trying to leave as well as those innocently fishing. It is probable that dozens of attempts to escape ended in tragedy, but no one was keeping records of the dead – or of the living for that matter. After the war, Norwegian historians picked up and preserved a good number of individual stories, but no attempts to flee were recorded during these first three weeks.

The first phase of escapes began in early May, and continued during the rest of the fighting until the capitulation. A few of these are to be found in Norwegian records. Seventy years later, the new digital British Newspaper Archive opened a Pandora's box of additional information and stories. To a limited extent, in the earlier years of the war, local and national newspapers continued to publish war news without severe censorship. Editors still had discretion and did try usually to conceal sensitive information such as names, numbers, dates, places of departure or arrival, military units and so on. Such information could be and sometimes was fed back to the enemy; arrests and worse could follow. Sometimes, however, there were indiscretions, an example of which was a report in the *Aberdeen Press & Journal* of 17 May. It gave titles, full names and other details of three professionals on board an escape boat; hopefully the Gestapo were not reading.

The first confirmed arrival of refugees on British soil was on 4 May as described in the *Daily News* (London) the following day, and is worth recounting as the anodyne report reads like a fashion statement that completely belies the horror that lay behind it:

> Among fourteen Norwegian refugees landed at a Scottish port yesterday were four women and a boy of eleven who, with his mother, had escaped from the Germans. He and several others in the party were dressed in ski-ing suits and lumber jackets. One of the men who fled from Oslo as the Germans had marched in had covered 40 miles on skis.

A report was syndicated all over Britain on 6 May. The fishing boat *Jåbæk* had made land at Baltasound on 4 May after a crossing of two days. The skipper, Peder Godø, had been asked to evacuate M.R. Turner, who had been the manager of the British Aluminium Company in Norway for 30 years, along with his Norwegian wife and daughter. The departure was planned to be from Ålesund, and the Germans had already entered the town when Peder arrived. Other desperate people struggled to clamber onto the small boat, two Norwegian Navy officers included. Everyone had just dropped everything in the moment and run towards *Jåbæk*. With twenty people crowded on board, Godø set out amongst other boats which were being machine gunned from the air. He thought he was the only one to make it away. There is no record of what happened to the others.

It is only about 200 miles from western Norway to Shetland and it is surprising that some of the earlier escapes chose not to go there. Several boats went further north to the Faroe Islands, almost twice the distance; perhaps there were fewer ships and aircraft in that direction. On 4 May, the *Disko* and *Koralen* together left Brattvåg on the west coast well laden with twenty-six and twenty-one refugees respectively, half of whom were children, and reached Thorshavn three days later. A hero of escapes to Faroe emerged at the same time, 75-year-old

Ole Solbjørg who owned three fishing boats. Absolutely outraged by the Nazi invasion, he decided to do something for the war effort. He resolved that his three boats would be useful to the British, if nothing else to keep fishing for the Allies, and he determined to take the boats over to Faroe himself, one by one. On 3 May, he left Ålesund with the *Utvær* with a crew of refugee volunteers. This three-day voyage to Faroe was uneventful, and as soon as he arrived he began to prepare to go back to collect the next boat. The Faroese laughed at him when the old man said he was returning in a 20ft open boat with a small inboard motor. A young man stepped forward bravely offering to go with him and the two cast off four days after Ole had arrived. No one really expected to see them again – there were 450 miles of open sea ahead. About half way back, a severe storm struck; the motor was swamped and gave up. Solbjørg was a wise old man of the sea, so he threw out two sea anchors. They were still fighting for their lives, and so he improvised a third anchor from some old pieces of canvas. The storm eventually subsided and they carried on by rowing and under sail. They eventually reached Måløy, where they put in to get the engine going again. Absolutely determined to get home that day, they finally reached Ålesund. At last at home, the old man went to his own bed and slept for 36 hours without stirring.

The next boat on Solborg's list of gifts for the Allies was *Eldøy*, currently residing at Flekkefjord at the south west about 400 miles away, having been marooned there by the invasion. About a week later, Ole and some volunteers went to fetch it back to Ålesund. By this time, the conflict was over in southern Norway and there was less danger of getting caught up in the fighting. Nonetheless, German aircraft were shadowing them and at Ålesund one repeatedly circled overhead. To put the air observers off, Solbjørg started to make fake preparations as if for a fishing trip, but luck intervened in the form of a thick sea mist. *Eldøy* quickly cast off and set course for Faroe. This time Solbjørg remained on the quayside as he still had to retrieve his last boat, *Gå På* which was moored on the adjacent island of Hessa at Skarbøvik. Local gossip about the first two boats had reached the Germans who ordered the police to 'stake out' the *Gå På*, and a detachment had landed on the island. Ole and his volunteers were tipped off and stayed out of sight. Approaching midnight, the police decided to call it a day and departed; they probably weren't that enthusiastic. Without delay, *Gå På* set off into the dark and made Faroe three days later. This time, Ole could not return to his own bed as he knew he was a marked man, and he had stepped aboard to deliver his gift in person.

Ole Solbjørg survived the war in exile and returned home to Ålesund on *Gå På* in 1945. Aged 80, he had by then acquired some celebrity and he was greeted with a civic reception, speeches, flags and music. Later he was awarded the St Olav Medal with Oak Branch, a medal specifically designated for exceptional contribution during the war. For their dangerous idle talk, the locals around Ålesund quickly learned their lesson, and they went on to organise and support around forty escapes during the war. Norwegians, fond of nicknames, accorded their district the sobriquet *Lille London* (Little London).

As the fighting was still raging in the Narvik area the main hub of activity on the opposite side of the North Sea was the Sound of Bressay in Shetland. This channel of water lies between the mainland harbour of Lerwick and the island of Bressay, which protects it from the open sea. Its situation as a natural harbour and refuge gave it significance as a major naval base in both world wars. The desperate situation in Norway from April to June 1940 unleashed a frenzy of activity. The Sound had to be protected at the north and south channels by mines, nets, land-based torpedoes and coastal artillery. The mainland and the island were bristling with ant-aircraft gun batteries and barrage balloons. The population of the Shetlands was doubled by the arrival of 25,000 military personnel. The invasion of Norway had brought the Luftwaffe much closer and raids were happening with greater frequency. To picture the scene, as far as the eye could see the water was crowded with navy ships, merchant vessels, fishing boats, flying boats, damaged warships that had returned from Narvik, sunken wrecks and now increasing numbers of small boats that were arriving with refugees. Between 9 April and 10 June, fifty-one civilian refugee boats escaped from Norway, and of these twenty-four arrived directly at Lerwick. Another eight arrived on the island of Unst, some 50 miles further north. It's not clear why they chose to arrive up there. Perhaps the wise skippers were familiar with those waters or perhaps they figured that Lerwick would be just too dangerous. The Unst arrivals were redirected and escorted down to Lerwick, where all the boats were gathered in.

As the month of May progressed, fighting came to a close in the west and south of Norway. Those needing and wanting to leave gathered in groups looking out for a boat. All boats had a 'mixed bag' of people on board – the Norwegian skipper and his crew, sometimes with their wives and families, other fugitive Norwegians, soldiers, sailors, Jewish refugees and even a few German prisoners. It was a matter of 'all comers welcome' and a scramble to get as many as possible squeezed on board. A succession of heavily loaded boats continued to arrive throughout the month and up to the final capitulation of Norway on 10 June.

An unusually full report appeared in *The Scotsman* on 8 May, the day after a heavily-laden small fishing boat arrived at 'a Scottish port'. It was crammed with thirty passengers – fifteen men, seven women and eight children. A teacher of English had the ear of the reporter, giving more details than usual. He and some of the others had been in a town that was being flattened by the Germans. They had grabbed outdoor clothing and knapsacks and had left in a hurry. Their journey to the coast took a week, during which time they were constantly dodging the enemy who were 'snapping at our heels'. Others joining the group reported that the German planes had machine-gunned refugees fleeing towns and villages and, as if for fun, had shot up a field of sheep. Another time they fired at two old men fishing from a boat on a lake. They reached the coast where they got onto their boat, but the planes were still flying around firing at everything. As they set out, the planes must have run out of ammunition and flew away. They were lucky and the luck stayed with them for the rest of their crossing.

Some escapes were made 'by request', in this case by the British Consulate in Bergen (the city was under German control from day one), which wanted a passage for a consular officer along with several boxes of papers important for the Allies. The request came to Mons Storemark, a redoubtable fisherman on Fedje, a westerly island about 50 miles from the city. He needed a volunteer crew for the one-way journey, and he sent word to his friend Kåre Høsteland who lived on the mainland at Masfjorden about 20 miles to the east. Høsteland and a friend were so keen to get to the Allies that they rowed 10 miles to one island, which they crossed on foot, and then they borrowed another boat and rowed another 20 miles to Fedje. Kristian Røre, an engineer, and another Fedje man wanted to come along as well. Kristian later left an account of these events and the audacious plan.

On 9 May, Storemark and his crew set out in the fishing boat *Wailet* heading eastwards to intercept and 'flag down' the north-bound coastal ferry from Bergen. This was a bit like stopping a bus and was done from time to time. They came alongside the ferry. It was packed with Germans, but the brave British consular officer was on board at the rail with his precious boxes which he calmly lowered by rope down to *Wailet* from the deck, being watched by many eyes. He then climbed down himself and calmly explained that the Germans had been in the middle of a documents check. Storemark cast off, turned about and headed for open sea. The Briton's relief was soon forgotten as they ran into heavy seas and sea sickness. Approaching landfall after two days they were blanketed by fog and the passenger became extremely worried that they would founder on rocks. He stationed himself at the bow and after hours of his watch he was the first to cry 'land'! Storemark's navigation was so accurate that the little boat was at the north channel for Lerwick. On arrival, Storemark was summoned to confer with 'senior Naval officers'. He was thus to become one of three very different men who launched the first offensive operation back to Norway.

Most of the refugees were just grateful to get away from the fighting and the continuing danger. Many were consumed with rage at what had happened to their country and wanted to pick up arms and explosives, turn around to re-cross the North Sea to bloody Hitler's nose. There was, however, at that stage no military group planning anything for the Norwegian refugees. Such wartime situations often throw up an eccentric entrepreneur to get something going and in this case, there were two. You could almost say 'enter stage left' when describing James Lawrence 'Mouse' Chaworth-Musters of Annesley Park, Nottinghamshire. He was one of those British aristocratic characters whose special qualities contributed so much in devious and irregular ways to the conduct of the war. Having studied medicine and geography he became a zoologist and explorer. The nickname 'Mouse' was acquired after a new species he had discovered in Afghanistan. He was one of 'that dying breed of gentlemen scientists who did not need to work for a living'. When young he had inherited a Norwegian farm at Surnadal (inland from Kristiansund) where he spent much of his time, learning to speak Norwegian in the local dialect, a great advantage. At the outbreak of war, at the age of 38, he rushed back to Norway to become Vice-Consul at Bergen and it is probable that that he had been already recruited by British Secret Intelligence Service (SIS). He was at work during the invasion when the Germans arrived at the front door, so he quickly nipped out the back. Crossing the vast mountains to the north on skis and foot for several weeks, he headed for the isolation and security of Surnadal. He needed to get back to Britain to carry on with his war work, so he next set out for the coast to find a boat, picking up three wandering British soldiers en route. They reached the coast at Bryggja near Måløy, where he persuaded Edvin Nore, skipper of the fishing boat *Reidar* to take them over to Shetland. They made land at the Outer Skerries on 12 May.

'Enter stage right' came 40-year-old Major Percy Wilfred Theodosius Boughton-Leigh. As a young man he had served for a while in the Coldstream Guards, and from 1934 he was a solicitor. He re-enlisted at the outbreak of the war. Little is known about how he came to be in Lerwick at that time. Being a bit on the old side for regimental duties, he must have volunteered for special operations. Certainly, later on he went straight into the Norwegian section of SOE from July onwards. He, an army officer, and Chaworth-Musters, a civilian, worked together from May 1940 onwards. They adsorbed Mons Storemark into their embryonic plans to launch the very first raid back to Norway. This was fully six months before the inception of the Shetland Bus and fifteen months before the first 'Bus' mission.

Fresh from his own adventurous escape, Chaworth-Musters is the one credited with having initiated the raid. The mission was planned at great speed and not a lot of precision. Storemark was allotted the command of a handsome 70ft Danish schooner, *Hospitset*. He was joined as crew by Olav and Oskar Leirvåg from the Mastrevik area north of Bergen. They arrived on 20 May in a small boat *Snål*, in which they had rescued Colin Campbell the British Vice-Consul in Oslo and five British stragglers who had been in the mountains for weeks. *Hospitset* was to take a group of saboteurs with radio transmitters, supplies of arms and munitions to Haveland about 100 miles north of Bergen, there to wreak havoc with enemy communications. The eleven saboteurs were Norwegians, all civilians, recruited from earlier escapes and they had to be given a crash course in radio procedures, weapons training, unarmed combat, silent assassination and use of explosives. Their course lasted for under two weeks. It was less than adequate, to the point of being foolhardy. Oskar Leirvåg noted, not with amusement, that they hadn't been given proper boots; one man was even wearing patent leather shoes! In great haste they left on 30 May arriving at Haveland on 1 June. On the way over, they towed *Snål* so that she could be returned by Storemark to her owner; after doing so he returned to the fishing life at Fedje. The saboteurs unloaded their cargo and set up an arms dump, but before they could do anything at all they had to re-equip themselves with outdoor clothing and boots before they could move out. Over the next week the main party blew up a pipeline, attacked a power station and downed telephone lines. Something went wrong with an attempt to blow up the main Bergen railway line. It is not known what happened. There was a sense of mistrust in the air, which later became manifest as a betrayal. They made a decision to withdraw only ten days after they had arrived. Another unknown is why they did not use *Hospitset* to get away; perhaps it was being watched. It seems that they needed another boat.

Oskar Leirvåg was the saviour of the group; he also had another agenda. Evidently rattled, he decided that he needed to get his family out of danger as well. A favour came from a friend, Ivar Duesund, who offered the loan of his boat, *Gneist*. It was a favour given with risk and with dreadful consequences. Hastily gathering his family on board *Gneist*, Oskar then picked up ten out of the eleven saboteurs (one of them had failed to rendezvous). They left on 10 June just nine days after landing and got back to Lerwick without trouble. Back in Norway, however, the suspicion of betrayal became manifest. The departure of *Gneist* was reported and led to the arrest of Deusund by the Gestapo, along with the remaining saboteur Karsten Wang. They were sent to a concentration camp at Ulven near Bergen where sixteen months later they were executed. Oskar Leirvåg remarked dryly that there was a 'lot to learn' about future return trips to Norway.

The would-be warrior Chaworth–Musters was still a civilian. It's not known what his next involvements were, but it is likely he was in on the ground floor of SOE as part of SIS when it was launched in July. Early on he met Captain Martin Linge, who had been evacuated as wounded on a British hospital ship. The two, being of like mind, went on to be the co-founders of No 1 (Norwegian) Independent Company, the famous Norwegian commandos. Chaworth–Musters acted as an interrogator at the London Reception Centre, screening incoming refugees to weed out spies and gather intelligence. Doing this work, he was in an ideal position to identify potential recruits for No 1 Company, and later for the Shetland Bus. With his linguistic skills, he also acted as a liaison officer between SOE and the Norwegian government in exile, not always as easy as you might think. Whatever his mysterious status was during 1940, it was not until 4 March 1941 that he was given a commission as a Lieutenant (Special Branch) Royal Navy Volunteer Reserve. The Norwegians thought rather better of him and awarded him the King Haakon VII Liberty Medal and the War Medal, and much later they erected a statue of him at the family farm at Surnadal.

The professional soldier Major Boughton-Leigh remained in Norway Section of SOE and was involved in the establishment of No 1 Independent Company and the Shetland Bus. His shadowy presence and his quiet contribution have been underestimated subsequently, but the Norwegians recognised his contribution and he was also awarded the King Haakon VII Liberty Medal.

Whereas the *Hospitset* raid was designed to be an offensive skirmishing mission, a second initiative which followed in its footsteps was different in that it was to do with intelligence gathering. Sigurd Jakobsen from the large island of Karmøy, north west of Stavanger, had started a resistance group on the island shortly after the invasion. He was joined by four 'rogue' British servicemen (they had been separated during the fighting), a Royal Navy Captain Ware (Intelligence), a Colonel, a Pilot Officer and an Able Seaman. How they came to be there isn't known, but they must have had a radio transmitter. Working together, they observed and collated German shipping and troop movements, sending information back to Britain. As the Germans began to prevail and Allied forces were being withdrawn, they decided to get out. Jakobsen had friends, Bjarne Hagen and Magnus Tangen, who owned the 60ft fishing boat *Vest*. They left Karmøy with the four Britons on 17 May – ironically Norwegian Independence Day. Jakobsen kept a diary that many years later revealed this story. The crossing went well until a submarine suddenly popped up beside them causing much alarm. Hastily they prepared to throw their secret observations and charts overboard, but all was well when the red ensign was run up and the challenge was shouted in English. With the realisation that a senior RN officer was on board, they were then escorted by the submarine and by a plane overhead directly into Lerwick.

As with the *Hospitset* raid, they had the intention to turn *Vest* around and go back to Norway with arms, explosives and all equipment necessary to continue the operations they had been doing before. So the three Norwegians, Jakobsen, Hagen and Tangen also undertook training in everything required by agents in just three weeks. They set out on their way back to Karmøy on 4 June and started transmitting three days later. On that very first transmission they sent the position of a German convoy moving up the coast that was bombed soon afterwards.

The intelligence unit on Karmøy grew to twenty young men working hard to gather vital information about German shipping and troop movements to transmit back to Britain. 'Every day there were new questions from the management in England.' The Karmøy resistance men called themselves the '*Haugesundgjengen*' (Haugesund Gang), a term which was echoed the following year on the other side of the water by the celebrated '*Shetlandsgjengen*'. It all came to an abrupt end on 7 August. They were betrayed by a Norwegian Air Force officer who had decided to support the Nazis. In a planned Gestapo operation, eighteen of the twenty were arrested simultaneously. Only two escaped – Bjarne Hagen and Magnus Tangen – who were out on their boat. In the nick of time, Sigurd Jacobsen got a message to them and they managed to get away, going straight back to Lerwick. Of the eighteen who stood trial, ten were sentenced to be shot without delay. They were surprised therefore when the sentence was not immediately carried out. Days turned into agonising months, during which time some of the prisoners were forced by the Gestapo to clear unexploded bombs. After this work or possibly as a result of it, their sentences were commuted to ten years in a concentration camp in Germany, from where they were liberated eventually in 1945.

This was the final act of the two attempts to turn escapes around and take the war back to Norway. Their objects were noble, but their tragic outcomes will have been salutary for those who organised the two excursions, and to those who started to organise the Shetland Bus the following year.

The little *Leive* was an inshore fishing boat only 25ft long, yet it brought twenty-one people to safety in dramatic circumstances, as reported at length (some would say too much length) in the *Shetland News* of Thursday, 16 May. One of the escapers was a journalist and this may explain the revealing detail in the story. British units which had been in action at Tretten on 23 May were completely overwhelmed by superior German forces, and the order had been given 'every man for himself'. One group of sixteen soldiers were in the mountains for fourteen days being stalked by Germans, whilst being sheltered and fed by local Norwegians. Eventually they reached the coast at Måløy where their escape was organised by the owner of *Leive*, Adolf Kvalheim, and the skipper Thomas Melkevik. They were joined by two crewmen and the journalist. Leaving on 4 May all went well enough until, almost in sight of land, the engine gave up. They tried to sail on westwards into a rising wind but could make no progress. The next problem was that they began to run out of drinking water. Melkevik had to make the almost unthinkable decision to run with the wind back to Norway, which they reached at Bremanger four days after they had set out. After repairs and re-provisioning, they were on their way in less than 24 hours. It was dangerous to loiter in harbour with a consignment of soldiers. This second crossing went without a hitch, and they arrived in Shetland on 12 May to a 'marvellous reception'. In journalistic idiom, this was conceivably a 'double crossing'.

Not all boats brought so many people. That May one of the smallest boats to cross the North Sea took two determined men to Scotland from the Finnås area of the island of Bomlo (to the south of Bergen). This boat was one of the only boats photographed in the course of an escape, leaving an iconic image (used on the cover of this book). The older man, aged 30, was Johannes Baldersheim, a local fisherman, disgusted by the invasion and the behaviour of the aggressors. He doubted that his own motor boat was fit for the open sea and made a surprising swap for an *oselvar* (a small rowing boat made of just three broad planks each side), just sixteen feet long. The one advantage was that the boat was brand new. A younger man, Peder (Per) Magne Klepsvik aged 20 agreed to accompany him. They busied themselves with preparations, cutting slivers of cork and hammering them between the planks to prevent leaks, gathering together a compass, ropes and canvas, food and water. The villagers deemed them to be crazy, suggesting that it would be simpler to make up two coffins as a shorter route to heaven.

Approaching midnight on 16 May, family and friends gathered at the Finnås jetty to see them away. Johannes set a course, not for Shetland but for Kinnaird Head Lighthouse on the north east Scotland (north of Peterhead), as he feared that they would be lost in the Atlantic if they overshot Shetland. Without any wind they rowed carefully through a minefield, worrying endlessly about passing German planes which, however, chose to ignore them. Perhaps they were not spotted as the boat was so tiny, just a speck on the ocean. Oddly it was Baldersheim the professional fisherman who suffered most from seasickness in the heavy swells. Their food and water became contaminated with the lashing sea spray. The pair actually rowed most of the way across but as they came closer to Scotland the wind got up and they were able to run with a jury-rigged sail. During the fifth night they saw the lights of a plane but they still held back from signalling at it with their flashlights in case it was an enemy aircraft.

The following day the wind dropped and they ran into a haar. In the murk they saw a warship circling and then coming closer; the ensign showed it was British. This was HMT *Lord Plender*; a large trawler converted and armed for anti-submarine warfare. At first the warship had thought the tiny object was the conning tower of a submarine, and prepared to do battle. Realising their mistake they came up alongside, with one of the crew taking the photo of Baldersheim and Klepsvik, so immortalising their incredible feat. 'Where do you come from?' came a cry from the ship. Before answering that question, Baldersheim answered with another, asking, 'Where are we?', and was delighted to be told that they were just two miles off Kinnaird Head – that was exactly where he had set his course. The trawler wanted to take the two on board but with typical Norwegian stubbornness, Baldersheim insisted that they wanted to complete their journey under their own steam. This caused consternation with the British who eventually prevailed. The Norwegians agreed to be taken on board provided their boat came too. Once on deck, the two were 'treated like admirals'. In the captain's cabin they were offered drams of whisky, turned down by a teetotal Baldersheim but gladly taken by young Klepsvik. Utterly exhausted, he soon passed out 'flat on his back'.

Lord Plender was on its way north to Orkney, and the pair had another 125 miles to go before being landed at Kirkwall. About a week later, a Norwegian broadcast from London ran thus:

This is London. There are many from Norway who come over to England in these days. We cannot greet everyone, but we make an exception for two young people who came rowing over in a small boat of 12 to 13 feet (sic). This greeting is from Per, who says that everything is fine with them both.

Nearly as small as the Finås *oselvar*, the small rowing boat *Roald* arrived at Lerwick on 1 June 1940 with Peder Grane from Askvøll, entirely on his own, having taken three days to row across. Only four solo attempts were made and two of these never arrived. Two other tiny boats with just two men in each arrived in May 1940, *Porat* and *Skarv*.

On Sunday, 12 May the *Newcastle Sunday Sun* carried a story with really far too much information; its readers were desperate for news from across the water. The story began towards the end of April, just about the time at which British forces were in retreat from central Norway. One of the last significant actions took place in a valley at Otta on 28 April, where British soldiers of the Green Howards gallantly held up greatly superior forces, but with no air cover they were then told to fall back. In the confusion that descended, groups of soldiers became separated and lost in the mountains, hunted by the Nazis. Six men were discovered by a lone Norwegian who was escaping from Oslo, and who had trekked nearly 200 miles from there over the mountains. Being an experienced mountain man, he offered to guide the soldiers to the coast where he was heading; it was about another 200 miles away. As they went along, he gathered in another group of ten (including an officer), and then a third group of twelve. The Germans were still hunting these stragglers on land and from the air. At one point the party managed to hide unseen as an enemy patrol passed them on the other side of a lake, in plain sight. They were spotted by a prowling plane and luckily the Norwegian and the officer stopped the men from firing at it. They had a much better chance hiding in the woods. Over the next week, they dodged German troops and police, and the Norwegian found them shelter and food from friendly locals. They had to leave behind one soldier in the care of a doctor as he had severe frostbite of his feet.

Nearing the coast, they began to join up with other refugees, another dozen Green Howards, four political refugees, some Norwegian Navy and Air Force escapers (about twenty including a senior officer in the defence staff) and other Norwegians who wanted to get away. All in all, there were about seventy people hoping to get to Britain. The Oslo man was instrumental in organising two fishing boats with their crews to take the whole consignment across to safety and they arrived at a 'northern port' on 12 May. The heroic 'Oslo traveller' arrived with no money and few possessions. The Green Howard soldiers who he had saved clubbed together to give him what they could, and their officer gave him an open letter commending him to be given assistance wherever he went in Britain. It's not hard to say that he also deserved a medal.

Towards the end of May, five men huddled around a table in a café in the Torvet district of Arendal on the south coast. In the aftermath of the invasion, they had one aim; to cross over to Britain and join whatever armed forces they could so that they could fight back against the oppressor. They were planning an escape by boat and if they wondered where to start the owner Ole Ellefsen was keen to be of help. Indeed, although he would not be going himself, he was keen be involved and provided a boat, fuel and supplies. He regarded himself as the sponsor of the escape. On 25 May, the five set out from Arendal in a 21ft motorboat heading for Aberdeen, but without great navigational skills. Out in the middle of the North Sea the engine cut out and they drifted for about eight hours before they could get it going again. During the drifting they must have gone well off course, as they arrived not in Aberdeen but at Skegness (south of Hull) some 300 miles to the south. It was 1 June and they had been at sea for seven days. After the war, some or all of them must have returned to the café in Torvet and presented their Norwegian ship's flag to Ole Ellefsen as a token of thanks. Until that visit Ellefsen would not have known if the crossing had been successful or if the men had even survived the war. The happy reunion prompted Mrs Ellefsen to make a unique souvenir of the courageous escape. She embroidered the flag with yellow thread to show the route of the escape with the names of the escapers listed. She then added her husband's name as, after all, he had sponsored the escape. The flag is now on display at Arendal's Kuben Museum, a poignant reminder of local endeavour and bravery.

Just three days later, on 28 May, another boat left Arendal, a small sailing boat called *Lady Nancy* which belonged to Reidar Stray. He had been approached by three others wanting to get across to the Allies and he decided he would go with them in his own boat. Unfortunately, *Lady Nancy* was a bit of a sieve and they had to put into Mandal to caulk the planking. The next problem was a violent storm in which everything got soaked, and then a greater threat – a German plane. Stray threw out some fishing lines and they waved, indicating that they were fishing. The plane went away and that was the last of their troubles. Five days later they came across a trawler from Grimsby well down the English coast, which escorted them into port.

Captain Peter Branston of the Sherwood Foresters was in command of sixteen members of his regiment, and they were completely lost in the mountains. They had become separated from their unit after the rout at Tretten in the central valley of Gudbrandsdalen on 23 April. 'Every man for himself' had been the order, but it was wiser to stay in groups. We don't know what then happened to them, but it was a whole two weeks later on 8 May that they bumped into some helpful Norwegians at Årdal, in the middle of the mountains about 100 miles west from Tretten. It is possible that they had tried going north but had found Gudbrandsdalen overrun by Germans and had turned west and become lost in a white wilderness. Clearly they had travelled a lot more than the 100 miles. They didn't have proper winter clothing or equipment, very little food and only one pair of skis. Now they were among friends and for the next seventeen days their entire journey to the coast was managed by relays of brave Norwegians; in total over twenty of them were involved. Never leaving the group the Norwegians fed and clothed them, provided them with shelter and even summoned two cobblers to repair their tattered boots. They moved by night and lay up by day to avoid detection by the Germans. On day four they had to make a decision to leave four men at Avdalen because their condition was so poor. A lone Norwegian refugee also joined the group which now numbered thirteen. Most of the journey was on foot in snow for which they fashioned some crude wooden snow shoes, bound on to their boots with twine. No one could doubt the difficulties they faced in the second week when they climbed through a mountain wilderness up to the Jostedal Glacier which they crossed with specialist mountain guides. When they descended to sea level, they were taken by motor boat where possible. By this time the Norwegians were calling them '*Gruppe Branston*'. They eventually reached Florø on 25 May and enjoyed the luxury of a few days' rest until a boat was found in the form of the fishing boat *Livlig*, whose skipper and crew had volunteered for the job. Casting off on 28 May, the *Gruppe Branston* had been on the run for five horrendous weeks. Fearing that they might not survive the voyage, Captain Branston wrote a letter which he handed to someone in Tirdal on the understanding that it would be sent if they failed to make it. The letter was addressed to the 'Officer Commanding, Sherwood Foresters, Normanton Barracks, Derby', as from Tirdal Norway and dated 28 May 1940. Absolutely to the point and no more he said, 'The following left here on the motor boat *Livlig* today....' and he goes on to list the names of the twelve British soldiers and their numbers, concluding, 'If any are still reported missing please inform the War Office on receipt of this communication. (signed) P.J. Branston, Capt 8th Foresters'. Happily, the crossing was successful and the letter remained at Tirdal, being kept as a souvenir. It still survives in the local archives today.

Further north, at Ålesund, the skipper of *Breisund* was preparing an escape with six locals when five British soldiers turned up. It was 26 May and the soldiers had been on the run from the Gubrandsdalen area for a week. They had covered about 350 miles across the snow-covered mountains, all the time evading German troops and spotter planes. They must have been exhausted and they must have been relieved to lay their heads down on board *Breisund*. But was this a matter of the frying pan and the fire? The sturdy fishing boat ran into a gale as it neared Shetland and, approaching the island of Unst, it ran onto rocks and began to sink. They launched their 12ft tender into the surf and somehow all eleven passengers managed to get into it. They rowed it to a tiny uninhabited islet, from which they were later rescued. They had all survived, but they had lost everything. *Breisund* broke up in front of their eyes and the wreckage spread all over the broad beach of Haroldswick Bay.

As May turned into June it became obvious to everyone that the total collapse of Norway was imminent. The evacuation of the remains of the expeditionary force was being completed 1-3 June. During these last days, Norwegians desperate to get away, and stray military personnel who had missed their evacuation, crowded together onto small boats, while the Germans tried to stop them.

Ottar Nøvik, the owner of the 69ft *Kaare II*, had already tasted action when he took his boat to help with the evacuation of Kristiansund at the end of April. The historic little town wraps itself round an inlet formed between three adjacent islands; its attractive tightly packed waterside buildings were almost all wooden. In four days from 28 April, the Luftwaffe totally destroyed 800 out of 1,300 buildings, and severely damaged the rest. That there were so few casualties (only six) is due to the rapid and efficient evacuation of almost all of the 12,000 inhabitants by boat to nearby communities and *Kaare II* had been in the thick of it. These appalling scenes made Ottar think about his own extended family, scattered along the coast, and their destinies in this terrible war. So he organised three little boats to pick up family groups and take them to Tromsø which, at that time, was still not taken by the invaders and still, with King Haakon, was the effective seat of government. The family was dispersed around the city waiting for a lull in the fighting, but it was not until 9 June, just after the king had left, that Ottar decided it was time to go. Twenty-three members of the Nøvik family (including eight children) crowded into *Kaare II* and they were off, heading for Skålefjord in the Faroe islands, wanting to go onwards to Britain. As they left the coast they were strafed by a German plane, picking up some holes in the boat and their lifeboat. At that stage of the war, the Faroese were uncertain of their political status and refused to allow them to land. They moved on to Tórshavn where the decision to turn them away was upheld. Considering their options, they made a bold choice – onwards to Canada. They left on 30 June and encountered horrendous weather forcing them to take refuge for three days at a small island off the south of Iceland. Eventually they landed on 16 July at North Sydney Harbour, Nova Scotia, to a fanfare of media interest, demonstrating all the bullet holes in *Kaare II*. They had covered over 4000 miles in five weeks. They were beaten to Canada by the larger wooden coaster *Grimsøy* which had a much more comfortable voyage, leaving from the far north at Honningsvåg on 9 June. As well as eighteen refugees it was carrying a cargo of aluminium important to build planes for the war effort.

One of the very last escapes as the fighting was coming to an end was preceded by an astonishing series of events that actually began eight weeks earlier in the first hour of the first day of the invasion. Bjarne Hagen made a series of four amazing escapes during this time. To use the ancient adage of a cat with nine lives, he described how he used up four of them. He told his dramatic story in an interview filmed at the Marinemuseet at Horten in 2003.

He had been on the run for two months, managing to get away on about 9 or 10 June. A merchant seaman, Hagen had been pressed into service on the old coastal defence ship KNM *Eidsvold* at Narvik just a week before the surprise attack on 9 April. At 04.15 am, the German cruiser *Wilhelm Heidekamp* signalled an unprepared *Eidsvold* with a request and then an order to surrender, both of which were refused. Three German torpedoes were launched at short range and one found the ammunition store on the Norwegian ship. It exploded, and the ship split in two sinking in under a minute; it was 04.47 am, thirteen minutes before the planned start of *Weserübung*. Hagen was one of only eight survivors out of a crew of 183. He was pulled out of the icy sea and taken on board the German cruiser. He was so angry that he decided he wouldn't be a prisoner under any circumstances, and a little later he jumped overboard to try to swim to the side of the fjord. Soon, however, he became hypothermic and was fished out a second time, unconscious. This time he was sent along with another survivor from *Eidsvold* straight to hospital in Narvik, where the two soon thawed out and recovered, under the watchful attention of German soldiers. That night there was a heavy bombing raid on the city and in the alarm and confusion they managed to slip past their guards, finding a hiding place in the nurses' home. In a clever move, they exchanged their uniforms for those of Red Cross volunteers, figuring that the best place to hide was in plain sight in the hospital. They made themselves useful and stayed as auxiliary helpers for several weeks. After this, Hagen and his companion melted into the turmoil and destruction that pervaded the once beautiful city, lying low and living hand-to-mouth.

In early June they joined up with a group of twenty-one other young Norwegians either trying to avoid capture or just determined to get away and set about searching for a vessel big enough to get them away to Faroe. In the last week of the fighting, they found a suitable fishing boat, but the skipper was reluctant and started to manoeuvre his boat away from the quay. These were desperate men and one of the group produced a machine gun, giving a burst across the bows. The skipper rapidly changed his mind, and soon they were on their way. They reached Tórshavn without difficulty and there they were directed back to Scotland. They landed at Port Edgar in the Firth of Forth on the east coast, having travelled around 1,800 miles. Port Edgar had just become the headquarters of the new free Norwegian navy, and Hagen was again pressed into service. It was 20 June 1940 and he had been perfecting escape and evasion for ten weeks.

The fighting ceased at midnight on 9/10 June and the formal Capitulation document was signed at 5.00 pm on 10 June at the Britannia Hotel, Tromsø. The Norwegians had fought for 62 days, the longest resistance to German invasion to date (later surpassed by Russia). But the war was not over for Norway. It still had a revered king, a government-in-exile, and free Norwegian forces would soon be formed. The fight back was just about to begin. Since the start of the fighting on 9 April, 51 small civilian boats (as far as is known) had carried around 700 refugees to safety through the thick of it. This was only just the start of a much larger *Englandsfeber*. This 'fever' was to incubate over the rest of 1940. It continued into the next year and was to reach a true 'fever pitch' during the summer of 1941.

Chapter 3

The New Regime
(June–September 1940)

Vidkun Quisling did not find himself as Statsminister of Norway after the Germans took over the country. He had tried to tell Hitler in December 1939 that Norway was ripe for an immediate and easy take-over and this had directly led to Operation *Weserübung*. But Norway had unexpectedly and fiercely resisted for 62 days, and significantly Germany had suffered a loss of almost half of its surface fleet. Perhaps the Führer was not amused. Quisling's party *Nasjonal Samling* (NS), however, quickly moved into the police, civil administration and the labour unions, but interestingly the overall party membership hardly increased at all.

The power was devolved upon Reichskommissar Josef Terboven on 24 April just two weeks into the conflict. He was a particularly unpleasant career Nazi whose position could be likened to that of a Viceroy. He had almost total control of everything that happened in Norway until the end of the war, and he lived a life of regal style at Skaugum, the palace of Crown Prince Olav and Princess Märtha. The army garrison was under his control, but the actual command remained vested in General Nikolaus von Falkenhorst, who had organised the invasion. This led to friction between the two because Terboven wanted to rule by well-tried Nazi principles of fear and ruthless enforcement, whereas Falkenhorst wanted to win over the population by means that were more reasonable. For example, he said that if an elderly lady was crossing the road, then she should be helped by a soldier of the Wermacht. Neither approach was effective with the people.

Within the population in the wake of the fighting came a plethora of confused and conflicting emotions, ranging from relief, acceptance, and collusion at one end of the scale to grief, outrage and defiance at the other. The great majority of 'good Norwegians' (their term, often used) were in the second group. Their country was smouldering, the dead had yet to be buried, prisoners were being rounded up and the Nazi apparatus of power was being asserted. It's surprising how quickly an atmosphere of distrust descended upon the country, and it was accompanied by a strong urge to get away. The escapes did not stop – they continued.

The remainder of June saw only two more escapes of boats well laden with civilians and military stragglers. July brought an unusual and celebrated example of these North Sea escapes, not because of the two fugitives who achieved it, but because of the little un-named boat that became a wartime propaganda celebrity. The astonishing story still resonates today, and the boat holds pride of place at the *Nordsjorfartmuseet* (North Sea Voyage Museum) at Televåg near Bergen.

It all began at the end of May in the area of Trondheim when three men, Aksel Larsen (aged 27), Hans Larsen (not a relative) and another were outraged by what was going on. They had witnessed the Allied landings at nearby Namsos, followed by the straggling retreats and evacuations. They were determined that they wanted to join in with fighting which was still going on at Narvik well to the north. First, they needed a boat, and they bought one from a friend. It was about 19ft long, an open *oselvar*, made as a 'three planker' (three broad but thin planks on each side). The type was also known locally as an Åfjord boat. It was in essence a miniature Viking vessel, and its great asset was its flexibility, which allowed it to bend with the swell and the waves, rather than cutting through them. In its previous life it had been used by the midwife for getting to island patients. It had no motor and they planned to row and sail it. They set out on their adventure, heading north for Narvik on 31 May. On the way they heard that the Capitulation had been signed, so they turned about and returned to where they started. Their desire to fight the Germans was undiminished and so they came up with a new plan; they would go to Shetland to join the free Norwegian forces (at this the third man dropped out). A direct route to Shetland was out of the question as it was about 750 miles. A better idea was to meander down the coast mingling innocently with fishing boats until they reached a nearer jumping off point. Aksel and Hans set out again in early June zigzagging down the coast avoiding attention from the new occupying power. They accepted hospitality from good Norwegians and on other occasions camped out and cooked on a primus stove. After a couple of weeks, they arrived at the tip of the Stad peninsula where they made final preparations for a dash to Shetland.

They left Stad on 4 July, still hugging the coast as far as Florø where they altered course for the lighthouse island of Utvær and struck out into open sea. With just sail and rowing they had a rough crossing, which included an encounter with a whale, eventually making land at Haroldswick, Shetland, on 11 July. The two had been on the move for six weeks since setting out. In his classic 1961 book *Åpen Båt* (Eides Forlag 1961) about the trip, Aksel wrote wistfully and rather movingly about his experience, here translated and paraphrased:

Sometimes I can still wake up at night and see bits of the journey clearly laid out for me. Hans is the one foremost in these memories. Hans sitting at the tiller rising and falling in rhythmic rhythm, hour after hour. Hans singing and whistling in tune with the primus stove and coffee pot. Hans who takes a stone and puts his arm over the side into the cold sea to bash in loose nails. Hans who kept the courage up for both of us with his indomitable mood and his self sacrificing qualities of friendship. The strongest image is of him, tired and awake, as he sits crouched down on the sheltered side, rolling and swaying with the boat's movement – and then he sleeps with the seawater simmering beneath. I can see seabirds flocking around, the dangerous breakers rolling in, a whale jumping and a shark lazily running alongside.

The human endeavour of Aksel and Hans was impressive, but it disappeared without trace. It was the little boat that drew the attention and achieved a celebrity status. Someone in the Norwegian government had the bright idea of using the boat and the story of the escape as a propaganda tool to boost morale in Britain. The boat was bought for 500 kroner (perhaps £1,500 today) and, somewhat bizarrely, it was sent on tour. It was displayed in Edinburgh, Manchester, at Harrods and Galleries Lafayette in London. It was a statement that Norway was not down and out, and that its young would go to great lengths to join the fight against Fascism. The boat eventually found its way back to the museum at Televåg, where it resides in pride of place. It is one of only two of the smallest boats to survive.

A remarkable post-script to this story arose fifty-six years later in 1996, as reported in the *Aberdeen Evening Express* of 16 August 1996. Two Norwegians, Trygve Michelsen and Audun Nordhus, decided to make a re-enactment of the historic voyage of the *åpen båt*. Their boat was a similar *oselvar* of 19ft with no motor, but with the advantage of modern technology. This was their second attempt – they had tried in June but had been driven back just 50 miles short of Shetland. Undeterred, they had another go, leaving on 7 July and running into foul weather which caused them to capsize and abandon ship on 10 July. They managed to get into their life raft but lost all the other equipment. When their routine radio contact was lost, a massive air and sea search was launched from Shetland and Aberdeen, but it failed to find them and it was scaled down after two days. On 15 July the overturned boat was found empty, but later that day the two men were spotted and rescued by a Shetland fishing boat. They had survived without food or water for five days. They had resorted to eating an uncooked seagull and stayed hydrated by licking the dew off the sides of the raft. Michelsen and Nordhus certainly proved that they had the same resolve and the same Viking DNA as Aksel Larsen and Hans Larsen all those years before.

To return to Norway in 1940, Terboven was trying to complete the takeover by political means. He believed that Norway could be subjugated by getting rid of the monarchy and then substituting a Nazi administration. The Germans had been liberal with propaganda decrying the royal family for deserting the country and he judged that the people would become compliant in following Nazi ideology. He observed that some politicians had urged the king to surrender during the fighting as a way of saving the people from further death and destruction, and he sought to capitalise on this with a propaganda campaign. The *Storting* (parliament) was turned into a puppet institution with the appointment of sympathetic politicians. On 27 June, Terboven forced the *Storting* to contact the king and demand that he abdicate. The matter was certainly considered by the government in London, as some felt that his continued defiance and calls to resist were placing Norwegian lives in continuing danger. There were profound constitutional implications if he was to step down. Haakon's opinion prevailed and it was a flat refusal, delivered to the *Storting* on 3 July, followed by a BBC worldwide broadcast on 8 July. Haakon recounted the facts and reiterated his outrage at the occupation of Norway. He called for the Norwegian people to rally round him and his government. He called for Norwegians to join the fight in Britain and to resist the occupation at home. It was, in effect, a reinvigorated call to arms.

While these events were unfolding, a boat, *Nordlys*, arrived from Bremnes (about mid-way between Bergen and Stavanger), bringing support and encouragement for the beleaguered monarch. Bernhard Håvardsholm, a significant figure in early Norwegian resistance, organised a group with several VIPs to cross on 6 July. They included Thomas Spence the British Consul in Stavanger (with his family), Major Gjert Ording an Adjutant to Haakon, and Haldor Haldorsen, a prominent politician. They arrived at Buckie (on the Moray coast) the following day and were whisked straight down to London as VIPs for an audience with the king. The delegation was able to assure him of the continuing loyalty of the Norwegian people and of their burning desire to shake off their Nazi oppressors. They told him about resistance that was already beginning to take shape. There can be no doubt that this information post-haste from *Nordlys* helped Haakon with his BBC broadcast that same evening.

Resistance, secret messages and codes always excite the imagination in wartime and they are often a matter of life and death. It was no less so with four young merchant mariners at Arendal, who were tasked with taking documents and codes over to Britain at that time. They were vital for communication between the emerging resistance movement and the newly forming free Norwegian forces. They got hold of very small sailing boat (no motor) called *Trilby*, and persuaded the German harbour master that they were taking a little summer sailing holiday, leaving on 14 July. They extended their holiday by breaking out into the North Sea and ran into horrendous weather. On the second day their sail blew out and away and they were left drifting and in despair. Rescue came from the depths as a submarine popped up beside them. Thinking that it was a German U-boat they threw the documents and codes overboard. This was too hasty, as the submarine was soon identified as being British, but all was not lost, as the four men had taken the precaution of memorising the contents. As it turned out, the submarine was heading not for a friendly coast, but for Norway on a mission and couldn't turn back. So the four Norwegians became part of the crew for the next eleven days, after which they returned to Newcastle. Their little holiday had lasted for a fortnight, much of it underwater.

If ever there was a story that illustrated the rage felt by a young Norwegian about the violation of his country it is found in that of a remarkable young man from Farsund (on the south coast), called Odd

Starheim. He didn't live to tell the tale, but his short life was more than enough to fill a book, (*Salt Water Thief, The Life of Odd Starheim*. E.O. Hauge, Duckworth 1958). The 24-year-old merchant seaman was living at home while taking a navigation course at the Marine College at Kristiansand. He was astounded by the lack of preparedness for the events of 9 April 1940. He immediately joined up into a rudimentary militia unit, which marched into the mountains and marched down again; they had surrendered to the Germans without firing a shot. His anger could not be assuaged, and so, with two like-minded friends, he began to think of other ways of fighting back. They began to gather intelligence about German positions and constructions, creating maps and taking photos. As their plans developed, they decided that Johannes Seland, who had been editor of the local paper until it was closed by the Germans, should remain in Farsund. As a journalist he was best placed to gather intelligence and could set up a resistance group. Starheim and his close friend Alf Lindeberg would cross to Britain with the material they had already accumulated, and they were joined by another student, Fritjof Pedersen, to help with the voyage. First, they needed a boat. They scraped money together and bought a 21ft open motor boat with a locally made Marna engine. They hid her in a small creek just outside Farsund. From a cliff looking down on the small vessel the three young men contemplated for a few minutes and solemnly christened her *Viking*.

Careful preparations for the voyage included a barrel of potatoes with a false bottom in which they hid their intelligence reports and a bag of corks to stick into any bullet holes. A compass was 'borrowed' from the navigation college in an overnight burglary, and a Norwegian flag was purchased. In high spirits, they set off on 11 August, but after a night of strong winds they were beaten back to where they started from. After drying out and a short rest they set out again on 13 August. The three recent graduates of Kristiansand Marine College plotted a course for Aberdeen, and, of all people, they should have been on target. Their main problems were heavy seas, being soaked to the skin and an engine breakdown. Dangers came in the form of a low-flying German bomber which mercifully did not attack and some free-floating mines. On 17 August they spotted Girdleness lighthouse at Aberdeen, right on the mark. With the engine now running, they proudly hoisted their Norwegian flag and motored into port. Whereas they had fostered a fantasy reception at 'the best hotel in Aberdeen' the reality was more prosaic; they were arrested and thrown into jail. This was by this time a routine procedure with incomers, to weed out potential spies. They were treated and fed well during their four days of interrogation, during which they passed over their cache of intelligence documents. During this time, details of their arrival and their particular war-like qualities had reached London and as a result a key player was travelling in person all the way north to interview them. He was Lieutenant Martin Linge, the charismatic Norwegian army officer who had joined the SOE at the time of its launch on 22 July. Linge was in Aberdeen just four weeks later, seeking to recruit these three youngsters straight off *Viking* into No 1 Independent Company (later to be known as Kompani Linge). They went at last to 'the best hotel in Aberdeen' to seal their acceptance. Starheim, Lindeberg and Pedersen had already been self-selected by their courage, and now they stepped directly into the cloak-and dagger world of SOE.

Suffice it to say here that Odd Starheim went on to make an almost unmatched contribution to the war effort in a series of missions, raids and other exploits in occupied Norway. On 1 March 1943, whilst escaping from an operation that had gone wrong (Operation Carhampton), he and his group hijacked a coastal passenger steamer *Tromøsund*, which was under German control, and set sail for Britain. The Germans were so offended that they dive bombed and sank the ship, machine-gunning the lifeboats killing everyone, perhaps seventy people. Starheim's body was one of only two found, washed up on the small Swedish island of Tjörn, where he at least had a decent burial. Posthumously Odd Starheim was awarded the War Cross with Sword, Norway's highest military honour. The British also awarded him a Distinguished Service Order (DSO) – a very rare recognition for a foreigner.

In a similar vein to Odd Starheim, Oluf Reed-Olsen (aged 21) was outraged by the invasion and was precipitated into action within days. He had some outstanding, some would say foolhardy, adventures and unlike Starheim he lived to tell the tale in his own book *Two Eggs On My Plate* (George, Allen & Unwin 1952). Reed-Olsen and a good friend, Kaare Moe, living at Bestum on the west aspect of the city of Oslo, began their resistance by stealing some dynamite and fuses with the intention of making mischief. Their first opportunity arose after they heard a BBC broadcast on 12 April urging the citizens of Norway to disrupt telephone and road communications. The next day by chance they ran into a group of volunteer fighters who, out of the blue, asked them to blow up a bridge vitally important to German supply columns heading west from Oslo. The bridge was on the coast road at the Lysaker River. That was it; they had to do it themselves on their own initiative, and they had to do it that night, 13 April 1940, just four days into the conflict. They were joined by Kaare's brother Leif as an extra pair of hands and as lookout. After several hours of watching and timing the sentry patrols, they could gauge when to approach the target. They scuttled onto the bridge with a ladder, climbed over the parapet and down the ladder onto to a platform at the base of the main concrete pillar. They placed their 64lb of dynamite, lit the fuse, shinned up the ladder and ran. They ran hard for fifteen minutes and stopped only when an almighty explosion rent the early dawn sky. The Germans were not at all pleased, and the ramifications of the sabotage were far reaching. Quisling came onto the Oslo radio news bulletin that day ranting in condemnation of the sabotage, with a threat of the exemplary execution of ten men (this did not happen). It was a foretaste of the vituperation that punctuated all of his utterances. On a national scale *Norsk Rikskringkasting* (NRK, the national broadcaster) repeatedly broadcast messages from prominent Norwegians decrying the attack, calling for an end to violent resistance. The event caused political change in that a German-backed Administrative Council was established on 15 April with a more conciliatory approach, and an intention of leaving

Quisling out. Regrettably the bridge was not brought down completely, but it was severely damaged. It stopped the military convoys for some days and slowed them down for months to come. In an amazing quirk of circumstance, the damage to the bridge turned out to be a life-saver for the saboteurs a few months later.

Reed-Olsen and Moe made contact with a 'British Navy Captain', about whom they knew little except that he was in contact with London and seemed to be 'secret service'. He was probably the Oslo naval attaché who had gone to ground after the fall of the city. He gave them some rudimentary intelligence tasks they could do, such as making maps and taking photos of German dispositions for which he equipped them with small cameras and supplies of film. They went about this with gusto. Reed-Olsen had a motor bike and displayed on it either a Fire Department or an Oslo Police badge allowing them to move about easily. An early task given by 'The Captain' was to get photos of a new German anti-aircraft gun. Brazenly and with great panache, Reed-Olsen sauntered up to the gun emplacement, feigning naïve curiosity. Proffering cigarettes and a smile he struck up a friendly conversation with the guard who became enthused to demonstrate the workings of the gun. His camera was under his hat which he doffed and discreetly clicked to get the photos, masking each shutter 'click' with a cough. It was an amazing piece of theatre. In July, the duo was asked to do a photographic survey of Forenbu airfield, now the main base in Norway for the Luftwaffe. They crawled under the perimeter fence and found themselves in the middle of a British bombing raid. With the Germans distracted by the damage and fires they were able to move around and get their pictures.

In August they were asked to return to Forenbu to examine a Heinkel bomber that had crash landed but was still largely intact. Under cover of darkness, they reached the wreck undetected and went about their business by torchlight. A very specific request was to inspect and remove the rangefinder. Reed-Olsen was a qualified pilot so knew what to look for. He carefully dissected the apparatus from the dashboard, but they needed photos of the exterior range-finding gear. To do this, they waited until dawn when they donned white mechanic's overalls and emerged wielding clipboards as if they were assessing damage to the plane. They got their pictures and took more of the airfield for good measure. Wisely, they hid the stolen rangefinder near the perimeter fence, and strolled along to find their exit burrow. So far, they had been incredibly brave, skilful and lucky, but that was ended by a single word – 'Halt!'

The airfield commander and his subordinates were none too kind to the young Norwegians. They were held under interrogation and soundly beaten whilst their films were developed, revealing their true intentions. The next stop was to be with the Gestapo in Oslo, and they were thrown in the back of a truck, pretending to be more beaten and injured than they really were, lying prostrate at the feet of four guards. They could catch glimpses of their progress through gaps in the canvas awning and they became aware that the truck had slowed right down to crawl across the still damaged Lysaker Bridge. Instinctively and simultaneously, they leapt to their feet, lashed out at the guards, and threw themselves out over the tailgate. There in front of them was the hole they had created four months before! They plunged into the river below and swam downstream to hide in the docks area. That night they slept in their own beds. Five days later they found the courage to re-enter the airfield to retrieve the valuable rangefinder.

BBC broadcasts from the Norwegian government in London were calling for qualified pilots to get to Britain to help form a Norwegian Air Force. Pilots were also needed to set up a training school in Canada. Reed-Olsen had been a commercial airline pilot until the invasion cost him his job. He and Moe were compromised by their recent exploits, and needed to move on before they were identified. They were restless to get away, so started to prepare an escape plan. The motor bike was sold and the proceeds used to buy a small boat of 18ft with a half deck, a sail and a very old Bollinger engine 'not guaranteed to work'. The boat had been stored on the slipway and it leaked like sieve when first put in the water. They hoped that the wooden planking would swell and seal the gaps quickly. A friendly boat builder who was helping advised them against trying the open sea. To get to the open sea they would have to sail all the way down the Oslo fjord and then all the way along the south coast. They devised a plan to make this section easier. They registered as commercial travellers and could use this permit to move along the coast. Next, they stole a map of the minefields they might expect to find and threw together all the food and equipment they thought they needed. On 30 August, Reed-Olsen went to say goodbye to his mother and she asked to see the little boat. After she had a good look at it and had given her approval, the two of them named the boat *Haabet* (Hope). This was after her father's old sailing barque of the same name. She presented the flag from the original *Haabet* to her son as a token of her support and to wish the two adventurers good luck. It was needed.

Reed-Olsen and Moe, commercial travellers without any sales samples, set out from Bestumkilen on 2 September. On board they had carefully hidden the results of their recent intelligence gathering with canisters containing 1,000 photographs. They found that *Haabet* sailed well and engaged in a race with a racing yacht crewed by some Germans, with bonhomie being exchanged between the two boats. At Kristiansand they went ashore to photograph German navy ships in the great harbour. Not long after this they were intercepted by a destroyer that had fired across *Haabet's* bows. A boarding party was sent over from the warship, and they had to dig deep into their resolve. Somehow a bottle of whisky helped them bluff their way through the search, and they had the cheek to ask for a tow back towards to shore. At Mandal, Rolf Gabrielsen offered himself as an extra hand and squeezed into the tiny boat. At Farsund, after foul weather, a break suddenly appeared, and they were off. It was 14 September, and they had already travelled about 350 miles, spending twelve days reaching open sea. Now the real challenges began. As the coast of Norway sank over the horizon two Heinkel 115 planes spotted them and came in low. The refugees pretended to be fishing and waved both Swastika and Norwegian flags together. The planes dropped a flare near them and gave a burst of machine gun bullets across the bows – and that was that; it was only a warning and the planes disappeared. After that fright, the rest of the sea voyage was just a matter of battling with appalling sea conditions, including the mainsail being split in two and a half capsize. On the 18 September, some way out from Aberdeen, they were spotted by a British Avro Anderson plane which circled and signalled that they would be rescued. The relief was immense; they settled down, had something to eat and lit their pipes, waiting for the rescue ship. It didn't come, but a violent wind from the west did, and it's hard to believe how cruel that wind became. What happened next, as described in Reed-Olsen's book includes every maritime catastrophe possible – lost sea anchors, another split sail, loss of the tiller, a capsize and a man overboard. All the food was soaked in sea water and all three men had suffered injury. Five days after the contact with the British plane, they saw a light. It was either the Lynvig or the Bovbjerg lighthouse in the Jutland area of west Denmark. Most people would have gone ashore readily and surrendered to the Germans, but they knew that could lead to certain death. Instead, they made repairs as they drifted southwards down the Danish coast, eating salty sandwiches. After about four more days, they set up a repaired rig and set a course westwards once more.

On 29 September, three British planes spotted the men lying in their damaged boat more dead than alive. The pilots indicated the direction to follow. They ran the Norwegian flag of the old *Haabet* up the masthead and prepared to be embraced by the Royal Navy. An un-named destroyer came along side and announced, to their bewilderment, that they were in the outer reaches of the Thames estuary. To their consternation, however, the captain said that they would take the men on board but not *Haabet*. There was no way that they could persuade the intransigent captain to change his mind. The three proud Norwegians refused to comply. *Haabet* was the only thing that they owned in the world, and it had been their saviour. They would complete the journey under their own steam in their own boat. As they obstinately cast off, the captain shouted through his megaphone, 'I've heard many stories about you crazy Norwegian Vikings, but it seems to me you beat them all! Good luck to you!'

Once again they were on their own again, making slow progress against the wind. Someone at the Admiralty must have been ashamed of the first encounter as, two hours later, HMS *Bedouin*, which was heading north on a course to Edinburgh, came along side with a completely different attitude, welcoming the men aboard as the true heroes they were. The intelligence dossier and films were recovered before *Haabet* was 'rafted' to the side of the destroyer. The sea had got up again and it was too dangerous to lift her onto the deck. The sea had the last word insofar as *Haabet* was concerned and she broke up against the side of the warship slipping away into the storm. Since they left Oslo, *Haabet* had carried them about 2,000 miles, and now she was lost. Reed-Olsen wrote, 'The North Sea had won at last and got a prize it had been toiling for over fourteen long days.'

The three exhausted men were claimed by an eighteen-hour sleep. As guests on HMS *Bedouin*, the three refugees were treated like royalty, but there was no quick return to the shore. As the ship was nearing Hull it had to make a diversion out into the North Sea to rescue the crew of a downed bomber, adrift in the same storm that had nearly claimed the three Norwegians. Only one man from the bomber survived, clinging to the liferaft. It wasn't until 4 October that the three remarkable young Norwegians were put ashore at Leith, Edinburgh. That was thirty-one days and about 2,500 miles after they had left home near Oslo. Apparently, they had endured one of the worst and longest North Sea storms in living memory. Archive meteorological weather reports on 18 September confirm that there was a 'deep depression to the east of Shetland, with a strong westerly … gale'. They learned that it was such a storm that the destroyer sent out from Aberdeen to rescue them that day had to turn back.

Oluf Reed-Olsen went on to fight his war. He joined the Royal Norwegian Air Service and helped to set up the Canadian air training school. But he craved action and so he went to train for the SIS and was parachuted into south Norway on 20 April 1943. Six months later he was on the run again and this time he decided to 'go east' to Sweden. Reed-Olsen received Norway's highest honour, the War Cross with Sword and the British Distinguished Service Cross (DSC).

Over that summer and autumn of 1940 there emerged another early precursor of crossings 'to and fro' in the way that the Shetland Bus followed. The brothers Hilmar and Gerhard Langøy of Mastrevik (on the Lindas peninsula north of Bergen) owned a brand new 36ft boat *Traust* and had a contract taking passengers from Bergen to the islands. Under cover of this legitimate activity they also squeezed in four return trips to Shetland in *Traust*, and a fifth one in *Stjernen* on 17 October that year. Locally these trips became known as *Nordsjøbus* (North Sea Bus), a name that was picked up for use as the Shetland Bus. In due course, the Langøy brothers entered the Viking legend of the North Sea. The first trip set out on 12 July in a great hurry from Utvær with two agents who were desperate to get away following betrayal of their mission. The boat was so new that the compass had not yet been fitted, and navigation was awry. Fortunately, a British plane picked them up and guided them in to Lerwick. Skipper Langøy turned around and went back, knowing that the Årstad-Brun Group in Bergen were desperate to get more fugitives away. On the second voyage in August, he took five refugees, the third voyage in September another five and the fourth trip on 16 September another nine. On the fifth of these crossings, in October 1940, the *Traust* broke down and was replaced by *Stjernen* in a truly dramatic series of events which is told in detail in the chapter which follows.

Chapter 4

Mackerel Fodder
(8 September–30 October 1940)

Knut Vidnes was walking home after work. As a journalist he worked for the newspapers which were day by day increasingly falling under German direction and censorship. By night he was in the business of the underground press, printing and distributing papers and pamphlets. This was a way of registering his outrage at the occupation of his country. It was important work, keeping people informed about the real conduct of the war and encouraging organised resistance. The Nazis were quickly alert to this, clamping down rapidly and hunting down the perpetrators. Arrest would lead to a death sentence or concentration camp and this was no idle threat – during the war, 62 Norwegians involved in the underground press were executed and 150 died in captivity.

Life in Oslo since the occupation just three months earlier had become for Vidnes a game of cat and mouse. A widower aged 35 he had less to lose than some and was prepared to take the risks. As a precaution, in case he had to flee, he assembled an escape kit of clothes and essentials, his passport and a wad of money all in a rucksack, and he sensibly kept this at the home of his aunt Josefine Tøssebro who lived close by in the same street, just in case his home was raided.

Approaching home, he was astounded to see 'Aunty Jos' on her hands and knees with a bucket scrubbing her front steps – she was very definitely not the sort of lady to turn her hand to such a domestic chore. Sensing something was amiss, he sauntered up and paused within earshot.

'Go inside, don't go home', she hissed under her breath, 'They're waiting for you'. There was no eye contact and nothing more needed to be said. That meant the Gestapo or the police. With his heart in his mouth, he took a breath, steadied himself and did what he was told. He stepped past her, went inside, grabbed his rucksack and went out through the back door. Knut Vidnes had arrived walking, but now he was on the run.

As a senior newspaper journalist and diarist, Vidnes kept and updated a record of his extraordinary journey over the next six weeks It is probably the most complete surviving account of such an escape in the Second World War. My introduction to the Vidnes family in 2016 gave me access to this unique record. This and the family's enthusiastic support were critical in my decision to go ahead with this book. Vidnes's story deserves to be told at length, as an exemplar of all the components that made such adventures so remarkable, and their effects so profound. It is an epic saga of Viking proportions. East or west? That was the first decision that he had to make. He had no obvious travelling companion at that time. There were not too many people wanting to leave the certainty of home for the unknown in the aftermath of the invasion. To the east of Oslo, tantalisingly close, lay the border with neutral Sweden. A distance of only 70 miles it was, by virtue of its proximity, a very dangerous proposition. Being relatively populous it was seething with German forces very aware of refugees taking the shortest route. Public transport was out of the question; he would have to walk. This would take at least two days if it was at all possible to avoid interception. The border was doubly difficult as the Germans were determined not to let people out and the Swedes were almost as equally determined not to let people in. Swedish neutrality was difficult to uphold under increasing Nazi pressure. Reports were rife in Oslo of people being caught, turned back or even shot and killed on both sides of the border. An old family friend in Oslo advised Vidnes bluntly, 'If you go to Sweden, you will get no further. You must take the North Sea route'.

On the other hand, to go west might seem to be even more risky. Some Oslo confidants thought that Vidnes would end as 'mackerel fodder'. It may seem to be counterintuitive to head west to the coast and to risk a sea crossing, but in their Viking blood Norwegians always had looked to the sea. Knut had been born and brought up in Ålesund, a remote coastal town difficult to get to by land; almost all traffic to and from came by sea. Everyone owned or had access to a boat, and for Vidnes the most comfortable decision was to head west and risk a North Sea crossing. In those early days after the occupation there were no organised or defined escape routes from Oslo. He would have to make his own plans as he went along.

It was on a sunny late summer day, Sunday, 8 September 1940, that Knut Vidnes started his great adventure. As he headed by tram and on foot towards the railway station, he looked around his adopted city of Oslo, now violated by the occupiers. Public buildings were all draped in huge Swastika flags and every flagpole flew that hated symbol. The city was covered in warnings and notices, so much so that Vidnes speculated that every German unit must have a dedicated sign writing section. Soldiers were everywhere, marching, singing and generally lauding it over the population. He had no official papers or permits allowing him to leave Oslo and travel to Bergen, so he endlessly rehearsed in his mind the reason he would offer if challenged. He did, however, have with him a bundle of documents and official letters entrusted to him to get to the Norwegian government in London. If caught, he would have to lose these in a hurry, and so he rehearsed for this scenario. As it happened, the train journey to Bergen went without incident. In these earlier days, the Germans were less efficient at their checks and there was no inspection on the journey with no one to dodge at the ticket barrier.

Bergen was a mess in the aftermath of the occupation, with bomb damaged buildings and ships sunk at anchor. Clearing up had not got under way to any extent, and there was an unpleasant smell of as yet unrecovered bodies. Vidnes was in a hurry to move on, but as a fugitive in the city, he could hardly just ask anyone for help and draw attention to himself. He did have cousins living in the south of the city and was worried about getting them implicated in his predicament. In the end, he decided that family was better than strangers, so he took the tram to go to see them. Of course he was warmly welcomed to stay with them, and the cousins would discreetly cast about for information.

By day, Vidnes meandered around the city centre and docks area, hoping to overhear or otherwise pick up information. He found a well-known café called *Kaffistova* (Coffee Table), where he could eat well and while away the time. The café was located close to the waterfront of the historic harbour at Bryggen, right at the heart of the city. The locals seemed to be unthreatening, it was free of Germans and the waitress was friendly. Small pieces of information were gleaned, but people were wary of informers, imagining them to be round every corner. The Germans were openly boasting that an invasion of Britain via the Scottish east coast was imminent. Back at home with his cousins the same anxiety pervaded, and with reason, for that very day the Germans had executed two Bergen residents accused of spying. Amidst the shock of this news came reliable information that the small island of Fedje was operating as a launching point for travel to Shetland. The island sits at the far end of a long chain of islands projecting north west from Bergen and is the most westerly island in Norway, just over 200 miles from Lerwick. So this was it then; Fedje was the next step to freedom

Vidnes' final day in Bergen was spent in preparation for his onward journey by coastal ferry MV *Prektig*. Using *Kaffistova* as a base for the day, he wrote letters to those he was leaving behind. He gathered and bundled up a collection of newspapers that he thought might be of interest to Allied intelligence and he re-secured the package of secret correspondence he had bought with him from Oslo. He looked up from his task and saw that some Germans had come into the café and they were clearly not there for the coffee. They advanced on two Norwegians at the far end of the room, and after a while the Norwegians were producing their papers. This made the hairs on the back of his neck stand up. He couldn't just get to his feet and walk out of the main door in front of everyone; he was effectively trapped. Making urgent eye contact with the friendly waitress at the till, she raised the side flap of the counter. Seamlessly Knut rose to his feet, retrieved his rucksack, stepped through the gap and slipped out through the back kitchen. The man with no papers made himself scarce in the nearby fish market.

It was Friday, 13 September. He was not superstitious, but this narrow escape was a bad omen. By the end of the next seven days, he had cause to doubt his luck.

Later that evening, Vidnes felt far from secure on board the ferry MV *Prektig* as it cast off. The boat was heaving with rowdy, inebriated, singing and shouting Germans. The atmosphere was oppressive and dangerous. His agitation was spotted by the steward who intuitively stepped forward to help, asking outright if Vidnes was heading for Scotland. Equally intuitively, Vidnes decided to trust him. The steward said that there was a control point ahead at Flotøya and that Vidnes' rucksack was likely to be of interest. He took it and stuffed it deep into a locker in his cabin covering it with clothing. Approaching the control point Vidnes' heart rate must have surged. The steward led him wordlessly to the galley and heaved a sack of potatoes out from behind the door. Vidnes inserted himself into the potato space as the door was fastened across him. He moved not a muscle and hardly dared to breathe as the German control officers inspected the ship. It was a huge relief as the steward unlatched the door and released him to sample the fresh air on deck, handing over the rucksack as they came into the harbour at Fedje. With a grateful thanks, Vidnes climbed over the rail and dropped down onto the floodlight quay.

Vidnes' main concern as he dodged past the disembarking and embarking Germans thronging the side of the ferry was where to spend the night. He was soon embraced by pitch darkness as he climbed up the hill towards a guest house that the steward had suggested. Alas, appearing out of the dark night, he was unceremoniously turned away. Stumbling upward toward the church silhouetted against the night sky he bumped in to a boy who helpfully directed him to the house of Anna and Hans Husa; she was the local midwife, he a fisherman. These were kind people, good Norwegians – he had fallen amongst friends. He could close his eyes and rest.

In the next days, Vidnes could take stock of his situation. The island of Fedje is small and its population was then around 600, subsisting on fishing and peat cutting for fuel. Already there were perhaps 100 Germans on the island digging and building fortifications because of the strategic position. The Germans were also on the lookout to recruit informers. Everyone was full of suspicion. One local hero, Mons Storemark, had been over to Lerwick with refugees in May and had returned to Norway with agents in July. He and his family were feeling ill-at-ease about their situation. It was unlikely that more trips from Fedje would happen in the near future. Gudmundsen, the island storekeeper, convened trusted friends to an informal council and the general view was that Vidnes should head further north as far as Askvoll to look for a boat. Gudmundsen had an illicit radio with which the islanders kept up with the war situation from London. At that time the news was all bad.

Vidnes could not leave the house by day, as this would advertise his presence to curious neighbours. To overcome this, on the Monday he was kitted out as a fisherman and taken to sea by Hans Husa.

The next day, a plan to move on was suddenly presented by Magnus Storemark, the son of Mons. There were reports that boats were leaving for Scotland from the area of Utvær about 35 miles north. Utvær was a small remote island with the most westerly lighthouse in Norway. Magnus Storemark was supplying a boatload of peat fuel for the lighthouse keeper there. The small open motor boat was already loaded to capacity and was on the point of departure. Without delay, Vidnes grabbed his few belongings and squeezed aboard. With the weather turning for the worse Knut Vidnes embarked on the next leg of his journey. Proverbially it would turn out to be a broken leg.

That journey was rough and drenching, ending in refuge in the lighthouse. In discussion, the lighthouse keeper and Storemark declared that there was no chance at all of an escape leaving from Utvær so the next day Knut crossed eastwards to the larger island of Solund where he could pick up the northbound coastal steamer. Once on board the MS

Atløy, he found himself surrounded by Germans, and overheard talk among them that they were making big efforts to catch boats heading for Scotland. This was confirmed by some Norwegian fishermen who were also on board. On arrival at Askvoll, the coastal steamer would turn around and return southwards back to Bergen. Weighed down by fatigue, doubt and low morale Vidnes decided to stay on board for the return trip. On Thursday, 19 September he disembarked at Bergen, and resumed the seat at *Kaffistova* which he had vacated in such a hurry only six days before.

Taking stock of his situation, Vidnes realised that his best bet was to return to Fedje where he had felt comfortable among the people who had befriended him, the Husas, the Storemarks and the Gudmundsens. There was the prospect of another interception on the ferry, and for this reason he decided to wait three days for a sailing when his former saviour would be on duty as steward. Leaving Bergen on Monday, 23 September, the trip was much easier with no searches as the control point at Flatøy had been hit by British bombers in the interim. The same night he was back with Anna and Hans Husa, very much relieved that he had returned to a safe haven. But just how safe was it? The Germans were tightening their grip on the island and were actively trying to recruit informers. Bored teenage boys who they could fill up with unaccustomed steins of beer in exchange for loose gossip were easy prey. In an uncomfortable incident, one such young man drunkenly shouted and taunted the Storemark family from right outside their house, broadcasting that it was known that Mons Storemark had been over to Scotland and that the family would suffer for it. Other lads decided to sober him up in the sea – and then it all went quiet.

Later, at Gudmunsen's store, islanders gathered in secret to listen to the radio from London and their king, Haakon. Vidnes kept a close record of this memorable scene:

When we heard the King's voice clearly and loudly in the little room it was as solemn as at high mass. The old men leant in closely to the instrument. The pipe was taken out of the mouth, and the blue smoke from shredded tobacco was allowed to rise up to the ceiling in blue plumes. It was gripping to see these old fishermen sitting there and listening so intently. Their hard lives had made them strong, but now more than one of them sat and wiped away an obstinate tear with a weather beaten hand.

As September slipped into October, a sudden opportunity arose to join a boat taking refugees from Bergen. In great secrecy, Olaf Langedal, an experienced and reliable fisherman on Fedje took Vidnes in his small boat *Aron* across to the archipelago of Austrheim about 20 miles to the east, accompanied by Magnus Storemark. This island municipality was becoming an assembly and jumping off point for Bergen escapes. Arriving after dark at the tiny village of Mastrevik, he was taken to the house of Ellef Lohne and his family who greeted him as an honoured guest, as they did with three other men who had arrived from Bergen sent by the Årstad-Brun export group. The term 'export group' became common terminology for those who worked together to organise escapes, working at considerable risk of betrayal, arrest and more – as will be seen. They were told that they were to be taken across by the Langøy brothers, who had been back and forth across the North Sea in their boat *Traust*. Five more Bergen escapers were picked up and an extra opportunist man jumped aboard meaning that the little boat was overloaded with twelve men on board. Nonetheless, with a flat sea and a bright moon, Langøy cast off with everyone in high spirits.

After a little while the engine spluttered and the speed fell to a snail's pace. They were just able to get to shelter amongst the small islets. As day broke, they had to cram in below decks out of sight, whilst Hilmar Langøy went in search of help. This came in the shape of a larger 35ft boat *Stjernen* which he managed to 'borrow' for the duration. These were desperate men fleeing from the clutches of the Gestapo in Bergen, and for them there could be no turning back. The two young men on *Stjernen* volunteered to stay with her as extra crew, and everyone from *Traust* transferred to the larger boat.

Could anything more go wrong? A German patrol boat started to shadow them and, with all the passengers below decks, they pretended to be fishing whilst effectively playing a game of cat-and-mouse between the numerous small rocky islands. Shaking off the German boat, they laid up in a hidden cove until evening came. When they crept out in the darkness, they almost bumped into the patrol boat, which turned hard about and began to give pursuit. The refugees began to fear that all was lost. Knut got out his pack of secret documents and added a heavy lead weight, ready to heave it overboard. Only Hilmar Langøy was unflappable and cried out, 'Don't worry, we will trick him this time as well!' With unparalleled skill, he steered *Stjernen* into a very dark and narrow canal between two rocky islets. It was impossible for the larger patrol boat to follow them. Emerging on the other side of the islands, Langøy increased speed and turned due west. It was 4 October, and they should be sitting down for a pint of warm Scottish beer in Shetland on the 6th.

The weather had other ideas, and so did the engine. With a rising sea they were suddenly without power and were adrift. *Stjernen* after all had not been prepared for this trip. Seamen do what they have always done in such circumstances – they 'make sail', in this case it was very make-shift using an old canvas that had not seen the light of day for a long time. A simple clearing of a fuel filter got the Rubbestad engine going, and the escape was on again. The onwards crossing was simply appalling, with horrendous seas and freak waves sweeping the boat. Most of the passengers were completely debilitated by sea sickness, and for the others the simplest task became a major challenge. Speed had to be reduced to save the ship from breaking up. A day and a night followed but as dawn broke there was no sign of land as expected. Langøy had suspected that the ship's compass was faulty, and he was also seriously worried that they had overshot the north of Shetland. Whilst he was considering what to do, the engine stopped again.

This time the problem was more serious; the engine could only be kept going at reduced power with someone continuously applying lubricating oil by hand. It wouldn't be possible to risk searching for land like this. As if to help him make up his mind the compass started spinning wildly, oblivious to the earth's magnetic field. In the face of opposition from almost everyone on board, Hilmar Langøy stepped forward and turned *Stjernen* about – next stop Norway. It's hard to imagine what Vidnes and the other fugitives felt on the return journey, but the sea has its own rules and Langøy had made the right decision. As it happened, he brought the boat safely and with great accuracy back to near where they had so recently left, just four days before.

The *Stjernen* needed major slipway repairs, and it was decided not to cancel but to postpone the escape attempt. The bulk of the Årstad-Brun party was to return to Bergen and lie low until new preparations were made. Vidnes and one other man decided to stay at Mastrevik where they were embraced with commiseration and kindness at the Lohne household. After a long exhausted sleep, they could attend to some basic needs such as washing and shaving, and washing their filthy clothes. It was not safe to go out of the house; a known informer was operating in the area. If a visitor came to the house the pair had to retreat soundlessly to a back room. One strange problem was that a trip to the outside toilet in daylight might be observed. An amusing solution was adopted; the one in need could wrap a 'skirt' round his waist and put a scarf over his head because as a woman he would attract no attention! Beyond this, there was just a matter of patience and waiting, waiting, to be followed by impatience and irritation.

At last, about a week after reaching Mastrevik, news came of passengers starting to arrive from Bergen and being distributed around several different locations to avoid attention. There were to be additional fugitives, a young woman included. Hilmar Langøy was in charge of shepherding the small groups onto *Stjernen*, which had to be done with great care. To dismay and some alarm one group was not at the agreed rendezvous and there was worried talk that the 'shipment' had been betrayed. Langøy had to make another deeply unpopular decision; to again postpone the departure whilst he and one of the

Bergen men went to the city to find out the truth of the matter. There was just too much at stake.

Some of the party remained on the boat and some were let ashore to be hidden by islanders. The missing passengers were located. Everyone had to settle down, stay low, stay quiet and ... wait – for another long day. Langøy returned from Bergen satisfied that the operation had not been betrayed, but he had been alarmed to learn that the Germans were being extra vigilant. He reported, 'the Germans had taken a boat south of Fedje ... there had been a fight between the Germans and the men on board and they had all been arrested.' *Stjernen* gathered up the passengers again and proceeded under cover of darkness to the final assembly point, the old whaling village of Blomvåg. On the way, they brazenly passed by their old enemy the patrol boat at anchor for the night. The manager of the station came to see them off, bringing with him the final passengers from Bergen, including another young woman, and a large box of freshly cooked lobster. That made a total complement of twenty-three – the skipper and four crewmen, sixteen male passengers and two women. The manager slipped the mooring lines, and at last they were on their way.

The delicious lobster feast on board was at odds with a worsening sea state. The chivalrous Norwegians had given the two women the only decent quarters on the boat, in the forecastle which is subject to the greatest motion in a storm. The two were the first to become seasick, followed by most of the other passengers. The fishermen were hardly bothered but they became concerned about the survival of the two women who became virtually unconscious. They moved them into the centre of the vessel. Vidnes was one of those who escaped the worst effects of the lobsters.

Stjernen had been properly prepared for this trip and there were no mechanical problems this time around. She was built to weather such seas and chugged along confidently throughout the following day. In the afternoon, and well over the half-way mark, the watch cried out 'Plane! Plane!' But whose was it? Everyone strained to see. It circled round and then banked into a low straight run at them, but there was no cannon fire. As it went overhead the Royal Air Force roundels signified redemption for the little boat. Everyone rose from their sick quarters and cheered wildly. Langøy raised two flags to the masthead – Norway and a special blue signal identification flag given to him on one of his previous crossings. Circling again several times the pilot banked his plane to give cheery waves and a 'thumbs up'.

For the first time in weeks, Vidnes felt he could relax and put his ordeals behind him. He could even enjoy the remaining 'home run' of his Shetland cruise. Approaching Bressay Sound in pitch black darkness from the south they were met by an escort vessel showing three white lights. Rafting up alongside the larger escort, there was a brief interrogation and there were a few formalities necessary to validate their identity. All this was done in a happy and good-natured way and everything was sealed by the welcome transfer of packs of Player's cigarettes. Half an hour later they stood on dry land on the quay at Lerwick, a land free of Nazi occupation, a land of hope for freedom for their beloved Norway. It was Friday, 18 October 1940, almost six weeks since Knut Vidnes had taken those first steps from Oslo.

In spite of the elation, it would be a mistake to think that their arrival in Shetland was a holiday. Any one of them could be a German agent, and that meant that every one of them had to be screened and kept under guard. The first 'immigration' checks were done by two 'charming' Royal Navy Officers. All passports (if carried), personal documents, driving licences, diaries, newspapers etc were laid out and inspected. Knut was concerned to hand over his packet of secret documents from Oslo, but that was deferred at this first brief inspection. Langøy and the crew remained on board, the two women were whisked off to the comfort of the Queen's Hotel, and the men were marched off to an army barrack room under the not too vigilant and cheerful guard of a section of seven Black Watch soldiers. After the privations of Norway and the horrors of the crossing the slap-up meal they were given in the sergeant's mess was a real banquet. Sleep came easily, followed by a long lie-in and a 'full Scottish' fried breakfast.

That day brought the second round of screening for Vidnes, accompanied by his Black Watch escort. The intelligence officer, Flying Officer Pearse, was at once interested in the secret documents and the cache of newspapers, and undertook to get them to London as soon as possible. At last the responsibility had been removed from Vidnes' shoulders; the heavy lead weight had not been required after all. Following this, they undertook a detailed analysis about what he had noted on his journey, aided by maps and aerial photographs. Finally, Pearse took the bundle of letters that Knut had collected during his tour of the western isles and promised to forward them onwards. The postman had delivered the mail.

The Norwegian Vice-Consul visited the group and explained that they would have to wait for onward travel to Aberdeen, as the ferry had departed the day before and it wasn't known when it would get back. More waiting, but as a consolation they were moved to more comfortable accommodation at the Royal National Mission to Deep Sea Fishermen, under the care and good cooking of Mr and Mrs Patterson. An extra treat was a march to the cinema in step with their Black Watch escorts. With uncanny congruity the film was called *Thunder Afloat*.

The following day, Vidnes, because of his translating ability, was invited to help with a meeting between Hilmar Langøy and a Commander Hewitt to discuss return crossings to occupied Norway. Langøy had already been back and forth three times and had ideas about setting up regular return trips. The size and type of boats needed, radio equipment, armament and other requirements were discussed over cups of tea. In effect, they were talking about the birth of what would become the 'Shetland Bus Service'. Hewitt was clearly interested and convened another meeting the following day. It was decided that Langøy would travel to London to share his ideas with the newly formed SOE.

Stjernen was to return to Norway without Langøy, taking the three volunteer crewmen under the command of his brother Gerhard. Commander Hewitt ensured that the boat was not only fully prepared for the return trip, but that also extra cargo of fuel, food supplies and even some luxuries were on board. All the men and the two women that the little boat had carried to Lerwick gathered at the quayside to offer thanks, bid farewell and watch until she had entirely gone from sight.

The low mood that followed the departure of *Stjernen* was lifted the following morning when the Shetland ferry SS *St Magnus* returned to Lerwick, in sight of the Seaman's Mission. It was time to move on; next stop Aberdeen, then Leith (near Edinburgh) and finally by train to London. Their experience of Lerwick and their onward journey was overshadowed by the reverberations of the war raging across Europe in late 1940. Lerwick had been bombed the day before their arrival, the harbour was full of damaged vessels and there was a collection area of boats that had escaped from Norway. The island, such an important naval base, was bristling with military defences. The *St Magnus* had been attacked on its way and continued to have air and sea escort on its voyage. At Aberdeen, the Norwegians had a ringside seat during a major night-time bombing raid, which contributed to the inevitable wartime travel delays. None of this, however, could suppress the rising optimism that they would soon be able to join the struggle to regain their country. They finally reached London on 31 October.

What then became of *Stjernen* and her crew, and what became of some of the other brave souls who had helped Knut with his escape? It took four and a half long years to find out. Gerhard Langøy and the three volunteer crewmen were arrested shortly after their return, along with another Mastrevik man who had been involved. Even at the beginning there was knowledge of an informer in the area. Ellef Lohne resisted several Gestapo interrogations and was poised to flee to Scotland with his family. A typical winter storm held them back and he, too, was arrested. The evidence against these six men wasn't strong enough for execution and they were transported to concentration camp in Germany. They survived, emaciated and damaged, to return home without any fanfare in May 1945.

On Fedje, the atmosphere of distrust and anxiety increased over the next months. Who would be next to fall to 'German executioners just around the boathouse corner' in Vidnes' words? Olaf Langedal gathered his wife Hanna and three children into his small boat *Aron* and was joined by nine others squeezing in. Amongst these was Olaf's niece Borghild Langedal who was on the run from the Germans in unusual circumstances. She had idly defaced a picture of the Führer in a newspaper by drawing a noose around his neck. The paper found its way to the Gestapo who were intent on an arrest. Nothing could better illustrate the pressure on the islanders. The party left Fedje on 16 March 1941 and arrived in Lerwick on the 18th.

Magnus Storemark hung on until 25 September when he and nine members of the Storemark family joined six others on the small boat *Feiøy*. They had a long crossing but arrived safely on 29 September.

After being debriefed and processed at the London Reception Centre, Knut Vidnes transferred to the Royal Norwegian Navy and because of his background in journalism and his language skills he was retained in London as a Press Secretary to the Norwegian government in exile, located at Kingston House in Princes Gate. He worked closely with King Haakon and helped with his morale boosting trips around Norwegian forces and organisations. He was also involved in the propaganda work of the Norwegian Information Office. It was there in London that he met his wife, Diana Cooper. The story goes that he spied her across the room at a dance, crossed the room and rather directly said, 'You will dance with me'. She acquiesced reluctantly as she was already engaged to be married. By the end of the dance, she had become re-engaged to the handsome Norwegian officer. Such is the stuff of family legend.

Vidnes came out of the war suffering from tuberculosis, and life was a struggle for him and Diana. Such was his relationship with King Haakon that the King sent him substantial personal funds to support him through his recovery.

Vidnes subsequently became a renowned film screenwriter and director living in Oslo. He died in 1971, leaving amongst his effects his meticulous account of his escape. Written in Norwegian as a journal it was over 40,000 words long, and needed some time to digest.

It was therefore consigned to the attic and obscurity for the next 40 years, coming to light when Vidnes's two sons, Robin and Jon both retired. Intrigued, the two decided to retrace their father's six-week journey following his route, tracing and thanking those families who helped him on his way. For the Scottish side of their pilgrimage, from Shetland to Aberdeen, they enlisted my help, and I caught up with them in Aberdeen in May 2016. The brothers captivated me with the story of their father's adventures. They told me of a sketch that their father had made on arrival in Shetland of Stjernen breaking through mountainous seas. After the war he had used this to commission a striking oil painting, so that he would never forget the experience.

Robin and Jon kindly agreed to share the journal and pictures with me. In due course Jon painstakingly translated the account into English for my benefit, and, more importantly for the benefit of the Vidnes family living in England. Their father's story is the most detailed and significant one to emerge in the evolution of this book. It helps greatly in the understanding of all the issues involved in making these escapes.

Chapter 5

Winter of Discontent
(September 1940–March 1941)

A ny misguided hope that the Norwegian people would meekly become subservient to Germany was wearing thin by the autumn of 1940. They were not showing any sign of adopting Nazi ideology and were frankly being downright awkward in the view of Josef Terboven. In a crack of the whip, he assumed what amounted to absolute power on 25 September 1940, in a series of rapid and drastic actions. He dismissed the interim Norwegian Administrative Council and appointed a Provisional State Council of hand-picked stooges. He issued a proclamation deposing King Haakon VII. He abolished the *Storting*, outlawing the government in exile, and he banned all political parties. Only Vidkun Quisling's *Nasjonal Samling* was exempted, but even it didn't have the total confidence of the Reichskommisar, as Quisling was not given any formal office. Leaving no doubt as to his intentions, Terboven took over the *Stortingsbygningen* (parliament building) in Oslo as his new headquarters.

For ordinary Norwegians, reality was setting in, and it wasn't pleasant. So much housing stock had been damaged in the fighting and bombing that accommodation was scarce and crowded. Food rationing was quickly introduced and became a great hardship in the cities, less so in country regions where food could be accessed directly from the land and the sea. A great proportion of the fish catch was confiscated on the quayside and diverted straight to Germany. Many people had lost employment with the invasion and there was general financial decline as Norway lost its export markets at a stroke. The earnings from the

Norwegian merchant marine, one of the largest fleets in the world, could not be sent home. Hardship for all was inevitable.

In terms of passive resistance, people hoped to make the occupiers unwelcome and uncomfortable. In its simplest form this was manifest as the 'Ice Front', whereby Norwegians would not speak or engage with Germans. If a German platoon marched down the street, they would turn their backs. They would not sit next to a German on a bus or train and would stand for the entire journey. This so enraged the Germans that they issued a law forbidding standing whilst there were empty seats. In the autumn, university students adopted the simplest of badges – a paperclip slipped onto a lapel. This spread like wildfire and became too widespread for the Nazis to do anything about it. The wearing of a red beret and red tipped matches showing in the top pocket of a jacket spoke of a burning fire to be rid of them. King Haakon's royal monogram 'H7' was easily daubed on public buildings, but to do that was getting more dangerous. Throughout society there was a practice of non-cooperation.

Active resistance sprang up spontaneously at the time of the invasion with a small number of sabotage operations. After the capitulation, there was a latent period during which people tried to work out the best way forward. People who wanted to take up arms (there were plenty left over after the fighting) and use them formed into local units. These became known as *militær organisasjon* (military organisation) soon to called Milorg. A first requirement was effective radio and intelligence communication with the Allies. After Churchill launched SOE in July, such a liaison became a priority. Incoming information could be picked up on the BBC, and Norway had around 500,000 receivers at the start of the occupation. The Nazis had a frenzy of confiscations and edicts containing dire threats that resulted in 470,000 sets being seized, the other 30,000 remaining well hidden. Radio transmitters were an absolute necessity, and some early shipments had been made in the summer of 1940, but in the autumn there were still great deficiencies in communication and effective command structures. Armed resistance could not be effectively coordinated.

Midway between passive and active resistance lay the dangerous path of the underground press. The risk lay at two levels – first, producing the newspapers and pamphlets, and second, distributing them throughout the country. The former carried a death penalty and the latter at least a spell in a concentration camp. That the underground press succeeded and lasted so well throughout the war is tribute to people such as Knut Vidnes.

However much Terboven and his henchmen wished that the Norwegians would just knuckle under, it was becoming clear that the opposite was happening. A heavy hand and a jackboot became more commonly used.

Winter months are not good for crossing the expanse of the North Sea. Already in September the tiny *Haabet* had run into dreadful weather. Even smaller than a motor fishing boat, a *seksaering* is a rowing boat about 16ft long with six 'rings' (rowlocks) for three oarsmen. Highly regarded amongst coastal folk as 'fit for anything', it was over optimistic to consider such a boat was suitable for a crossing to Shetland. On 4 October, four men set out from Husøy (between Bergen and Stavanger) in a 'six ringer' and were never heard of again. The archive weather report for 6 October shows a deep depression over east Scotland with gale force winds, so it is likely that it was the sea rather than the enemy that took them. There were only five other crossings in October. One was *Hugin* on 25 October with two 20-year-olds in a tiny boat. They had engine trouble in bad weather but managed to make it to Baltasound on Unst. Of four boats in November, *Pokal* carried a mixed bag of nine fugitives from Ålesund including four Norwegian officers and some civilians. This was the first consignment from the so-called Torsvik export group. The Torsvik Group was the first in Ålesund and also the first to be betrayed to the *Sicherheitspolizei* (Secret Police), being rounded up in May 1941. That action resulted in the execution of four men on 26 November 1941.

The day following the departure of *Pokal*, three young men from Oslo arrived in Ålesund looking for a boat but they had no prior arrangement with the Torsvik Group, no local contacts and could offer no credentials. They were treated with suspicion and given a cold shoulder. They were 17-year-old Marius Eriksen and his close friends Jan Løfsgaard (20) and Bjørn Bjørnstad (18). They were certainly an interesting trio, as history later revealed. Marius came from a well-known winter sports family in Oslo. At the age of 14 he had already been selected for the World Alpine Championships at Zakopane in Poland, where he attracted the attention of a young British girl who gave him a skiing scarf, later to be significant in his life. After the Germans had taken over Norway, his family had misjudged the mood of the country by inviting a former German skiing friend to stay. This caused disquiet within their neighbourhood which upset Eriksen. He started to conceive a plan to clear his family's name whilst at the same time pursuing a teenager's dream of becoming a fighter pilot. He was abetted in his dream by his two friends who also had ambitions of being pilots. All three had heard Norwegian radio broadcasts from London urging pilots to escape and come to Britain to build up an air force. Eriksen reasoned that competition skiing was excellent basic training to be a fighter pilot.

The youngsters needed no further prompting and made the long journey from Oslo to Ålesund, only to find themselves wandering aimlessly round the harbour area, friendless. In time they learned about a boat under German control that was being prepared to run some Abwehr (German Military Intelligence) agents across to Scotland. It was fuelled-up and ready to go and just thirty hours later, the boys set foot on dry land at Lerwick on 7 November 1940. They later declared that the Abwehr had prepared for them and had footed the bill.

Marius Eriksen was still just 17 and had to lie about his age and education to enlist for pilot training. No doubt his skiing celebrity helped. The other two were also accepted and the three were soon on their way to Canada for flying instruction. Eriksen's instructor and later commanding officer in 332 Squadron was Wilhelm Mohr, who was himself an escaper who had crossed with a group of pilots on the boat *Sjøgutten* in May 1940. He described the young Eriksen as 'almost too good', an expression that seemed to harbour a foreboding of tragedy. Young Eriksen took to the skies within a few months. Around his neck he always wore the skiing scarf given to him by the British girl at Zacopane in 1936; it was his lucky charm. Before his 20th birthday (8 December 1942) Marius Eriksen had become one of the youngest Allied fighter aces (with more than five confirmed 'kills') and went on to complete a score of nine before being shot down in May 1943. The foreboding was misdirected; he survived and spent the war as a prisoner of war in Poland where he had been in 1936. He still had the precious scarf around his neck to keep him warm. Jan Løfsgaard was not so lucky; he was shot down in January 1943. It was said that he bailed out and was shot whilst entangled in a tree. Bjørn Bjørnstad also became a fighter ace with a score of six, and he survived the war. These three young men made a remarkable contribution to the nascent Norwegian air force, and were accordingly recognised with the highest of decorations. Eriksen's achievement was recognised by the British who commissioned an official war portrait by the artist Erik Henri Kennington in 1942. Returning home after the war his celebrity and good looks propelled him into being a film star and model.

A fishing boat with seven on board left the island of Remoy near Ålesund on 13 November 1940, heading for Iceland. The crossing was itself unremarkable, and the star of the show was actually the boat, *Brattholm*, which was to become noteworthy later on in March 1943, when it was on Operation Martin for the Shetland Bus. On board were twelve men of Kompani Linge, armed to the teeth and with 8 tons of explosive on board. They were on a mission to incapacitate a German airfield. On arrival at the island of Karlsøy they were gratuitously betrayed, being trapped in a small inlet by a German minesweeper. In the fire fight that followed, they blew up *Brattholm*, one was shot and ten were captured (later executed). Only one, Jan Baalsrud, managed to get away. His escape to Sweden over the next three months is regarded as one of the greatest feats of escape and survival in the whole war. Baalsrud's story subsequently passed into legend that has been told in books, TV documentaries and films. It demonstrates beyond doubt the defiant resolution and bravery of the true Norwegian Viking.

The last boat of the year, *Igland*, arrived on Christmas Day 1940 bearing not three Wise Men, but three secret agents escaping from Bremanger.

That December was marked by Vidkun Quisling flying to Berlin to meet Hitler, a year after he had been there to urge the Führer to take over Norway. Now he wanted to plot the future direction of the country under his control, and he spent a week in Berlin trying to feather his nest. He offered to raise a Norwegian Legion for the Schutzstaffel (SS), and made an alignment to Nazi policy towards the Jews. Heinrich Himmler, head of the SS, paid a personal visit to Norway to make preparations for the new SS Legion, which was launched the next year. It was never popular and failed to recruit more than 2,000. It never achieved a major combat role, even when deployed to the eastern front, and it withered away into disbandment in 1943. That's not to ignore that, over the whole war, up to 15,000 Norwegians volunteered for some form of German service, from the Police to the Wermacht, the Navy or the Luftwaffe. Motivation and loyalty in wartime is a very complex subject indeed. Insofar as the 'Jewish Question' was concerned, Norway actually had a very small Jewish population to start with, just over 2,000. That does not detract in any way from their treatment by the Nazis and their NS supporters. Fortunately, about two thirds managed to escape, almost all with the help of the resistance. They went mostly east to Sweden and a smaller number went west over the sea, helped by the export groups. The less fortunate one third who did not get away were all gathered up and sent to eastern Europe where they suffered outcomes that are unpleasantly familiar. Only a handful of prisoners (twenty-thirty) survived and returned home. Quisling may have pleased the Führer and his henchmen, but he did not enhance his standing back in Norway.

New Year 1941 arrived and the desire to get to the Allies was not diminished – far from it, for it was to grow steadily to peak in August of that year. Age was no barrier to the attempt at a winter crossing, even if young age was foolhardy. In early January 1941, Kåre Iversen Hafstad from Kristiansand was to be found in the Bergen area. He was only 18 and it is not known why he was so far from home. He met up with a Dutchman, Paul Winnemüller, 23, and it's not clear what he was doing there either. In early 1939, Winnemüller had jumped ship whilst at Birkenhead and had travelled to London where he found he was in big trouble for breaking his contract. Normally he would have had his papers withdrawn for up to a year but he soon and surprisingly departed for Germany, even as war was imminent. This led to a strong assumption that he had been recruited as a British spy. Alternatively, he may have just been shipwrecked off the Norwegian coast whilst on a supply convoy. Whichever way he got there, he wanted to escape and so did Hafstad. The pair stole a small motor boat and set out on 13 January. It's not known how far they had got, but they were caught, arrested, tried and sentenced to death. They were held in concentration camps until the following 26 February 1942 when they were taken (with four others) to the island of Håøya in the Oslo fjord, where they were all executed.

The departure of the fishing boat *Mars* from Herøy (south of Ålesund) on 18 January 1941 was notable not for the manner of the escape, which was fairly straightforward, but for the subsequent achievements of the four young men on board. The skipper August Nærø was just 21 when he and three friends from the village of Straumane – Mindor Berge, Gunvald Bergsnes and Ivar Brekke – stole (or they would prefer to say 'borrowed') the sturdy boat and set out into the unfriendly January sea, arriving at Baltasound two days later. They were not so much fugitives as volunteers very keen to join the fight back against the Nazis. This eagerness was picked up by Major Leslie Mitchell and Lieutenant David Haworth RNVR at Lerwick, the progenitors of the Shetland Bus. The Bus had yet to be formally established, had no base and was still tentatively operating from Lerwick or Cat Firth about ten miles to the north.

The four men who had crossed on *Mars* needed little persuasion to turn around and return two weeks later on what could be described as a prototype Bus operation, taking the agent Karl Johan Arsæther on a mission, and back to Shetland with him just three days later. Having proved themselves, the four went on to become the backbone of the forthcoming early Bus crossings. Nærø was the only one to survive the war. Berge (along with Per Blystad) was taken at sea by the Germans in August 1942 and never heard of again. Brekke died in action in December 1942 and Bergsnes, who had transferred to the merchant marine, fared no better, being lost at sea. Even the boat *Mars* made a contribution to the war effort, being selected for North Sea ferry work for British SIS out of Peterhead (this was separate from the Shetland operations), and she didn't survive long, being attacked and sunk with all hands in April 1942.

Less fortunate in their crossing were four other youths aged 16 to 19 who almost perished when they set out from Bergen in a small open rowing boat (no sail or motor). About half way across they met a storm that turned them back towards Norway. Exhausted, soaking, short of water and food they were aimlessly drifting around close to death when the fishing boat *Sildøy* spotted them, eight days after setting out, They were rescued and taken to the nearby island of Karmøy a good 100 miles south of Bergen. The islanders restored them to life over the next week before they returned home to anxious families a fortnight after they left.

Winter weather also nearly claimed *Rypa* which left from the northern community of Stockmarknes on 18 January. There were thirteen people on board and the course was for Lerwick. They ran into a storm and progress was hampered by a faulty compass, causing them to overshoot Shetland completely, heading for Faroe. Turning south they went in a big loop to the west of Shetland and Orkney, and made land near Cape Wrath on the Scottish mainland, after eight terrible days at sea. They landed at Durness Bay and they had barely got ashore when the poor old *Rypa* broke up and sank.

Around this time, in January 1941, the following edict was posted all over Norway –

ADVARSEL
Forbindelse med fienden
straffes med doden
Bergen den 20 Januar 1941
Der Admiral der noregischen Westkuste

The translation being –

WARNING
Contact with the enemy
Is punishable by death
Bergen 20 Jan 1941
Admiral of the West Norwegian Coast

In various forms of wording and in increasingly threatening detail this notice was posted in every port, fixed to every boathouse and pinned in the wheelhouse of every registered vessel the length of Norway. No one could possibly miss the message. It only put into words what they had already been practising, but it is an indication of the frustration the authorities felt in failing to stop the North Sea crossings.

This would not be any sort of deterrent to Leif Andreas Larsen, a natural leader of men who had formed an early resistance group operating in the Bergen area. From early February they had been hunted by the Gestapo and needed to get away. Eleven of them, along with a fugitive bus driver from Oslo, retreated to the small island of Turøy, out to the west of Bergen, and camped in a boathouse. Larsen soon had designs on the 35ft fishing boat *Motig* and started to make preparations. Unfortunately, the two owners of the vessel turned up and were alarmed to find their boat being readied to sail. Larsen was not a man to be crossed and successfully put his case for taking the boat. After all, he argued, the boat really belonged to the *Fiskeribanken* (the Fisheries Bank). Leaving on 9 February 1941, the twelve men had a rough but otherwise uneventful crossing. It is worth recording Larsen's own feelings about their arrival off Lerwick. 'To the men gathered in the tiny wheelhouse, the morning's landfall marked the beginning of a new life, an escape from oppression and an opportunity to fight back with real weapons.'

Leif Larsen was quickly recruited into the Norwegian Naval Independent Unit, at that time part of SOE, later to become the formalised Shetland Bus. David Howarth, one of the founders of the unit described Larsen as 'one of the most remarkable personalities of the entire Second World War'. He went on to perform extraordinary feats in fifty-two missions across the North Sea. He survived the war and became the most highly decorated Naval officer amongst the whole of the Allied forces. Amongst the many honours Norway awarded the War Cross with Two Swords, and the British awarded a Distinguished Service Medal and Bar (DSM), a Distinguished Service Cross (DSC) and Distinguished Service Order (DSO). Only his Norwegian nationality got in the way of a Victoria Cross.

The lengths that people and communities would go to keep an escape secret and then to cover up afterwards are demonstrated in the case of Arne Grönnningsoeter and his family, living on the island of Gossa, located between Ålesund and Kristiansund. Grönnningsoeter was the teacher of navigation at the Fisheries School, where the Director was Sven Somme, a cog in the local intelligence and resistance. The Germans were building an airfield on the island and there was a strong Nazi presence – and not much goodwill. Everyone was very careful with what they said or did and there was even an overtly Nazi teacher infiltrated into the school staff. Only Somme realised what his old friend was up to as he acquired a 28ft fishing vessel with an engine home-made by the island blacksmith. Grönnningsoeter very discreetly stored up fuel and supplies, as he perfected the operation of the unusual engine. On Saturday, 17 February 1941, Arne Grönnningsoeter, his wife Elsa, four-year-old son Elias and an older boy from the school disappeared. The Grönnningsoeter family and the Fisheries School could be dragged in if the Germans found out what was going on and wanted to make reprisals. So Grönnningsoeter and Somme had made a plan to cover up the escape. Grönnningsoeter asked for the Monday off for a long weekend to visit some friends. When he did not return, Somme widely broadcast his concern that they had got into trouble in the dangerous waters of the outer Skerries. On the Wednesday, he formally asked the Mayor for an organised search and he reported the loss to the police. On Friday, he posted an obituary notice for the tragic family and the next week the school held a large memorial service for the community. Everyone was in mourning, but that night Somme confided in his wife and at last was able to have a good laugh. His old friends were by then safely in Lerwick after a five day crossing. The home-made engine served them perfectly.

Winter had not lost its sting as the small 28ft motor boat *Kantonella* slipped away from Haugesund on 20 February with nine people on board. As they made very slow progress heading west, there was a hurricane heading east across the north Atlantic, which arrived at Shetland on 27 and 28 February, as shown on the archive weather reports. They must have very nearly made land before disaster struck. In early March, two bodies and the wreck of the small boat were washed ashore at Yell, Shetland and a week later four more appeared. None had any identification and the local residents of Gossabrough buried them side by side in Mid Yell Churchyard. They placed a common gravestone to the six unknown Norwegians, tending to the graves over the years. After the war it was found that there had been nine men on the wrecked boat. Many years later, on Norwegian Constitution Day, 17 May 1980, relatives of the nine men arrived to give them their identities back. A handsome new memorial stone was unveiled in the churchyard, proudly carved with their names, and with a bronze plaque describing the circumstances of the tragic wrecking of *Kantonella*.

In early March, a group of refugees from Bergen crossed the fjord to the ferry terminal at Kleppestø and climbed aboard a small motor boat *Norge I*. Heading towards the sea in heavy snow, they had been asked to pick up some more people at a remote location near the lighthouse at Hjelteskjæret a couple of miles along the coast. It was a trap; shots rang out just as the new passengers were boarding, and they were surrounded by Germans. To show their intention, the Nazis threw down the unconscious body of the organiser who had been betrayed and picked up the night before. Herman Steinfeld had been brutally tortured to reveal the details of the escape. All of the fourteen escapers received long sentences in concentration camps where two of them died. Crucially, one of them was found with a written message from a secret agent who was traced by the police and arrested on 14 March. He was Erling Christian Martinsen, a brave man indeed, who was operating a radio transmitter and running an intelligence network. He was sentenced to death but managed to escape from the Ulven prison camp and got back to Britain via Sweden. Not deterred, he joined Kompani Linge, learned their tricks and went back to Norway in the spring of 1942. He was recaptured and sentenced to death, and on this occasion after being held for another year, he paid the ultimate price for his outstanding bravery.

Another remarkably brave man was Joachim Holmboe Rønneberg who became recognised and admired around the world as the leader of the famous 1943 raid that became the subject of the blockbuster film *The Heroes of Telemark*. That raid was only one part of an incredible contribution that he made in the war; although as a modest man he decried the attention he received. He would not associate himself with the film. He was awarded Norway's highest honours, a DSC from the British and awards from the USA and France. From a prominent Ålesund family, Rønneberg was very keen to escape to Scotland with the intention of joining the Norwegian Navy. He crossed over in the small boat *Sigurd*, leaving Ålesund on 13 March 1941 without any drama, in contrast to his later exploits. On the eve of his leaving, he wrote a letter to his parents, which deserves reflection. After an explanation as to why he has to leave, he thanks his family and asks for their understanding. He ends:

> I hope you'll forgive me for keeping you out like this and leaving without saying goodbye – it's really hard – but that's how times are. Live well then dear mother and father and brothers. Now be more careful in words and actions than ever. You will probably always follow me wherever my path takes me in the world.

Instead of the Navy, he was recruited by Martin Linge into No 1 Independent Company – it was an excellent choice.

A potentially cataclysmic coincidence nearly overtook the escape of *Myrland* with ten people on board, planning to leave the port of Svolvær in the Lofoten Islands (within the Arctic Circle). All hell broke loose at 06.45am on 4 March 1941 as they found themselves at the receiving end of the first Allied Commando raid of the war. This was Operation Claymore, launched from a British navy task force, landing 500 British commandos and 52 Norwegians of No 1 Independent Company in simultaneous landings on four ports. Without any foreknowledge, the escapers found themselves in the middle of a naval bombardment and fierce fighting. It must have been a dreadful shock. Later that day, the British allowed *Myrland* to leave as planned and they headed post haste to Faroe, delayed but delighted.

Operation Claymore achieved complete surprise and considerable success. The principal aim was to destroy the fish oil factories of the Lofotens. Fish oil was still, in those days, vital in some processes for making explosives. Great plumes of smelly fishy oily smoke ascended over the islands. Eight German merchant ships were sunk and one warship, *Krebs*. Of the greatest significance was that a set of rotor wheels for an Enigma code machine was recovered from *Krebs* before she sank, vital for the work of Bletchley Park. The task force returned with 228 prisoners of war, 10 Quisling collaborators and no less than 314 Norwegians. A Norwegian press release said, 'Hundreds of young men immediately lined up on the shore. This was the chance of a lifetime and they meant to take it … (they were) youngsters all anxious to get into the fighting services in one way or another.' In Britain, there was unaccustomed and widespread media coverage of the raid; some positive news was allowed past the censors, after the disasters of the previous year. Perhaps the best overall outcome was a tremendous boost to the morale of the British, the Norwegians and the other Allies, as the first successful demonstration of the fight back against Nazi Germany. Churchill was delighted.

Reichskommissar Terboven, on the other hand was outraged. He arrived in Svolvaer the following day and ordered the immediate arrest of 100 people, anyone thought to be complicit in the raid, and family members of those who had left to join up. Eighty-four of these ended up in the concentration camp at Grini. Then he ordered the burning of ten houses thought to be homes of escapers. It was the shape of things to come. Finally, he imposed a crippling fine on the municipality. The 314 young Norwegian refugees arrived in London on 8 March in high spirits and were treated to a reception by the government, at which they received a rousing speech from the king. They would not hear about the reprisals for many months.

Something unusual happened with the weather in mid-March 1941. The archive weather charts show high pressure circular isobars coming to settle over the North Sea from 9 March onwards. That means settled weather with milder winds, and it must have been welcome to those Norwegians waiting for a chance to get away. Over the next twelve days the North Sea was in slumber, and a dozen boats took advantage with uneventful escapes. The benign weather was confirmed in an account by Herman Eilertsen from the island of Øygargen lying seaward of Bergen (told to me in Scotland in 2007). A merchant seaman, he had managed to get home at the time of the occupation and found there were no prospects for him on the island. He burned with desire to join the free Norwegian forces. On 16 March, he and four friends 'borrowed' a 30ft half deck motor fishing boat, leaving at midnight. 'We were incredibly lucky with the weather at that time of year. The sea was calm, and there was a thick fog to hide us from the Germans'. On arrival at Lerwick two days later, they were not received as readily as some of the others arriving as facilities were over-stretched. Instead of a decent meal, a beer and a bath they were directed to get back into their boat along with six additional refugees, given some fuel and supplies and told to continue by sea down to Buckie on the mainland. There were now ten crowded on board, including two women, for whom there was to be no privacy. They had another 200 miles ahead, taking two days. 'We had to make the best of it for Norway, and we were in high spirits', he added, uncomplainingly. What the girls may have said is not known.

The good weather came to an abrupt end on 21 March when a deep depression with tight isobars, indicating very strong winds, swept down from Norway. A robust and purposeful former pilot boat called *Kristine* had been bought by Ingvald Rødi to take twelve fugitives from the island of Karmoy, just to the north of Stavanger. They set out on the day before it struck. In those days there was no way of knowing about such violent changes in advance, and *Kristine* didn't get far, literally breaking up in the hurricane off the Feistein Light. Some wreckage was found later and only five bodies were recovered. Leaving a day later and from further north at Ålesund the small motor boat *Reidulf* with seven on board suffered the same fate, probably on the same day and in this case nothing was found at all.

Almost all Norwegian boats were either rigged for sail or at least carried a sail, mast and rigging that could be put up if needed. All seafarers were able to make their way by sailing, providing there was wind. Additionally, in the great Norse tradition, most were expert strong rowers. Nearly all boats excepting the smallest also had some sort of engine often made locally and of low sophistication, so that they could be easily repaired, often whilst the boat was at sea. Fishermen generally acquired a good basic understanding of their engines and had a rim of black oil under their fingernails. On the smaller boats they were usually single cylinder engines with an external flywheel whirring at low speed, emitting a very characteristic 'tonk tonk' exhaust noise. You could hear and recognise a Norwegian boat a long way off by its exhaust note. The flywheel was turned by hand to get the motor going, often resulting in torn flesh when the engine was being difficult. Because of the heavy flywheel spinning a gearbox was not included, and to go in reverse required a variable pitch propeller controlled by its own lever. The engines were really designed for inshore work, not for crossing more than 200 miles of difficult sea. In many of the escapes these motors seemed to have given trouble, either because of overheating or because of fuel filter blockage caused by stolen fuel of uncertain provenance. In almost every case the crew managed to get the engine going again – but not in the case of *Ulebrand*, from Haram which had been stolen by a group of seven, setting out on 16 March. On the third day, its engine caught fire, setting the boat well alight and causing extensive damage. The passengers must have been terrified. Drifting helplessly, they were lucky in two respects; Shetland was just over the horizon (they didn't know it), and they were spied by a trawler which towed them into Lerwick.

Not so lucky was *Reidar* which left Ålesund on 25 March with fourteen on board and which suffered an unfixable engine failure not far out into the open sea. Exposed and vulnerable they drifted back towards the coast where the boat ran aground on an uninhabited islet just off the island of Vigra. They managed to scrabble ashore. Luck returned as they were spotted by islanders and rescued, and luck continued as they were offered another try on a boat, *Njal*, leaving Vigra the very same night. Undeterred by their frightening experience half of them took the chance and left with *Njal*. Two of the others went three weeks later, on *Dolsøy*. The remainder probably thought better of the whole experience.

Egil Johansen and Harald Nilsen from Bergen, both 21, could be described as reckless youths heedless of the dangers of the sea, but that would be inconsiderate of their extraordinary bravery. Like increasing numbers of their friends, they were focussed on joining the free Norwegian forces. They were competition rowers and athletic sportsmen so they were not daunted by heading out into open sea. The problem lay in their choice of vessel, a two man sea going kayak which belonged to Nilsen. They prepared the fragile craft as well they could, adding a keel, a mast and a sail. They erected canvas spray screens in front of the cockpits. In the protected inland waters around Bergen the kayak flew through the water, performing well especially if the sail was hoisted, but the North Sea was another matter. Their recklessness conflated with the righteousness of their cause – to get to fight against the Nazis. They were not to be deterred, and they thought they could do it in six days.

Setting out in early April all went well to start with as they headed out into the open sea as darkness came down. With a following wind in their sail, they thought they had done well overnight, but when they looked back they could still see the mountains behind them. On the third day they were roused from exhaustion by the sound of a plane headlining towards them. It was a floatplane skimming the waves and it was heading straight at them. As it lifted over them they could see the hated Swastika, but the pilot didn't attack them, simply firing off a flare. Perhaps he was saluting their courage. Another German plane, a Heinkel, intercepted them and they waved their paddles as if they were lost; that plane also left them alone. But perhaps the two planes had gone back to base to summon a patrol boat? They frantically tried to get away from that position just as the sea rose up against them. After an exhausting night they realised that they must be a lot nearer to Norway than to Shetland, so they decided they had better turn back. Now they were in the coastal tidal race that was sweeping them southwards, and they were too weak to do anything about it. Luckily the fishing boat *Astrid* spotted them before the Germans did and plucked them, nearly senseless, with their kayak from the sea. Later, delivered to the village of Sotra and laid in comfortable beds, Johansen and Nilsen slept for fourteen hours before waking none the worse for their experience. They completed the last ten miles back to Bergen in their kayak under their own steam, such was the resilience of their youth. In due course, Johansen crossed over in September and Nilsen in October, meeting again in London. Johansen later flew in Catalina flying boats from Woodhaven (opposite Dundee on the River Tay) which were involved in anti-submarine warfare and also in flying agents to and from Norway. Nilsen trained as a Spitfire pilot in Canada before returning to Britain to engage the enemy.

These two young men, surprisingly, were not the only ones to wriggle into a kayak in an attempt to escape. On 28 May 1941 two young men from Alvastradkroken, north of Stavanger set out after intensive preparation and training over several months; they were lost and nothing was found. In August, another two men set out from Ryfylke and were lost without trace. Also, on 20 August, a student, Andreas Saxe, set out on his own from Ålesund. He worked his way down through the coastal islands to get to a suitable jump off point for the crossing. After ten days he had only got as far as Stad, having covered about 100 miles and from there he turned to the west heading out to the open sea. Eight days later the empty kayak drifted ashore about 20 miles to the south. Anyone who has considered the North Sea, even on a benign summer's day cannot fail to have respect for the deep swells, the swift currents, the white topped waves and spray. That any young person could contemplate kayaking through that for a minimum of 200 miles is unfathomable; that they were prepared to risk it stands as a measure of their determination and courage.

During that winter of 1940–41 the story of one landing in Scotland from Norway that was not strictly a refugee escape deserves to be told. The three arrivals were not Norwegian, they were spies sent by the Abwehr. They travelled not by small fishing boat but by a flying boat and a rubber dinghy. Nonetheless, the intention was for them to melt into the stream of genuine fugitives from Norway and the Abwehr planners chose as the landing place the town of Buckie in northern Scotland, where several hundred ex-patriots from Scandinavia were living. But it seems that the Germans weren't particularly clever with their spies; to start with, they hadn't a clue as to how refugees were received and processed on arrival on British shores. It became a litany of ineptitude aspiring to the point of comedy.

In the early hours of 30 September 1940, a woman and two men paddled ashore at Portgordon (next to Buckie), in their rubber dingy. The dinghy had been launched from a German flying boat which had come from Stavanger, along with three bicycles with which they were supposed to cycle on their way but actually the bikes were swept overboard in the surf. The leader of the three was the beautiful but enigmatic Vera Schalburg, once a genuine Russian countess. In the absence of their bicycles, she decided that the three would split up. She and Karl Drukke would get a train from the nearby station, whilst Werner Walti would go on foot to the next station along the line.

Schalburg and Drukke sloshed into the station at around 7.30am with wet trousers and shoes, with salt and sand on their suitcases. It was not very clever and was not unnoticed by the stationmaster and the porter. Clearly not knowing exactly where they had landed, Schalburg asked for the name of the station – it was Portgordon (names had been removed from stations for exactly that reason), and then she didn't seem to know in which direction Aberdeen was. Drukke opened his wallet to buy tickets, not realising that he was offering a very high denomination note. He then sat down, withdrawing a large continental sausage from his pocket and began to cut pieces from it with a knife. At this early hour at tiny Portgordon station, the large sausage was an absolute giveaway, a luxury not seen since before the war. The stationmaster told the porter to keep the couple engaged whilst he phoned for the local policeman, Constable Bob Grieve, who lived at the Police House on the waterfront, just five minutes away. Grieve wasn't fooled by their claims of refugee status – Schalburg claiming to be a Danish refugee (cover name Vera Eriksen), and Drukke from Belgium (cover name Francois de Deeker), both with London addresses. What on earth were they doing nearly 600 miles away at this hour? Their unsophisticated fake papers would fool no one. He marched them to the police station, sending for the Police Inspector at Buckie. A search of their luggage revealed a loaded Mauser pistol, ammunition, a flick-knife, radio equipment, other espionage paraphernalia, large amounts of money and – another incriminating German sausage. Soon their poorly concealed rubber dingy had been picked up by the coast guard, concluding the evidence gathering. Well and truly caught, Vera Schalburg decided to change her stance and mitigate her circumstances. She gave the name of an MI5 officer in London to vouch for her, which was a very odd thing to do. She then volunteered the existence of the 'third man' Walter Walti (Swiss cover name Robert Petter) disclosing that he was already on his way to London. She was effectively betraying him, selling him out to buy her freedom, even perhaps her life.

Meanwhile, Walti had achieved more success in boarding an Aberdeen train from Buckie station, whilst drawing attention to himself by offering a high denomination note. Aberdeen police just missed him but confirmed his onward departure for Edinburgh. He arrived at Waverley station ahead of the police tip-off and having several hours ahead before the evening train for London he decided to leave his suitcase in the left luggage office and set out to see the delights of the ancient city. Acting with commendable speed, Detective Superintendent 'Wee Willie' Merrilees and a large posse of men swept through the station, to find that their man had gone. But they did check the left luggage office, easily identifying the suitcase still damp and crusted with sand and salt. Within it was a complete radio transmitter. Merrilees quickly donned a porter's uniform and directed a comprehensive stake-out of the station, using men in plain clothes and borrowing the services of some WRVS ladies to make up couples to blend in more naturally. At last Walti returned to reclaim his suitcase, and in the act of so doing was gripped at the collar by the friendly porter, Merilees, soon assisted by three others. As they attempted to relieve him of his briefcase Walti protested that he was a Swiss citizen. When this didn't have the desired effect he pulled a flick knife on them, a futile gesture as he was quickly overpowered. In the briefcase and the suitcase was a complete inventory of espionage equipment, including a loaded Mauser pistol. The efficiency of the railwaymen, the police and of Detective Superintendent Merrilees was in stark contrast to that of the bungling trio.

Against all prevailing security protocol, the *Daily Herald* got hold of the story and published it on the front page of the edition of 2 October 1940, with a headline 'Armed Spy Caught at Station', albeit that the identifying details had been hidden. In a brief but dramatic description the police 'found him at the railway station a few moments before the London train was due to leave. Hundreds of people on the platform were unaware that the first Nazi spy to be caught in Scotland since war was declared had been trapped'. The reporter got his scoop, but the editor would have got it in the neck for such a flagrant breach of the rules.

Leaving Drukke and Walti aside, it's astounding how badly this incursion was carried out, particularly as Vera Schalburg turned out to have quite a record as a spy; she could be described as being a professional. Of Russian birth, she had been raised in Denmark where she trained to be a ballet dancer, moving to Brussels and Paris where she became a member of the risqué dance troop, the Folies Bergère. At the age of only 18, in 1930 she married a down-at-heel Russian emigré, Count Sergei Ignatieff. He was a spy for the 'white' Russians with a penchant for drug dealing, no doubt a bad influence. By the mid-1930s she had thrown her lot in with the Abwehr, becoming the mistress of a senior officer, Hilmar Dierks. It is believed that she was sent to London in 1938 to seek out British upper-class people who were sympathetic to Nazism. Vera, as a multilingual Countess, was quite capable of moving in such high circles with ease. When she was arrested, she had no less than three legal passports and three illegal ones. Her list of aliases was impressive – she was born Vera Schalburg (in Siberia), her married name was Ignatieff, she then used Eriksen, Von Stein, Von Wedel, and, most grandly of all, Countess Vera de Cottane de Chalbur. So why, when she was actually the senior spy in command of this operation, was it such a fiasco?

It seems probable that she intended it to fail and to switch sides. When the case came to court in June 1941, it was announced, without explanation, that she would not appear. The other hapless fellows did not help themselves during their trial (even when offered eminent barristers to defend them) and were found guilty of espionage. They received a punishment that today seems shocking; they were hanged at Wandsworth prison in August 1941, the penalty for spying. At least they had the benefit of a trial, unlike the summary justice meted out by the Nazis in Norway. Vera clearly came to an agreement with her captors and gave much information to British intelligence. She agreed to spy on Germans held in internment on the Isle of Man. It was enough to spare her life and at the end of the war she disappeared into obscurity, probably with a new identity. She did have six passports to choose from.

As that winter turned into the spring of 1941 Norway faced up to an unpleasant first anniversary on 9 April, that of the invasion of their country. Like most predatory military regimes, Germany was probably looking forward to a celebration and some goose- stepping parades. What happened next was far from a party.

Chapter 6

Escape and Retribution
(April–July 1941)

A pril Fools' Day 1941 was not forgotten by Norwegians, who used their sharp humour as a weapon to ridicule the occupier. The newspaper *Hamar Stiftstidende* carried a spoof Directive that all men and women must report to have their hair shorn to boost raw materials for the production of felt. The fake Directive was accompanied by a final enforcement order for photo identity cards to be used from that day. There were no short haired girls in the pictures.

The anniversary of the invasion on 9 April 1941 was anticipated by Terboven with a raft of warnings and edicts, including the prohibition of flags, wearing black arm bands, laying wreaths, singing, displaying or wearing of national dress or emblems, gathering or demonstrating. The response of the Norwegian people was to bring everything to a coordinated and peaceful halt at noon on that day. For 30 minutes the whole country observed an absolute silence. It was as if the Ice Front was a nationwide glacier. All work, travel, music, speech or indeed any interaction just stopped. Wherever they were, people stopped, turned their backs on any Germans and stood still. A bus or train would stop and not one person would utter a word. The nation was in mourning on a grand scale. It was simple, effective and it irritated the invaders considerably. Some brave souls did wear arm bands and laid wreaths and they were immediately arrested. The first edition of an underground newspaper *9th April: Must Never be Forgotten* appeared that day. In the evening, Haakon broadcast to his people – the message was 'hold steady'.

Terboven and Quisling had at one time probably hoped to have a grand goose-stepping victory parade on 10 June, but the experience of 9 April indicated that any celebration would be a bad idea. Instead, there was just a total clamp-down. But they could not control packed church attendances at which protests were made and the National Anthem was sung at maximum volume.

In the spring of 1941 two words entered in the Norwegian language, but in completely the opposite meaning to the one intended. The NS party decided to delegate the word *Jøssing* to be used as a derogatory and insulting term for anti-German critics who aspired to an Allied victory. The word derived from the people of Jøssingfjorden who, even before the German invasion, had demonstrated their support of Britain in a naval incident in the fjord. The Norwegian people in their contrary frame of mind embraced the word not as an insult but as a fanfare of their defiance. It became widely used in parallel with the term 'good Norwegians' and it was used in the title of the underground newspapers up and down the country – *Jøssing, Jøssingen, Jøssingtidende, Jøssingposten.*

Vidkun Abraham Lauritz Jonssøn Quisling undoubtedly wanted his name to go down in history as the heroic leader of his people. Instead, his people turned his hated surname from name to noun, with the term 'Quisling' entering an international lexicon to describe someone as a collaborator and traitor of the worst order. The word has long outlived the man himself. It was not the legacy he had dreamed of.

The restrictions and controls on everyday life were accompanied by incrementally punitive food rationing. All foodstuffs which were imported before the invasion were now stopped. The occupying forces had first call on home produced foods, and a large proportion of fish, meat and dairy products were requisitioned for export to Germany. That left little for the Norwegians, particularly in the cities, where queues were omnipresent. Fishing and farming communities fared better as they could at this stage still subsist on home produced food, but later even this was seized and rationed. Norwegians have the highest per capita coffee consumption in the world and it is hard to imagine how it was when the ration reached 10g a week. All sorts of unpalatable substitutes for coffee and other foods were devised. When Norwegian refugees were interrogated and de-briefed on arrival in London, hunger was almost always mentioned as a contributor to leaving. That spring and early summer, the escapes began to gather pace.

Three brothers Mons, Gunnar and Jonas Habbestad with their friend Herman Habbestad were planning to leave the island of Bømlo in their father's fishing boat *Liv*. Their father, Emanuel, was in hospital and was unaware of the plan, probably just as well, as the boat was his livelihood. Mons, the eldest, was just 21, but wise enough to be suspicious when asked to meet another man said to be keen to join them. Being cautious he put the meeting off for a couple of days, whilst the four made urgent preparations for the crossing. On receiving confirmation that the stranger was indeed a Gestapo agent, the four youngsters left in a hurry on 21 April reaching the Shetland Outer Skerries two days later. At the same time, a much smaller boat left Fosnavåg with another five young men. The boat was *Sjøblomsten*, an open boat just 22ft long. They completely overshot the north of Shetland, ran out of fuel and were found drifting near Faroe by a fishing boat which took them all the way back to Aberdeen, where they were landed on 27 April after five uncomfortable and worrying days at sea.

Amongst the boats leaving there was one vessel heading in the opposite direction, the Norwegian destroyer HNoMS *Mansefield*. In an operation called 'Hemisphere' or '*Øksfjordraidet*' it should be described as more of an experiment, rather than a full-scale raid. Almost unknown, it deserves mention because it was an all-Norwegian operation, planned by the Norwegian navy, using a Norwegian ship and landing ten Norwegian SOE commandos. On 8 April, undetected, *Mansefield* entered Økfjorden in Finnmark (near the top of Norway). The commandos completely destroyed the fish-oil factory and the raid was logged as a complete success but it was undermined by tragedy. They had hoped to capture the director of the factory who was a Quisling collaborator. He managed to escape, but in the shoot-out his wife was killed. Sitting in her lap, her young daughter survived. It could be that this accidental tragedy is the reason that this raid received no banner headlines, just scant attention in the newspapers, at a time when the press was looking for something good to say. Later, Norwegians who were not uncritical of such events, remembered the little girl in a book about the tragedy.

With the advent of spring, the weather improved and many of the crossings went without major problems. The unexpected, however, could always arise and anything not bargained for could lead to discovery and great danger. The Nielsen export organisation at Ålesund organised for twelve people to leave on the *Signal* on 13 May. They hadn't got far when they ran hard fast on rocks at Runde and were dangerously exposed. After a few hours they managed to free themselves and once again set off, seemingly without further trouble until the engine stopped and they were drifting without power about 60 miles out from the coast. They were yet again at risk of discovery by German aircraft or patrol boats. Their fortunes changed for the better with the chance arrival of a Norwegian fishing boat, but this was no ordinary fishing boat. *Vita* had been an escape boat herself almost exactly a year earlier during the fighting (8 May 1940) and had become one of the first six boats taken on by the embryonic Shetland Bus operation. She was now on active service and was on the return leg of one of the initial trial runs. The almost million-to-one chance meeting of these two Norwegian boats in the open North Sea and the rescuing of the hapless refugees could be said to be due only to divine intervention.

There were two export groups in the Ålesund district that were independently helping people to escape – the Torsvik Group and the Nielsen Group. It was very dangerous work, as at every turn they were exposed to infiltration and betrayal, as proved to be the case. The Torsvik Group led by a lawyer, Harald Torsvik, worked closely with the Odell Group in Oslo, which sent 'export traffic' up country to Ålesund (about 350 miles) for onward dispatch for Shetland. Odell was an intelligence and radio transmitter unit (run by British SIS), supplying vital information directly to London. It was penetrated by the Sipo in May, and it was only a matter of time before they tipped off their local agent in Ålesund, the infamous Finn Kaas. On 26 May, Torsvik and others (not all) of his group were arrested by the Gestapo. Between the Torsvik and Odell Group there were subsequently five executions, and three men were sentenced to concentration camp.

Three weeks later, on 17 June, Obersturmführer Finck arrived in Ålesund with a list of hostages to take in reprisal for those who had escaped through the district. The police refused to make the arrests and had to be forced to do it under duress by the accompanying soldiers. Finck spent that day rounding up the first fifteen men and the round-up of hostages continued over the following days. On 20 June, a curfew between 21.00 and 05.00 was imposed. On 22 June it was announced that the total of seventy to eighty men, young and some quite elderly, were to be loaded onto a ship and sent to the infamous concentration camp at Grini. There was an immediate uproar as almost the whole municipality turned out into the streets, converging on the route between the police station and the docks. Thousands of people tore down Nazi flags and signs; they sang the National Anthem and chanted anti-Nazi slogans. A human wall was formed at the historic Hellebroa Bridge blocking the route to the ship and the bus was surrounded. The situation began to look very ugly as more German troops arrived. It was the prisoners themselves who defused the situation, urging the crowds to disperse before anyone got hurt. The crowds followed the buses to the waterfront, singing as the prisoners were stowed aboard. The Nazis were very angry, fixing bayonets to chase and disperse the population.

The Nielsen Group were now concerned for their own safety. Clearly local informers had given the Germans the names to go for. The two principal leaders of the group, Svenn Neilsen and Martin Ertresvåg began to plan their own escape, buying a suitable boat from the Ertresvåg family. Neilsen, Ertrevåg and five others boarded and set out on 2 July, but they did not get far. A German *Schnellboot* overtook them and settled across their path – they were caught in the act. One of the group, Marino Nilsson, was released immediately, thereby revealing himself to be a traitor. Kaas and Nilsson had between them betrayed and closed down both the export groups in Ålesund with devastating efficiency. Kaas decided to make himself scarce and enlisted in the Norwegian Legion SS, honing his unpleasantness on the eastern front for three years. He returned to Oslo in 1944 to re-join Sipo in Oslo with the task of infiltrating the burgeoning Milorg organisation, specifically a unit known as 'the Oslo Gang'. He succeeded, causing the deaths of several of the key players. Nilsson was not finished yet. He moved down to Bergen to start again in his treacherous activity.

In peacetime a hijacking can be described as one of the most heinous of crimes with some justification, no matter what the cause being promoted. In wartime, the piracy or hijack of vessels at sea is regarded as a more legitimate activity. But even then, the issues are more complex. Take the case of the icebreaker *Isbjorn* which was employed in keeping open the ice-bound passage between the island of Svalbard (which lies between north Norway and the North Pole) and ports to the south. Svalbard was at that time in German hands and was the source of much needed coal for Norway and the Reich. Her captain no doubt thought he was doing an important task. On the other hand, there were some men amongst the miners on that desolate island who thought they would be better employed joining the free Norwegian forces to fight the Nazis. It cannot have been pleasant being a miner in one of the most remote and cold places on earth. A group of eight of them boarded *Isbjorn* at Longyearbyen on Svalbard on 29 May, requesting a lift to a settlement a short distance down the coast. Once at sea they pulled out handguns and hijacked the ship, much to the annoyance of the captain who against their expectations didn't turn out to be a 'good Norwegian'. He refused to comply with their demand to head for Iceland, the nearest place in Allied hands. It was about 1,500 miles away, at least six days sailing. The miners had no navigational skills, there were no westward charts on board and they had no idea how to go through the ice fields. Joined by two of the crew, they pressed onwards. On the third day the boat ground to a halt. The captain, the engineer and the five other loyal crewmen refused to help unless the hijackers got out of their way and stayed in the aft cabin. It was a trap – as soon as they went in, the door was slammed and locked. The captain turned about and headed back towards Svalbard, notifying the District Governor who in turn summoned police from Tromsø. The eight miners and two crewmen were arrested, taken back to Tromsø and handed over to the Gestapo. Suffice it to say that they suffered 'extreme torture' over the next few weeks. At their first trial at the German Navy court in Tromsø, one of them was sentenced to death and others were given long prison sentences. They were offered remission of sentence if they agreed to join the SS Regiment Nordland, but to a man they all refused. The perceived leniency of the navy court and the obstinacy of the men in refusing the job offer with the SS led to a demand for a re-trial. They were transferred to Oslo and underwent a second trial at which the outcomes were predictably much worse; five of the miners and one of the sailors were sentenced to death and were executed and the rest were sent to a concentration camp. This shocking outcome marked the most northerly escape attempt in the war.

Towards the end of May 1941, a large group of twenty-three refugees assembled on the island of Giske and boarded the boat *Lill*, but they didn't get far as the engine was useless. They asked the skipper of a local fishing boat for a tow to which he agreed but only after he had finished his day's work; they would have to bide their time. They had to cram in below decks in case of observation from the air or from the shore. Only a few could get fresh air at any one time. At last, the other boat finished fishing and gave them a tow to a quiet anchorage on the nearby island of Vigra. Even there they were not safe, as a coastal patrol float plane circled around inquisitively and decided to touch down nearby. Surely they were under scrutiny by the two airmen; had they been betrayed? They kept out of sight and held their breaths for half an hour, when the plane started up and flew away. The pilot had probably been just enjoying a smoke break. Two of the men had gone to find another boat and very quickly came back with *Nordhav*, a much better vessel. The owner's nephew came as skipper. They had no more misadventures and reached Lerwick on 30 May.

Lill meanwhile was to be recycled for another escape and her engine had an overhaul. Two girls, Aud Herfjord and Else Wartdal, were keen to be on board as they wanted to join their boyfriends who had escaped that spring. *Lill* was ready by 24 June when she set out with fourteen on board. Once again, the engine gave trouble, but this time there was no turning back. They hoisted sail, running with the wind all the way across, taking six days; the two girls were reunited with their boyfriends and a double wedding followed.

Whereas the original Vikings navigated by the sun, the stars and dead reckoning, and modern seafarers have the miracle of global satellite positioning, at least the twentieth-century Vikings had the magnetic compass to guide them – or not, as the escape attempt of Paul Kråkenes shows. He and his friend Arthur Byrkenes were of a mind to cross to Shetland and were encouraged to do so by the local schoolmaster Harald Hundevin. They lived in the remote fishing village of Byrkenes (on the mainland opposite Fedje). Hundevin was working for the Årstad in Bergen, and the Gestapo had got scent of his activities. He needed to get away, and wanted to take his girlfriend Olava Einbærholm with him. Kråkenes had a 21ft open motor boat and made some preparations, which included 'swinging the compass', a term which means a procedure for adjusting the instrument. The four travellers set off in early June 1941 from Byrkenes, and like many who did the same they found the experience unpleasant. The young lovers were dreadfully seasick, whilst the two fishermen grappled with the engine which kept failing. They drifted for long periods, and one day turned in to another without seeing land. Kråkenes knew that something was wrong and decided they should turn around and run for home.

Eventually they saw the Utsira lighthouse and headed for that, passing safely by some German fortifications that were under construction. They found a discreet landing place, got the engine repaired and then returned to where they had started out several days before. Kråkenes was mortified by the failure, and then he twigged what had gone wrong. For the journey he had placed a metal barrel of fuel in the middle of the wooden boat. This had completely disrupted the compass operation. Hundevin and his fiancée now thought better of trying to escape and 'went to ground' instead. Kråkenes and Byrknes still wanted to cross over, but on a larger boat – and their opportunity arose later with *Soløy* at the beginning of August. Kråkenes eventually ended up as part of the Shetland Bus crew.

The fishing boat *Ulstein* reached freedom on the Shetland island of Mid Yell on 24 June 1941. No one would have believed that a 21-year-old farmer's son who was amongst the seventeen on board would be given a State Funeral by Norway seventy-eight years later. This was the remarkable Ragnar Leif Ulstein, without whom most of the boats and people in this book would not be remembered. He was born in the island municipality of Ulstein (not far south of Ålesund) and like many of the local young men he yearned to be able to free his country from the yoke of occupation. The group planned an escape and 'borrowed' *Ulstein* for the duration. All did not go well as they hit bad weather and the engine gave trouble. They were blown well of course to the north and had to put in to Vevang (near Kristiansund) for repairs, which took several days before they could continue their crossing. After reaching London, Ulstein soon fell in with Martin Linge and was to become a key member of Kompani Linge. He had a distinguished war record. But there was a price to be paid back at home. His father and uncle, Julius and Matheus Ulstein, were arrested and sent to Grini concentration camp.

After the war, Ulstein's sword was exchanged for his pen, and he became the leading chronicler of everything to do with resistance by Norway against the occupation in its widest context. He compiled the first lists of boats that escaped that form the very basis for this book, keeping adding and revising throughout his long life. He dedicated his life to examining the cost of war in human terms, with the positive message that it must not happen again. Ragnar Ulstein died on 3 December 2019. A full State Funeral at Ålesund was accorded by the Norwegian government, which took place on 13 December. It was attended by Crown Prince Haakon, the Minister of Defence, the heads of all three armed forces and thousands of local people.

Four young men in Stavanger, Kjell Endresen (20), Johannes and Olav Thorsen (22 and 20) and Inge Steensland (18) spent early July planning to make a run over to Britain. With the incautious optimism of youth, they at first intended to row and sail across in a *bindalsfæring* belonging to the Thorsen family. These pretty little boats built in the region of Bindal (near Namsos) are shaped just like miniature Viking ships with the bow and the stern swept upwards. They are good to sail and row around the coast, but they are not ideal for open sea. The four boys were persuaded otherwise and found a 27ft boat with motor and a small cabin, scraping enough together to buy it. It was called *Sjøgut* (Seagull). Olav applied for a job at Sola, the new German airbase, solely for the purpose of relieving the Luftwaffe of some fuel so they had an extra 100 litres on board. Telling anyone who wanted to know that they were going mackerel fishing, they left Stavanger in the late afternoon of 10 July. They reached the tiny islet of Håstein, quite well out into the open sea, to wait for darkness to descend. They found that there was a German guard hut on the island, but it was unoccupied that evening. In their excitement, they decided to mark their leaving with a wanton act of vandalism towards the enemy – they turned the place upside down. Although they had thought of setting it on fire, common sense intervened – the beacon would draw unwelcome attention.

A cover of rain came in overnight as they left the coast and made good progress until dawn, when they were buzzed by a German patrol plane. Pretending to be fishing, they turned and headed back until the plane lost interest. After that it was only the engine that caused concern, as on so many of these crossings. After three days they ended up in Sandend Bay, just ten miles east of Buckie. All four young men were soon recruited by Martin Linge. Kjell Endresen became one of the most cunning, evasive and long serving SOE radio agents, operating in Norway under the codeword *Blåmann* (Blue Man). The other three left Kompani Linge after the upset of the Måløy raid (see Chapter 12) and transferred to the air force.

Such was the worry about reprisals against his family if he made an escape attempt, that Arne Olsen Melkevik decided to adopt a false name – he became Arne Nipen for the rest of the war. He was a crewman on the fishing boat *Ingeborg*, working out of Televåg (to the south west of Bergen) and told his skipper he wanted to leave on another boat. The skipper abruptly blocked the move, but Nipen was not to be put off. Resenting the skipper's attitude, he and three friends decided to 'borrow' *Ingeborg* to make an attempt. As a crewman Nipen didn't know much about navigation and his brother gave him a crash course in reading a compass and following a bearing. The designated departure evening of 21 July came, and Nipen's friends failed to show up. Furious, he set out find them, and find them he did, much the worse for wear and in the arms of their girlfriends at a dance. Yes, they wanted to come, and yes, they wanted the girls to come (the girls were keen); but no, Nipen would not entertain the idea of women on board, an ancient superstition of bad luck amongst sailors. The four friends left later that night, and as the boys sobered up Nipen kept a steady course good enough to arrive off Lerwick in just 24 hours.

Having met and been charmed by Martin Linge, Arne 'Nipen' signed up for SOE training, but very soon transferred to Shetland, one of the early recruits for the Bus service. He had a very impressive war service, undertaking fifty-nine missions back to Norway, and being decorated with St Olav's Medal with three Oak Crosses. Probably his greatest award, however, was to be married to Scalloway girl Barbara

Christie. In the years after the war, and after his death, Barbara, still living in Norway, became a de facto goodwill ambassador between Shetland and Norway. It was Barbara who was invited to unveil the Shetland Bus Memorial in Scalloway in 2003.

A resistance cell in Oslo had a collection of ten people being hunted by the Gestapo, desperate to get away. Such cells which had previously been somewhat locally ad-hoc had by now been gathered under the umbrella of Milorg which coordinated the overall resistance movement. The central leadership of Milorg was located in Oslo, and the organisation became formally recognised by the government in London. In due course, it became integrated with SOE and SIS, although there were early dysfunctions in these arrangements. By the end of the war, the membership numbered about 50,000, a quarter of whom were women. This Oslo group had an 'export route' via Smola, an island municipality offshore from Kristiansund some 350 miles and several days to the north. It also had a radio connection with London, and able to make an arrangement for a boat from the Shetland Bus to pick up ten fugitives on 26 July. This seems to be the first time that a pick-up by the Bus was requested. If not successful on this occasion, it was formative in that the pick up of refugees later became a routine of the Bus service.

The ten from Oslo duly turned up at the rendezvous at Smola, but the Shetland vessel did not show up that day or on 27th or 28th. This must have been a very anxious time for the waiting passengers, so they purchased a 33ft boat to continue their escape under their own steam. They set off on 30 July and on the following day they were spotted by a German patrol plane which gave them a burst of cannon fire across the bows. They had no option but to turn around for Norway, the plane escorting them for the next two hours; it meant business. It departed for its base, probably to refuel, and returned to maintain contact. The almost certain danger now was that a surface patrol ship would intercept them or that an ugly reception committee would be waiting for them on the coast. Twilight descended and it seems that the air surveillance was lost overnight. With tremendous luck they made it back undetected to Hustadvika, a remote and wild coastline about 80 miles south of where they had started. Clearly the ten Oslo refugees had experienced too much excitement, as they didn't make another sea attempt. Instead, they decided to keep their feet firmly on land, and made successful escapes eastwards to Sweden.

The Oslo ship-owner Gabriel Smith was at his London offices when the Germans invaded Norway, so he was unable to get back home. A former naval officer, he had founded his own successful family shipping company, Belships. He was ideally positioned to be of service to the Norwegian government when it arrived in London, joining his half-brother, also Gabriel, who was head of Navy Intelligence. Back in Oslo, his 19-year-old son, Gabriel Smith Jr, had been looking forward to joining the family company but the Germans had put a stop to that. Instead, young Gabriel became involved with the resistance in Oslo, and because of this work he was able to get a message through SIS from his uncle Gabriel in London. He learned that his father was ill and was dying. This unsettling news made him determined to make the journey to London. In July, the head of his resistance cell called him in and at the meeting he met up with Sverre Haugbråten, another resistance man who had the Gestapo after him. He had quite a story to tell. Whilst being arrested by the Gestapo, there had been a fracas in which he was injured, enough to be sent to hospital, from whence he had escaped. It was paramount that the two young men, for their different reasons, must get away as soon as possible.

The route by sea was the quickest and surest way of getting Smith back to his father, and this required the long journey up to Ålesund to get a boat. After the Neilsen group betrayals the people in that area were in disarray and not a little jumpy. Smith and Haugbråten were offered for sale an old regatta sailing boat of 20ft length, the *Irene* or *Reeni* as she was known locally. It had no engine and sail was the only option. Neither of the young men had much sailing or navigational experience. They had no choice, so on 27 July 1941 the two sailing novices set out for Shetland some 390 miles away. In heavy seas, they enjoyed good progress over the first three days when joyfully, as the light faded, they spied land ahead. Joy was soon overtaken by despair as a violent wind whipped up, fierce enough to break the mast at the bottom taking the whole rig, sails and stays overboard with it. The tiller was also broken. The dead weight in the water threatened to pull the boat into a capsize. They had the sense to realise that if they simply cut it loose they would be rudderless, without sail and utterly at the mercy of the sea. Tying a rope around their waists they took it in turns to go over the side into the water to sort out the wreckage, cutting and retrieving useful materials. They managed to erect a new mast using the boom, fixed a make-shift sail, spliced on a temporary tiller – and they were under way again. Later, with a following wind, they even managed to fly a small spinnaker sail. This had taken all night and at daybreak they were exhausted. They crawled into sleeping bags and recited the Lord's Prayer.

They awoke to find their prayers answered – the storm had abated, but they had no clue as to where they were. There was nothing they could do but to press on in a westerly direction and that was for another four days. They were found and rescued by a patrol boat and taken into Peterhead on the Aberdeenshire coast. Goodness knows where they had been in the interim, as they had been at sea for eight days – it was now 4 August. After this incredible ordeal it must have been undignified to be taken to the police station, but the Consul from Aberdeen came quickly and smoothed their onward journey to London. Smith was able to be with his father just before he died on 11 August. It is not surprising that both these brave and resourceful men were selected for special operations. Gabriel Smith became a Lieutenant in No Ten Inter-allied Commando and was killed whilst storming a vital island at the mouth of the River Mass on 14 January 1945 – cruelly close to the end of the war. Sverre Haugbråten joined Kompani Linge and was wounded during the Måløy raid in December 1941. Later he survived a sinking by a torpedo attack – but he did at least survive the war.

Leaving on the same day as *Irene* from Ålesund on 27 July 1941 was another small sailing boat, the *Good Hope*, from Arendal on the south coast. Six men from the area were desperate to cross to Britain and set out that evening. If they thought that the name of the boat would bring them luck, they were dreadfully mistaken. The following morning, after they had sailed west for only about 50 miles, they were spotted by a reconnaissance plane. Not long after, a German patrol boat came out from Kristiansand, they were boarded and arrested. Why the plane singled out a sailing boat from the usual licensed coastal fishing boats will never be known. It's possible, even probable, that there had been a tip-off from an informer. Whatever the reason, the outcome was terrible. At a Navy Court Martial in Oslo, five were sentenced to death, four being executed at Håøya Island in March 1942 and one in Berlin the same year. The sixth was sentenced to fifteen years at Sachenhausen concentration camp in Germany, where, in the dreadful conditions, he contracted tuberculosis and died shortly after the war had ended.

Nazi thinking was that brutal treatment, execution and hostage taking would deter others from following suit. At home in Germany a whole nation had been subdued and made compliant by a mixture of ideology, propaganda and state terrorism. The Nazis simply did not understand that such methods did not work in the countries that they had seized by force. In fact, there was an opposite effect. Nazi ideology was rejected, propaganda was ridiculed and terror hardened resistance. Occupied and oppressed nations were prepared to take the risks and make the sacrifice of lives in order to fight back for the freedom of their peoples. The more the Nazis cracked the whip, the more they experienced a reaction. This was certainly true of Norway where the retribution delivered in the summer of 1941 was actually followed by a dramatic increase in westward escapes.

Chapter 7

Summer Days on the Scottish Coast
(July 1941)

Most of the escapes we know about have been recorded from the Norwegian point of view. After the war, Norwegians had incentive to find and record these events, and we have Ragnar Ulstein to thank for forming the bedrock of the information. The circumstances leading up to an escape attempt and the following of extraordinary adventures have been gathered from Norwegian accounts. The families and loved ones of those who headed off into the cruel North Sea had a need to know what happened. The Norwegian nation needed to recognise their contribution.

There is less known at the receiving end, in Scotland and elsewhere – what happened when an escapee turned up on the doorstep. In the great narrative of the war, the arrival of a boatload of unidentifiable potentially dangerous foreigners could be exciting on a local basis. But such landings were subject to press restrictions and a need for secrecy. Mostly, but not always, they faded into ephemera or total obscurity. The following two examples from north east Scotland, which happened in July 1941 can be told in much more intimate detail. This is as a result of my personal involvements locally, and my interactions with the families involved. My entanglements with these two stories were crucial to the evolution of this book. They show how the arrival of Vikings on our shores could have enduring outcomes decades later.

A thick wall haar was extending up and down the north east coast of Scotland. Sometimes when it was approaching from seawards it would have the appearance of giant snow–covered arctic cliffs. It was impenetrable and dangerous for small boats. But this morning, Monday, 28 July 1941, it did not stop teenager George Craig and a gaggle of his friends from scrambling over the foreshore at Old Portlethen. This was the school holidays, and surely the haar would lift later. What happened next that morning George would remember for the rest of his days.

The group thought they could hear voices and climbed toward the sound. There in the murk they could make out a small boat lying up against the Moat Rocks. It was a white boat with a single mast, a furled red sail and small forward shelter or cuddy. Some of the boat was covered in green foliage; why would that be? They could make out four men waving for attention.

'*Hei! Kamerat*!' was called out. Well, that sounded German to the boys – the enemy. Much alarmed, they quickly regained the beach and ran full pelt up the brae to the Coastal Defence Force lookout hut. That day it was manned by 'Mossie' Christie, whose morning cup of tea was rudely interrupted. An army veteran of the First World War, Mossie liked to portray himself to the village children as a fearsome warrior brandishing his ancient Lee Enfield rifle. It was generally suspected that he had no ammunition. He was clad in an ancient army battledress worn with a contradictory navy 'cheese-cutter' peaked hat. The boys urged him to challenge the intruders. When they reached the rocks, the old man knew at once that this boat was not local. For a start, it didn't have a Scottish registration number, it was displaying VA 92 L. Then there was that peculiar awning of branches and greenery. To the old veteran, this was certainly suspicious. Returning to his hut as quickly as possible he alerted his headquarters at Aberdeen, and within an hour, reinforcements started to arrive. The village not had such excitement since the start of the war.

By then the alarm was over. Locals had helped to get the little boat away from the rocks and across the tiny bay to the shingle beach. An older man amongst the four, by the name Samuelsen, had reasonable English and declared that they were in fact Norwegian. They had set out from Farsund in south Norway four days earlier, aiming for

Aberdeen, just about eight miles to the north. They were out of fuel and had drifted down the coast in the haar. He was delighted to find that he was so close to his destination. Everyone could now relax; these were our friends! There were congratulations, much laughter and a great general bonhomie. George said that most of the village had turned out and that it was 'as if there was a carnival on the beach'.

Climbing up to the village the younger Norwegians took the steep direct route, whilst the older Norwegian took the easier but longer path. To the amazement and amusement of all those accompanying him, Samuelsen suddenly burst into song, one well known to all Scots – the *Bonnie Banks of Loch Lomond.* I'll tak the high road and ye'll take the low road, and I'll be in Scotland afore ye...' He may be forgiven for getting the high road and the low roads mixed up.

In the beginning the young escapers had hired the boat for a two week 'summer holiday', and some holiday it was; it had ended up as a village fête on the tiny beach at Old Portlethen. What happened in between was the stuff of a typical North Sea crossing adventure. The story began barely a month before, and lay in the companionship between Carl Berthelsen, aged 25, and his younger friend Kåre Langfeld Jensen, aged 19. Berthelsen's medical student days in Copenhagen had been disrupted by the war and he had returned home to live with his aunts at Lunde, a few kilometres to the west of Mandal, close to the remote family farm of Brattestø. He was working as a country vet's assistant. Jensen was living with his parents in Mandal and was working there as a mechanic. As elsewhere in Norway, young and old were enthused by *Englandsfeber*, and the two began to talk about making their own crossing to join the free Norwegian forces.

In the middle of July, they fell in with an unusual and most would say dangerous recruit, Kåre Kirkvaag aged 22, for he wore an NS badge on the lapel of his police uniform. Kirkvaag was both charismatic and contradictory at the same time. From a well known Oslo family, he had secretly run away from school to sea as a teenager. After returning home, he completed his schooling and gained a pilot's licence. In late

1940, being noted for his right-wing views, he joined the NS. In early 1941 he joined the police and was posted to the Farsund district. He became acquainted with the other two through Jensen's sister Else, who thought he was unstable and untrustworthy; 'now anything could happen' said Else. Could he really be trusted?

Nonetheless Berthelsen and Jensen took Kirkvaag into their confidence and shared their plans. There was a hair's breadth between confidence and betrayal. In the event, it proved to be a shrewd risk. Kirkvaag was able to use his uniform to move freely around the district. In retrospect, it was probable that Kirkvaag was using the cover of his NS and police credentials whilst pursuing his own agenda for adventure and to help his mother country. He remained steadfast to his new found friends.

Mandal, sometimes known as 'The Pearl of the South', was not only an attractive holiday destination, but also a busy fishing port reflected by the three salmon depicted on its coat of arms. It was a centre for the light engineering industry, including the well-known Marna marine engine factory, whose small one-cylinder engines powered so many of the coastal craft. The harbour lay packed with small workboats.

One such craft lay at a mooring available for holiday hire. It was 21ft long, painted white, with a mast but no sail and a small Marna engine. It had a small forward shelter. It belonged to a police constable named Olsen who was known to be a Nazi sympathiser, often renting the little boat to Germans for a holiday. This boat caught the eye of the three escape plotters. After all, where was the crime in stealing it from a Nazi? As one policeman to another, Kirkvaag, with his NS badge, aroused no suspicion as he hired the boat – there may even have been a discount. It was Friday, 17 July and the rental was for just two weeks.

Within hours, the three young men were aboard and under way. Motoring westward for barely an hour they pulled into a remote bay where the Berthelsen family farm was situated. In the ancient wooden farmhouse Brattestø they collected whatever could be of use and spent their last comfortable night for ten days. They were irreversibly committed now. The south coast in that part of Norway is a nautical maze of small islands, Skerries, narrow fjords and tiny inlets. Moving westwards, adverse weather drove them into port at Farsund on Sunday 20th. It had become clear that, although all three of them had a lot of coastal boating knowledge, they really lacked proper seagoing experience necessary to tackle the North Sea.

Through a family friend at Vanse, an introduction was made to a master mariner, Jacob Samuelsen, aged 55. Samuelsen, a married man with a family, was burning with desire to get into the fight against Germany. On the spot he offered to act as their skipper. Such was the secrecy required that he didn't even discuss it with his wife Margrete, simply gathering some things together and leaving a note saying he would be away for some time. No doubt he was also concerned for the welfare of the three young erstwhile fugitives. Under his direction, further preparations were made for the journey over the next few days. A sail was obtained and a wheel fitted. Food and water were stowed. Their vital but small supplies of fuel, much of it 'borrowed', were deemed to be insufficient. Kirkvaag had the audacity to go to the nearby Farsund airbase then under construction, where he charmed some aviation fuel from some of the air crew. All the fuel was decanted into a couple of glass carboys and hidden from sight. Finally, a fake fishery district registration number VA 92 L was applied. At every juncture, the curiosity of strangers had to be diverted by a web of pretence.

At last, on Thursday, 24 July with the weather being favourable, the little boat VA 92 L set out at first light. Two of the four were designated to hide in the cuddy, so that to observers there were just two fishermen working their lines. Passing through the bridge narrows at Farsund, they were momentarily picked up by a German searchlight but appeared to be innocent enough. About ten miles out to sea they were spotted from the air by Messerschmitts patrolling from the new air base. Circling round the boat, they fired a burst of their machine guns to the seaward side, close enough to be a real worry. It was clearly signalling that they must turn back to shore. 'We were chased back to the land by German fighter bombers,' recalled Karl Berthelsen many years later, making rather little of the absolute terror they must have felt. Much alarmed, they scuttled back towards Farsund with a new concern that troops or police would be waiting for them and would soon unmask their plans leading to arrest and more. They dodged past the port and found a small island on which to hide.

As they lay up that day, hoping not to be discovered, they re-appraised their options. The ruse of being fishermen by day had proved to be dangerous. It would be even more dangerous to call off the escape as by now they were up to their necks and sure to be caught. To avoid being spotted from the air or from a patrol boat, it would be better to use the hours of twilight and darkness. At that time of year and at that latitude, the hours of twilight and darkness are only brief, but it would still be a better option. As an additional flourish, they cut some small branches and greenery to camouflage the whiteness and shape of their boat. They set out once again that same night, and this time they cleared to a safe distance from the coast. The full voyage of VA 92 L, destination Aberdeen, distance 400 miles, was on.

The following day was pleasant enough but there could be no relaxation. They had to keep watch in six hour shifts, on the lookout for aircraft, patrol boats and of course for free floating mines detached from their mooring cables. One of these was spotted in time and avoided, a menacing horned sea monster. That night the sea got up and incapacitated Jensen and Kirkvaag with sea sickness for most of the rest of the crossing, so that the burden of all the alternate six-hour watches fell on Samuelsen and Berthelsen. There was an argument about the discovery that there were only two life jackets aboard. This was settled by the wise old skipper Samuelsen, who threw both jackets overboard to even up the chances of survival amongst them all, a typically Norwegian solution. Next, they ran into thick haar and slowed to a halt as the engine failed. Samuelsen raised the sail and Berthelsen then tried for hours to get the old Marna engine going, until his hands were bleeding from turning the flywheel – but it remained unresponsive. The aviation fuel from the airbase was too rich and had overheated the engine. It did restart some hours later after cooling down. Onward through the haar they progressed until on the dark foggy morning of the fourth day they realised that there were nearing land. First there were some insects seen on the water, and then they heard waves breaking on a shoreline. Next, they could actually smell the scent of dry land and finally they heard the giant foghorn of Girdleness known locally as the 'Torra Coo' (Torry Cow). It was called this as the area was named Torry (just south of Aberdeen) and it sounded just like a bellowing cow. Years later, Carl Berthelsen reminisced, 'As we neared the coast we felt (sic) the smell of the heather.' The accuracy of Samuelsen's navigation was astounding considering that his only aid was his old compass and he was effectively blindfolded by the fog. Moving away from the unseen and threatening coast, he allowed the boat to drift down until a window in the haar allowed them to make land at the Moat Rocks.

Their ordeal had ended happily in a cheerful carnival on the beach at Old Portlethen. The village crowd swept the four excited but very hungry Norwegians to the door of a traditional thatched cottage where they were served lashings of bacon and eggs the like of which they had not seen for a long time. Meanwhile, Army Intelligence from Aberdeen and Police from Stonehaven had arrived; they were waiting outside. So, after their breakfast the four were arrested with due ceremony and courtesy; after all, they really could be spies. Everyone climbed into a lorry and nearly the whole population turned out to wave them off. As they went by road, their little boat was towed down the coast to meet them at Stonehaven. There they were locked up in the police gaol, but they were treated kindly, fed well and were able to rest after their long journey. That evening they were let out to go to the pub, though of course accompanied by their gaolers. The nearest one was the Ship Inn, situated on the harbour front from where they would have been able to see their little boat and raise a glass. They were interrogated by military intelligence and by the police. On 30 July, they were interviewed by the Norwegian Consul in Aberdeen. On the following day, they travelled under escort on the train to London to be handed over to the London Reception Centre at Wandsworth.

A lasting memento of the heroic escape of VA 92 L was made by a friendly policeman at the station, who carved the wooden box of the compass that had guided the little boat across the sea. The inscription read –

OVERFARTEN TIL
(the crossing to)
BRITAIN
24 – 7 – 41
J SAMUELSEN
C BERTHELSEN
K L JENSEN
K KIRKVAAG

Seventy-one years later the compass and the boat were to be reunited at the Marine Museum at Lista in south Norway.

Back in Norway, the absence of the escapers was quickly noted. The boat had been intercepted by aircraft on the first attempt and this would have created an alert. Kirkvaag had gone 'absent without leave' from his police duties. Within a few days, enquiries had begun across the whole region and thence to Kirkvaag's family in Oslo. They were mostly conducted by the police, under German scrutiny. All family members and acquaintances were visited, and notices seeking information were posted. The great secrecy of their plans paid dividends, as, in truth, no one had anything to say, and no arrests were made. Only Margrete Samuelsen suffered, and it is not clear why; Jacob had not even told his wife that he was leaving, apart from the note on the table. It may well have been because an agreed coded radio message from London confirming the arrival of the party had been received (after some months' delay) by a contact of Jacob's in the Vanse district. Perhaps this signal was intercepted. Whatever the cause, Margarete was evicted from her house in January 1942 with only her personal belongings. Her daughter Lillemor was unceremoniously thrown out of her hairdressing business. Such was the petty spite of their German oppressors.

So what of the four men, the mariner, the student, the engineer and the policeman who were so keen to be of service to their country? Jacob Samuelsen the master mariner once again returned to sea as a ship's captain and 2 December 1943 found him as master of D/S *Norlom* at anchor off the coast of Italy at Bari. In the infamous Bari Incident, his convoy was attacked and many ships were hit. An American ship carrying a secret cargo of mustard gas as well as ammunition exploded showering the harbour and the surrounding town with gas and toxic liquid. Samuelsen was rescued but died slowly and in great distress a few days later. The harrowing death of Jacob Samuelsen cast a dark shadow on the story of a man who had left his wife and family at home with just a note on the table. He was a man willing to risk everything to look after his young companions in the little boat VA 92 L and to join the fight to free his beloved Norway.

Having proved their initiative and their bravery, Carl Berthelsen, Kåre Jensen and Kåre Kirkvaag were all early recruits selected by the charismatic Martin Linge for Independent Company 1. Kirkvaag was badly injured in a night time parachute jump and had to leave. With his pilot's licence, he was able to transfer in a training role to the Royal Norwegian Air Force in Canada, where he remained during and after the war. Berthelsen and Jensen were rapidly trained in of special operations and returned to Norway just five months later as part of the celebrated Måløy Raid of 27 December 1941. Jensen was later killed in action at Spitzbergen in 1944. Berthelsen was disturbed by the events of the Måløy raid in which Martin Linge was killed and he left the commandos. He also transferred to the air force at the Norwegian ministry of defence in London. In 1942, he married Joan Dudley who he had met in a tearoom at Henley where the new Norwegian commandos were being assembled. Leaving the air force as a Major at the end of the war, he stayed living in England working at the Norwegian Embassy.

A typical small 22ft open boat arrives at Scapa Flow in August 1940 with Axel Wadel at the helm. He and his four companions had crossed 450 miles from Flekkefjord, south Norway. (*Imperial War Museum (A 877)*)

The tiny 18ft *Haabet* carried three men from Oslo in an epic 2,000-mile voyage in September 1940. Continuous storms blew them to-and-fro across the North Sea. After twenty-seven days they were finally rescued in the Thames estuary. (*Nordsjøfartsmuseet, Televåg, Norway*)

Four of six on board the 22ft *Cathinka II*, who crossed 550 miles from Kristiansand in August 1941. They outwitted German observers by switching boats at the last minute. (*Arkivet Center for Peace and Human Rights, Kristiansand, Norway*)

Hugin was typical of the larger fishing cutters from the Norwegian west coast. It carried ten escapers to Shetland in August 1941. (*Nordsjøfartsmuseet, Televåg, Norway*)

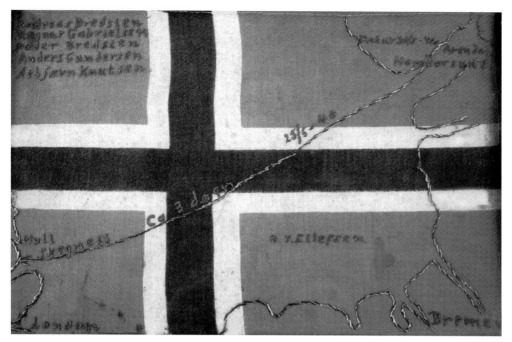

A 21ft boat from Arendal was blown off course and ended up in Skegness in May 1940. After the war their flag was embroidered with the names and route of the five escapers on board as a memento of their gruelling ordeal. (*Kuben/ Aust-Agder Museum, Arendal, Norway*)

The 27ft *Axel* was typical of the middle-sized fishing boats. Gerhard Skorpen and his sweetheart Sina Dragsund, pursued by the Gestapo, feigned their own deaths and fled to Scotland on *Axel* in November 1943. (*Ragnar Torseth: best endeavour*)

Above left: Knut Vidnes was on the run for six weeks from September to October 1940. As a journalist he wrote the most complete account of any escape. Becoming a naval officer, he worked in the Norwegian Information Office in London, supporting the intensive propaganda effort. (*By kind permission of Robin and Jon Vidnes*)

Above right: Knut Vidnes' escape ended with a horrendous crossing in *Stjernen* in October 1940. He commissioned this painting so he would never forget the experience. (*By kind permission of Robin and Jon Vidnes*)

The enigmatic Vera Schalburg was the spy with six passports. She posed as a refugee coming ashore with two others at Portgordon in September 1940. When caught, she changed sides to save herself. (*Little Norway, Buckie, Banff, Scotland*)

A German Räumboote intercepts an escaping fishing boat. The danger and drama are captured in this illustration for *Sphere* magazine, October 1942. *(Illustrated London News/Mary Evans Picture Library)*

Below left: An important message for British teenagers was conveyed in this Puffin storybook by bestselling author Kitty Barne in 1942, accurately covering all the issues involved in an escape across the North Sea. *(Author's collection: reproduced by kind permission of Puffin/ Penguin Books, Random House)*

Below right: Described as 'almost too good', Marius Eriksen was a world-class skier at 14, an escaper at 17 and a Spitfire ace at 19. Along with two friends he stole a boat belonging to the Abwehr in November 1940. This official war portrait is by Eric Henri Kennington, 1942. *(Imperial War Museum (ART LD 2321))*

Above left: Thirteen men from Flekkefjord celebrate arriving at Montrose in September 1941. A remarkable group, they made significant contributions to the war, with six of them not surviving. (*Arkivet Center for Peace and Human Rights, Kristiansand, Norway*)

Above right: Norwegian humour during the occupation. Hitler is seen helping Quisling to keep his balance on the ice. This brazen magazine cover escaped Nazi censorship at first because the Germans did not get the joke, but when the penny dropped, the magazine was shut down and the cartoonist sent to a concentration camp. (*Norsk Uskeblad: Egmont AS, Oslo*)

Overcrowded with forty-two desperate people, *Blia* was lost without trace in a hurricane in November 1941. A 1995 painting by Ants Lepson imagines the last moments. (*Nordsjøfartsmuseet, Televåg, Norway*)

Carl Berthelsen was an erstwhile medical student and later a Kompani Linge commando. With three others he hired a 23ft open boat at Mandal in July 1941 for a 'summer holiday', which lasted for over three eventful years. (*By kind permission Berthelsen family*)

Below left: A tiny 3HP Marna engine that propelled many of the smaller southern boats, such as that of Carl Berthelsen. Usually reliable, they did not like stolen aviation fuel and often overheated, causing many anxious crossings. (*Author's collection*)

Below right: The compass that guided Carl Berthelsen and companions to Scotland in July 1941. While the escapers were held in Stonehaven jail, a policeman carved their names and the escape details on the box as an enduring memento of their daring flight. (*Vest Agder Museet, Norway*)

An MF11 floatplane in Stonehaven harbour, similar to the one stolen from the Germans in Norway which landed at the same place in July 1941. It was the only known winged escape. (*Stonehaven Heritage Society, Kincardineshire, Scotland*)

Below left: Abelone Møgster, the 58-year-old escape organiser who spat defiance at the Gestapo, was arrested in June 1942. She inspired the female prisoners in the German concentration camp, where she became known as the 'Angel of Ravensbrük'. She later survived one of the notorious 'death marches'. (*By kind permission of the Von der Fehr family, Norway*)

Below right: Cinema sent Norwegian propaganda around the world. This blockbuster encapsulated the horrors of occupation, sinister betrayal, a small boat escape and a returning commando raid, as well as a tragic love story. (© *1943, renewed 1970, Columbia Pictures Industries, Inc. All rights reserved. Courtesy of Columbia Pictures*)

Carl Berthelsen never forgot the little boat VA 92 L that had so dramatically but safely carried them to freedom in 1941. Forty years later and still living in England he was surprised when he was contacted by a letter 'out of the blue' sent by a Søren Brandsnes (another escaper) in Norway who told him that he had found the boat that summer at Stonehaven where she was still working as a fishing boat. But there were doubts – could this really be the same boat after so many years? It construed that, after arrival, VA 92 L had been auctioned off by Captain Clark, the Port Captain, had been renamed *Thistle*, and had indeed remained at Stonehaven ever since. It had passed through several hands and was now owned by Robert Ross.

On 18 May 1982, Robert Ross welcomed Carl Berthelsen and his wife Joan at the harbour to be emotionally reunited with the boat, as reported in the local paper. The boat was much cherished and noted to be in fine condition.

Three decades onwards, 28 July 2011, exactly 70 years to the day after the escape, Carl Berthelsen's sons Ole John and Martin and their wives found VA 92 L for the next generation. She was lying at the side of the quayside at the small fishing village of Johnshaven, fifteen miles south of Stonehaven. The interim years had not been kind to the old boat. She left fishing in Stonehaven in the 1980s and came to Johnshaven for a refit and a new engine. When completed, she was lowered by crane into the water and kept on going down all the way to bottom. Too many of the old iron rivets had corroded away beyond redemption. She was lifted out again to the spot where the Berthelsens found her. She fell to the ownership of the Johnshaven Heritage Society, whose chairman Donald Marr launched a public appeal in 2005 to find out more of its history and to raise funds to restore her. Sadly this did not progress. At the end of that decade I had become involved and, by then, had collated most of the known information about the escape and subsequent history of *Thistle*. Following my contacts in Norway and with their advice, a permanent home had been offered at the Marinemuseet at Lista, very near to where she had come from. The timely arrival of the Berthelsen brothers put the seal of approval on these arrangements.

Newspapers and television news had by now latched on to the story. On 7 February 2012 on the quayside at Johnshaven hundreds of villagers, schoolchildren, sea cadets, the Norwegian Consul, the Lord-Lieutenant, and Norwegian naval visitors assembled to wish 'Bon Voyage' to *Thistle*. A large dram of whisky was poured over her bow, a pipe band marched up and down the quayside. These scenes and her final journey back home were closely followed by the media on both sides of the North Sea. A common theme in the commentary was that 'the stolen goods are being returned home'.

VA 92 L or *Thistle* is one of only two of the small boats to have survived and is on display in Norway at *Lista Marinemuseet*, Vest Agder, south Norway.

The publicity around the story of *Thistle* interested 86-year-old Bill Black, a former resident of Stonehaven. He had a story to tell (previously unknown) and wanted help in sorting out some details. The *Dundee Courier* put him in touch with me and I was soon investigating. But let's begin in July 1941 at the beginning of Bill's story as it unfolded. Bill's pin sharp memory has allowed us a unique glimpse of life as it was for a teenager in wartime Scotland when he was at the receiving end of escapers from Norway. The story is so detailed and so unusual you could give it a name of its own name - 'Vikings have Wings'.

War has a habit of exploding into everyday life totally unexpectedly and with devastating consequences, and this is what happened one January day in the small east coast town of Stonehaven. The town comfortably wraps itself in a curve around a picturesque bay at the south end of which lies a small harbour sturdy enough to withstand the full force of the North Sea, and attractive enough to draw artists from far and wide.

Here, on Sunday, 26 January 1941 a local man found a suspicious object on the sandy beach. Two obliging teenagers offered to take it along to the coastguard hut further along the beach, manned by auxiliary coastguard William Findlay Black. Shortly after they delivered the mystery object, the hut disappeared in a large explosion; all three were killed instantly. William Black was 39 years old and he left a widow, Jane, and four young children. No one knows what the suspicious object was, but it must have been a booby trap device known to have been deployed by the Nazis, in the guise of everyday objects. They were distributed by dropping from the air or by releasing them along the coast to wash up as flotsam. Known examples included oil and fuel cans, food tins and even large lumps of coal. Until this point, Stonehaven had been a quiet backwater in the war. This horrific event was a shock to the town, and it was devastating for the Black family.

The eldest son of the family, Bill, then aged 15, suddenly found himself the man of the house and was soon to be the main breadwinner. He had been earning extra money for the family over the last year by helping with salmon fishing in the bay. Now his wage was more important than ever.

Shortly after leaving school that summer, Bill went to the salmon fishing full time, aged just 16. He still hoped to take up an engineering apprenticeship when circumstances changed. The boat owner Gustave de Jonckheere was an interesting character. He was a Belgian who had married the Stonehaven nurse who cared for him when he was badly wounded in the First World War. He was a man who could turn his hand to many crafts. He had built the salmon boat with his own hands, along Flemish lines, elegantly tapered at both ends, 18ft long and with two sets of oars.

A July day that year, 1941, found Gustave and Bill checking their bag nets at slack tide – that point at which a high tide is just turning and the water is at its most tranquil. The sea was calm and there was only a mild breeze. They were only a few hundred yards from the spot where Bill's father had been killed just six months earlier. That proximity carried great poignancy for the teenager. No wonder that for the rest of his life Bill remembered so clearly every detail of that event and every detail of the event which was to follow that day.

Above the gentle sound of water lapping at the boat and the fishing tackle, the pair heard the distant sound of an aircraft out over the sea. They were immediately on alert. There were no commercial or pleasure flights at that time. A plane meant that the war was close at hand. Was it 'one of ours' or was it 'one of theirs'? Everyone – man woman and child – had by now seen the aircraft recognition posters and hoped to be able to identify friend from foe. Their eyes strained; this aircraft was unusual and was not recognised. It was flying very low over the water, and it had two large floats underneath. It became apparent that it was coming absolutely straight at them. It was not at all clear what was intended. Was it going to touch down? Was it going to strafe them? Was it aiming to run them down? The two readied themselves to jump overboard, but they held their nerve as the plane settled down on the water about 300 yards away.

Initially they felt some relief, but then the roaring aircraft with its huge propeller and its deafening noise continued to run straight at them! For a second time they again prepared to jump ship, but within yards the pilot cut the engines and the strange float plane drifted up near the small boat. Bill recalled that a 'dramatic silence' fell over the bay. One moment seemed to be their last, and the next bought incredible relief. The deafening roar of the engine was replaced by the gentle sloshing of water on its floats.

Now there was a chance to look over this floatplane. They still didn't know if it was friend or foe. It was a single engine biplane with two large floats and two open cockpits, both of which were occupied. It seemed to be two or three times the size of their tiny fishing boat. It was a patchy grey colour and where there should be recognition markings these had been painted over with a dirty orangey paint, possibly marine anti-fouling paint. There did not appear to be any armament with machine guns or bombs. The plane itself was in very bad condition with peeling paint and rust. 'A right old string bag,' said Bill. 'We were amazed it had been able to get airborne at all'.

By now the pilot had climbed out of the forward cockpit and scrambled downwards to the nearside float. He was not armed, and he called out a cheerful greeting in a language that sounded like German to Bill, once again on alert. Cautiously the two boatmen rowed closer to get alongside the nearside float. The second crewman followed down onto the float. He also was not armed; that was a relief. The two were wearing nondescript dirty old working overalls showing no military or other insignia. They appeared to be very young, in their early twenties, and seemed to be excited and friendly. Gustave relaxed and started conversing in some sort of mutual language with florid hand gestures, and an occasional English word thrown in. Turning to Bill, he said, 'They're Norwegians, not Germans! They just simply stole this plane from right under the noses of the Nazis over there and flew it straight over here!' The language was most probably German, as that is the most likely to be understood both by Norwegians and also by a Flemish speaker. After about five minutes, Gustave was reassured enough to throw a line across to the airmen, who pulled over and clambered into their little boat.

The two young Norwegians excitedly continued to chatter with Gustave. He must have gleaned a great deal of information about their dramatic escape – their names, where they had stolen the plane and the fuel from, the hazards they encountered. Bill understood not a word, and Gustave refused to reveal anything he had learned. He never raised the subject again that summer or for the rest of the war. The old war veteran understood the need for absolute secrecy in such circumstances in the middle of a war. He probably feared that young Bill might share too much with his teenage friends.

With the line attached, Gustave thought that they would try to tow the plane back into the harbour. The man and the boy manned the two sets of oars and bent themselves to the task. This wasn't going to work, however, as a fresh breeze had arisen from the south. The much larger plane picked up more of the wind and began to pull the 18ft boat backwards. At the harbour, two boys, George Leiper and his cousin William Pirie, had been 'messing about in boats' and had rowed out to investigate the noise and see the drama unfold. Realising that the attempted towing of the plane was not going well, they returned to find George's father and his uncle who had a fishing yawl which had a motor fitted. The two older men set out of the harbour and took the plane under tow, bringing it round the harbour breakwater and into a safe mooring.

Out in the bay, Gustave and Bill and rowed in to the beach with the two Norwegians and dragged their boat up the sand in its usual place. A waiting crowd of onlookers surged around them. Were they Germans? Were they spies? Where had they come from? Gustave, the old soldier, knew better than to give any information to anyone. He ordered Bill to say nothing and told the assemblage to keep back at a distance. In due course, the police arrived and moved the crowd well away. Without further ado, right there on the beach, Gustave and Bill were separated for questioning by a senior police officer. Gustave had obviously much more to say, but Bill was not allowed to hear that conversation. At the end of their grilling, they were together given stern warnings by the officer to not discuss the incident with anyone at all, on pain of committing an offence. Bill was made aware that by talking about this escape he could cause the Norwegians' families at home to be arrested by the Nazis, perhaps even executed. At this point the teenager began to realise the full significance of the daring flight of the two young men, scarcely older than himself, leaving behind everyone and everything they loved. Taking huge risks, they were obviously deeply committed to joining the free Norwegian forces. Who were they? Where had they come from? How did they do it? He yearned to know and, much later on, after the war, he tried to find them.

The two Norwegians were formally arrested by the police, as was the order of the day – after all, they could be spies, though Bill doubted this. Instead of being taken straight to the police station in the High Street, first they were taken a little further, down to the harbourside. The kindly-disposed bobbies took them into the Ship Inn, still in their grubby overalls. There, the publican, George Emslie, dispensed pints of beer and refreshments to the hungry and thirsty young men. They sat at a window together with their prospective jailers looking out over the harbour as the float plane that had delivered them from the clutch of the Nazis was being securely moored.

For Bill Black this was not the end, far from it. Whereas he kept to the order to keep the story secret for the rest of the war, his curiosity did not wane with the years. He became determined to try to find out the names of the two young Norwegian aviators, to meet them and learn more about their daring theft and escape. In the years after the war, he made several unsuccessful attempts to find out more through official channels. Later, he made two trips to Norway to try to find out the full story, but he drew a blank. It seemed that the Norwegian authorities simply did not know about this escape.

At every turn Bill ran into a problem – that everyone in the war at Stonehaven remembered the arrival of a similar float plane the year before, on 25 April 1940. The plane was a fully operational MF11 and had lost contact with its squadron during the early fighting. Low on fuel, it had touched down at Stonehaven as a 'bird of passage'. People were inclined to think that Bill was remembering this earlier plane and had become muddled, a considerable irritation, as he was so clear thinking. Fortunately, I was able to prove conclusively that Bill's story was valid (with some living witnesses). That was a considerable relief indeed for the 86–year–old, but so many years had passed that it was impossible to go further. The names and further details of the two brave young Norwegian aviators could not be found, nor was it possible to find any record of the theft of the plane. Bill Black had, nonetheless, identified the only known example of 'Winged Vikings', and he had demonstrated how such wartime incidents could have a life–long impact on a teenage boy.

Chapter 8

Fever Pitch
(August 1941)

June and July were quiet months in the scheme of things. A look at the numbers shows that in June just eight boats crossed (with seventy-nine people), and in July only sixteen boats sailed (with seventy people). The boats leaving in July were very small ones, carrying only four to five refugees each. It's likely that Gestapo and police successes at closing export groups and the newly exercised policy of arresting family members as hostages did for a while dampen the enthusiasm to risk a crossing. Another factor was that in the summer months, daylight hours are very long at these latitudes and so opportunities of setting out under cover of darkness are restricted and the chances of being spotted from the air or sea were much higher.

But nothing could hold back the '*Englandsfeber*' that had been incubating and which suddenly broke out, reaching its peak over the next three months. In August, 46 boats left (with 484 people), September 45 boats (with 722 people) and October 25 boats (with 421 people), which shows around a ten-fold increase in numbers. The boats being used changed to larger deep sea fishing cutters that could carry 10-15 passengers each, sometimes more.

Looking for causes behind this extraordinary increase in escapes, the only major disruption inflicted by the Nazis that summer was the final enforcement of the confiscation of radio sets, with accompanying threats. Nazis loved to keep records and statistics and a total of 538,000 radios were taken that spring and summer. In a country sparsely populated over a vast land mass, the loss of their radios was a considerable blow. It led to an explosion of new underground newspaper titles, more openly bringing news from London, with calls to arms from Norwegian Command. This growth in the underground press brought with it increased Nazi persecution. Otherwise, it was more of the same medicine – removal or arrests of teachers, academics, judges, local politicians, even clergymen, with replacement by NS stooges. The rationing screw was turning, particularly with dairy produce, and it was milk that precipitated the serious 'Milk Strike' that followed in September.

It is central to Norwegian culture to go into the mountains and islands to forage for wild fruits and berries. Even this was now controlled by regulation and by permit. The reality of this is illustrated in a small story about a group of around a dozen youngsters who in the summer holidays left Oslo for the mountains by train, to tramp their families' favourite harvesting grounds. After a day's toil, their baskets were full and it was time to take the train home. The exit barrier was not manned by ticket collectors but by a row of Gestapo men. They confiscated every last berry, along with the baskets. That sort of memory and the resentment dwells long in the mind of a war-time child.

Three young friends, Edvard Rieber-Mohn, Per Hysing-Dhal and Louis Pettersen were eager to get from Bergen to Britain. Edvard's father was head of Milorg in Bergen and asked the Årstad-Brun export group for help in getting them away. They were told to make their own way to Værlandet (an island about halfway between Bergen and Ålesund) to wait for others to arrive from Bergen. The wait extended for three long weeks, during which time the locals looked after them. More and more people arrived until there were twenty-eight in total (including six women) at the beginning of August. The little *Soløy* was a half-deck open boat only 27ft long and was really far too small for so many passengers. Before departure, the boat owner, the owner of a chandler's business, Sverre Brosvik, addressed those about to go with a pronouncement which later became well known. 'Those who do not dare to travel across the sea with *Soløy* are not worthy to wear the king's clothes.'

The passengers later wryly referred to his homily as '*Bergspreika*' (Sermon on the Mount). Brosvik did not go with his boat as he was still much involved with organising the escapes. His own departure followed all too soon, just three weeks later. Somehow all twenty-eight squeezed on board, and it is thought that this was the most heavily laden boat of its size to attempt the crossing. The passengers referred to the experience as being like 'herrings in a barrel.' They set out on 2 August arriving at Baltasound the following day. *Soløy* and the passengers were taken down to Lerwick for processing, where the sea had the last word on the matter as the little boat had in effect buckled under its payload, the rivets had sprung and she sank at her mooring on 5 August. It was a mercy that this had not happened during the voyage. *Soløy* had brought an important cargo with her – a fine fresh salmon for King Haakon, which apparently was flown to London. The shipment must have been described as a 'training flight', no questions asked. Of the three friends who started out at the beginning, Rieber-Mohn and Hysing-Dhal became pilots and supported SOE operations in Norway and in Holland. Pettersen was recruited into Kompani Linge. All three had outstanding war records and were highly decorated.

An unexpected opportunity presented itself to Alfred Langøy who was out rowing in his boat near the small island of Rongevær (near Fedje) – and he seized it. It was 12 August 1941 when he came across a 24ft motorboat, *Loyal*, on which there were four young men of his own age. They had set out from Fedje a few hours earlier. They exchanged pleasantries, and when he found out that they were on their way to Shetland, he asked to join them. In that second his destiny changed as he stepped over and into the larger boat and off they went. He took nothing more than the clothes he was wearing. After a couple of days, the fuel ran out. They were nowhere near land and what was more, they had no sail. They were, however, resourceful. They had taken four blankets with them, and they stitched them together with fish hooks and fishing line, hoisting the makeshift sail onto the mast. Another day or two of intermittent wind and calm found them drifting aimlessly not knowing where they were. Night came, and out of the darkness a ship appeared, then another and then many more. They were in the middle of a convoy moving up the Scottish coast. An escort vessel soon picked them up, taking them into the port of Leith, Edinburgh, on the morning of 17 August. The impulsive Alfred Langøy was ideal material for the Shetland Bus service, which he duly joined.

Another impetuous man was Ole Sæverud from the island of Bomlo (between Bergen and Stavanger). He had been in the Norwegian navy during the fighting and had returned to working on coastal ships, under the control of the Nazis. In early August, he had observed that several groups of strangers were arriving on the island from different places on that coastline, and he rightly supposed that they were planning an escape. Some of those arriving had already been through a considerable ordeal. They had bought a boat in Stavanger and had crossed to near Shetland (300 miles), when engine failure caused them to drift all the way back to Norway. Sure enough, on 13 August he observed them emerging from safe houses and other hiding places and climbing aboard a boat called *Svanen*. He counted and saw that there were no less than thirty of them. As *Svanen* was pulling away he mused that if they were so keen to get away, shouldn't he join them? On the spur of that moment, he asked his brother, Martin, to row him out to *Svanen*. They could hardly turn him away and they didn't. His only luggage was a spare pair of socks.

On the south coast in the beautiful coastal city of Kristiansand (formally laid out as a model city in 1641 by King Kristian IV) Edvard Tallaksen gathered together a group of five friends as would-be escapers. They scraped the money together to buy an old pilot boat, but as they were making their careful preparations, they realised that they were being watched by the Germans. In a clever move they lent the boat to some other youths for a holiday trip – provided they headed eastwards. The ruse worked and the observers turned their eyes in the wrong direction. But staying around wasn't an option as they could still be under surveillance and at risk. When he heard of their predicament, a retired army officer, Lieutenant Colonel Keim, donated them another boat – the much smaller open 22ft *Cathinka,* in which they made a quick getaway on 16 August. They made good progress over three days but went a bit off course, landing at Eyemouth in Berwickshire on 19 August. The *Berwickshire News and General Advertiser* of 26 August gives a charming insight as to the arrival of these young men. Within sight of land they had run out of fuel and were drifting when they were picked up by an Eyemouth fishing boat which brought them into port in the middle of a fish market. An eager crowd surrounded the seven Norwegians, keen to know all about them. Four of them were English speakers and were able to give preliminary information to the coastguards. 'Asked why they had tried to reach these shores the men were emphatic in their expressions of hatred against the Germans and added that the reason for their action was to be able to assist the fight for freedom.' A more pressing question for the young men was – were they hungry? A fishwife in the crowd cheekily called out, 'Have you brought your ration books?' to much amusement. The crowd led them to the door of a Miss Robertson where they settled down to a substantial meal. Admiringly, the reporter observed, 'Clad in yellow oilskins or navy woollen sea jerseys…all the men are tall and of fine physique and seemed only too anxious to get the opportunity of opposing the Germans.'

Among this boatload of fine young men, two of them went on to join Kompani Linge and to be awarded Norway's highest war decorations. Edvard Tallatsen received the War Cross with Sword and the British Military Cross with Bar and Birger Fjelstad the War Cross with Sword. They both had outstanding wartime exploits. Tallatsen, injured in a shoot-out in Oslo 1944 took his own life rather than betray his Norwegian countrymen. The little *Cathinka* was the bearer of some truly impressive young men.

You would have thought that Søren Brandsnes, aged 20, had enough adventures for a while. A merchant seaman, he was on the Norwegian ship the *Polycarp*, in an Atlantic convoy north west of the Azores, when they were intercepted by the German battleships *Scharnhorst* and *Gneisenau* on 15 March 1941. After the sinking of one of the ships the rest submitted and were taken as prizes, and that meant that all the Norwegian crewmen from the convoy became prisoners of war. They duly ended up in a huge prison camp for merchant mariners near Bremen, Marlag und Milag Nord. Surprisingly, 800 of these Norwegians were sent back to Olso in early May 1941, in a joint NS-German propaganda gesture designed to demonstrate a 'New Norway', welcoming back its citizens – no hard feelings. The gaunt prisoners were even treated to a special feast of roast pork, with photographers and the press relishing the event. But Brandsnes harboured no goodwill at all towards the Nazis and began to plan an escape to get back to Britain to re-join the war effort. He used his savings to buy a 20ft open motorboat. It was not in good order, so he recruited two friends to help repair and strengthen it for a North Sea crossing. When done, with patriotic enthusiasm they called the boat *Dronning Maud* (Queen Maud, King Haakon's late wife). They slipped away from near the Lindesnes Lighthouse on the southernmost tip of Norway on 17 August.

Like many of the smallest inshore open boats, *Dronning Maud* didn't like being out in the open sea where the stresses of the big swells and steep waves sprung the planking apart. Many, if not most, of the inshore vessels were held together with iron rivets and towards the end of their working life they were corroded to the point at which the open North Sea would break them apart. The three men rotated in three shifts, one steering, one bailing non-stop and one resting. At least the small one cylinder hot-bulb engine kept going, and after 58 hours they were taken onboard a coastal minesweeper and into Aberdeen. With its Norwegian flag proudly flying, *Dronning Maud* was tied up, half full of water, going quickly to the bottom. Søren Brandnes never forgot that little boat, hoping that it might have been saved and preserved in some way. In a demonstration of a Norwegian's attachment to his boat, exactly forty years later he returned to Aberdeen in 1981 to try to find out if it had been saved. Whilst making enquiries, he followed a lead to take a look at Stonehaven, just down the coast. There he was introduced to the surviving *Thistle*, (formerly VA 92 L), the beautifully maintained fishing boat. It was obviously and disappointingly not *Dronning Maud* (though the two were very similar). Brandsnes then made an effort to track down Carl Berthelsen (then working at the Norwegian Embassy in London) and it was he who alerted Berthelsen that VA 92 L was still extant and in use.

Kåre Iversen took to a seagoing life from the age of fifteen when he left school in 1933. 'I was brought up, you might say, with my feet and my head mostly in the sea,' he later remarked in his book *Shetland Bus Man*, (Shetland Times Press, 2004). His father Rudolf was a shipping pilot of the waters of Namsenfjorden leading 32 miles inland to the important northern city of Namsos. Iversen's first three years were spent on the pilot boat, learning from his father. Needing to spread his wings and earn better money, he became a peripatetic crewman fishing for salmon in the summer months and herring, halibut or cod further north in the winter. After the occupation he continued with the fishing and as he went up and down the coast, he started to make notes of German gun emplacements, fortifications and other constructions that he thought might be useful to the Allies. He would need to get across to deliver his charts and observations. In his own words after the war he said, 'I wanted to inflict as much harm as possible on the Germans and the Quislings. They came into our land like scoundrels. That was my motivation.'

In the spring of 1941, Iversen joined his father for the salmon season in their boat, the 42ft *Villa II*, in which he had a third share. In August they then gave the boat a thorough overhaul on the slipway – with a view to the long voyage that Iversen knew was ahead. He knew what he wanted to do but he didn't share his plan with his father. The time came for him to make his break for freedom with two others, Thorleif Grong (formerly a policeman) and Brynjar Hammer (formerly a sergeant in the King's Guard regiment) who were eager to come along. At the last minute, a young Swede calling himself Kåre Anker appeared, seemingly very anxious to join the fight against fascism. Something of an outsider, he was a 'strange sort of stranger', but in spite of these misgivings they decided to give him his opportunity. These three had never been to sea and 23-year-old Iversen was very much in charge, overseeing careful preparations. They slipped away from Namsos in the late evening of 19 August 1941, with over 700 miles of open and potentially hostile North Sea ahead.

On the third day they came under attack by a German flying boat. There were no warning shots across the bow; this plane was in for the kill. It flew round in circles coming in for bursts of machine gun fire over about 20 minutes, at the end of which it must have been low on ammunition. The refugees hid from view, two in the forward cabin and two in the engine room. The plane made an attempt to land near them, probably to check if anyone was still alive, but the sea was too rough, and it decided to leave them, probably thinking that all were dead anyway, or that the boat would sink from all the bullet holes. With a wooden boat like *Villa II*, the bullets would have gone right through. Amazingly, all four men were untouched, but *Villa* was extensively damaged. The wheelhouse was riddled with bullet holes, and there were holes along the waterline letting in water like a sieve. Most of the bullets had gone harmlessly through the sails, which were in shreds, but they could manage without them as the engine was surprisingly still running. They managed to plug the leaks with sacking coated in grease, after which they pulled themselves together and restarted their journey which went well enough apart from some remediable engine problems. On the fifth day, at dawn, the sea flattened and was full of seaweed, signs that they were near land. The 'strange' Swede, Anker, who had not been at all helpful on the voyage, now produced a bundle of English pound notes which he offered to the first man to spy land. This fell to Iversen who was standing on the roof of the wheelhouse, but the inducement was forgotten about in the excitement of finding a landing spot. They came ashore on the island of Fetlar, Shetland and were treated to a wonderful breakfast by the nearest farming family.

Even on that remote island there were uniformed and armed Home Guard soldiers who turned up with instructions to keep an eye on them and confine them to their boat whilst waiting for the escort vessel to take them to Lerwick. This didn't turn up for two days, by which time they were impatient to move on. On the journey down to Lerwick, the Swede appeared with the bundle of notes in a tin can, looking for some old nuts and bolts to weigh it down. Any hope of Iversen claiming the prize vanished as the can was thrown overboard. The Swede said 'that's forty forged English pounds', and offered no explanation as to how they were in his possession. Clearly, he didn't want them to be discovered when they landed. At Lerwick, where their papers were examined, the Norwegians were hardly surprised that Anker was addressed by a different name – Gustav Warholm. Their instincts were correct; the man was an impostor, probably a spy. He was spirited away, and later they learned that he was on the wanted list by Milorg back in Norway for working for German intelligence. Unfortunately, the taint of Warholm's arrival on *Villa II* rubbed off on Iversen, Grong and Hammer in case they had colluded in it. This meant that the boat was thoroughly 'turned over' and they endured a more prolonged interrogation than usual. They were detained at the reception camp for an extra ten days.

Kåre Iversen received training by Kompani Linge before returning to Shetland to join the Shetland Bus. He became one of the longest surviving members of the Bus, going on fifty-seven missions. He married a Scalloway girl, Christine Slater, in 1944 and stayed on in Shetland after the war. The well-known couple raised three daughters and, as the years went by, they became enduring custodians of the memories of the *Shetlandsgjengen*.

'*Omnia vincit amor: et nos cedamus amori*' ('Love conquers all; let us, too, yield to love') –Virgil's words could well apply to student teacher Klara Værøyvik. She yielded to her love for the fisherman Per Nybø in the face of opposition from her family and the dangers of crossing the North Sea in war time. Nybø was determined to join the war effort and Værøyvik was determined to stay at his side. It was 23 August 1941, and the pair was among thirteen men and six women climbing aboard the fishing boat *Solveig* on the island of Værlandet (mid-way between Bergen and Ålesund). Værøyvik's younger brother Trygve decided to come along too. Their father was on the quayside trying to persuade them not to go. Also boarding was Sverre Brosvik (he of the 'Sermon on the Mount' speech), his wife Matilde and son. Three weeks after waving off his own boat *Søløy*, the Gestapo had found out and were at his heels. His brother was the owner and skipper of *Solveig* and organised the evacuation in such haste that Brosvik's two daughters, who were away on holiday at the time, had to be left behind. Many islanders came to wave goodbye to the departing refugees. They wouldn't see them again for three and a half years.

The crossing was marked only by dreadful sea sickness and *Solveig* arrived at Lerwick on 25 August. Klara Værøyvik married Per Nybø in 1943 and they duly had five children. She completed her teacher training and was a founder of the Norwegian boarding school at Drumtochty Castle, Kincardinershire. Her brother joined the navy and tragically died on the very last day of the war, 7 May 1945, when his minesweeper was sunk in the English Channel by a U-boat. The sinking took place just two hours before the formal ceasefire. Sverre Brosvik became Norwegian Consul at Buckie from May 1943 until the end of the war, and he and his wife became well known and respected in the town. Almost unbelievably, he and Matilde spent the whole time until the end of the war not knowing what had happened to the two daughters they had to leave behind during their sudden escape. One can imagine the anxiety they carried for over three years, but in the end, they were relieved to find that the two girls had come through safe and well.

The port of Lerwick was overwhelmed with escapers towards the end of August, and there was a need to move some of them down to the mainland to relieve the pressure. The ferry service to Aberdeen was full to capacity, so the Norwegian Consulate asked the boat owners for help. Would they move some refugees down to Buckie on the Moray coast (a further distance of perhaps 200 miles)? Three boat skippers took on the task. The boats were *Villa II* (arrived with four on 24 August), *Solveig* (arrived with twenty on 25 August) and *Klippen* (arrived with 13 on 26 August). These boats had brought 37 people over, and now they were being asked to take 101 – nearly three times as many. No one demurred, and everyone crowded aboard in high spirits. The little convoy set out at 6.00 pm on 27 August, making slow progress overnight, as *Villa* had to give *Solveig* a tow several times because of engine troubles. *Klippen* disappeared into the dark. The following evening the *Villa* and *Solveig* rafted together and anchored on the north side of the Moray Firth. Some guitars appeared along with an accordion and in no time a *cèilidh* was under way, the six girls from *Solveig* being danced off their feet for much of the night. Next morning, they tied up at Buckie and were joined at last by *Klippen* which had got lost and taken a 'long route'. All 101 Norwegians were served an excellent meal in the Town Hall, following which the accordion and guitars had another outing. Next stop was Aberdeen by rail, an overnight stay and then on to the London train. There were so many of them that a carriage had been reserved, marked in large letters 'Refugees from Norway'. They were refugees from small remote island communities, and the next stop was the great metropolis.

The flight log of a Dornier DO18 flying boat discovered after the war tells us what happened to the handsome new 60ft fishing cutter *Hod*, that set out from Ulsteinvik (near Ålesund) on 25 August 1941. There were a number of groups in the area desperate to get away and the boat had been cut from its moorings at midnight by a taxi load of strangers. They quickly picked up about twenty fugitives emerging from their dark hiding places and set out. Later, in broad daylight they were spotted by the Dornier, a rather cumbersome flying boat mostly used for coastal patrolling. Its armaments were light – two light machineguns and two 50kg bombs under the starboard wing. It circled and fired across the bows – but this was ignored. The pilot decided to try a bomb run. He had only two available, and the chances of a hit were actually very low. *Hod*, however, received a direct hit and was blown to smithereens. The terrible fate of the refugees wasn't known for some time, until the body of a young woman (identified as coming from Oslo) and a wooden nameplate bearing the name *Hod* were recovered. Embedded in the wood were pieces of shrapnel that allowed the police at Ålesund to conclude that a bomb explosion was likely. Confirmation didn't come until after the war when the flight log was revealed. This was a salutary example of the risks taken in attempting to escape the clutches of Nazi ideology.

Happily, most of the crossings during that summer avoided or survived encounters with the enemy and did not run into trouble with the weather. The Gestapo and secret police were, however, tightening their grip on the export groups that were arranging for the departure of larger groups. These groups remaining in Norway took different but just as profound risks as those climbing into the boats. In fact, the arrests of these organisers far exceeded the 114 arrests of those caught during an escape attempt. The outcomes of the arrests were just as draconian.

Sigurd Årstad in Bergen had actively opposed the German occupation since the early days of the occupation. His Årstad-Brun Group in Bergen had helped many fugitives to travel to coastal communities to make their escapes. Now the Gestapo was closing in on the group and it was time for them to get away. Årstad, his wife Borghild and daughter Elen were amongst eleven people from the Bergen group who made their way to Fjell at the end of August. They boarded *Svanen II* on 28 August and were quickly on their way, landing safely at Buckie two days later. The Årstad-Brun Group had ceased to exist.

Fathers and sons don't always see eye to eye. With the polarisation of Norway after the occupation, Reinhardt Horn threw in his lot with the NS and was rewarded by being appointed Mayor of Nord-Vågesøy, a small island municipality down the coast from Ålesund. He was the owner of a fine fishing boat, *Vikingen*. His son Ingvald, aged 20, on the other hand was burning to get to Britain to join the Norwegian navy. One can imagine the tensions within the Horn family as Ingvald plotted his escape along with five other local boys. He registered his resistance by stealing his father's boat on 28 August 1941 and sailing across, landing in Baltsound three days later. Horn did indeed join the Norwegian navy, and served until the end of the war as an engineer. You can imagine that his father was apoplectic with rage. The fine boat *Vikingen* was returned to Norway after the war. It survives today, having had a complete restoration.

At the height of *Englandsfeber*, larger boats were being pressed into service, bringing thirty to forty people at a time. This meant that families and extended families started to leave together. One such example was the boat *Hitsøy* belonging to Nils Hitsøy from the lighthouse island of the same name (west of Fjell). With a veritable clan of thirty-two Hitsøys on board, Nils set out on 27 August. There were no less than ten men named Hitsøy on board. One was his son, five were brothers and the rest were cousins, most were fishermen. There were also four women and a child – everyone was a relative. Their departure must have made quite a dent in the population of tiny Hitsøy island and on adjacent Fjell. The boat ended up in Buckie where it spent the rest of the war fishing; fishing is what they did best, and it was important to keep landings up in the war. Family members became prominent in the community of Norwegians that had become established at Buckie.

Another family group was befriended by 13-year-old Douglas Allan of Arbroath (half way between Aberdeen and Dundee). Douglas liked nothing better than to mess around the east coast harbour with his friends. In those days there was no particular security at the port, just rudimentary rope and fishing net barriers and the boys were free to roam and explore. There was always something of interest with a war going on, and there was always a fish to be caught from the pier. On 4 September 1941, something of wonder to the youngsters arrived – a beautifully varnished and impressive wooden fishing boat came in and tied up, proudly flying the Norwegian flag. She was *Elieser* and had crossed over from the island of Vigra (near Ålesund). The skipper had been heading for Shetland, but bad weather had blown them considerably off course, so the journey had taken seven days. They had nearly run out of food and water over the last few days, but the first thing they were offered on arrival, to their amusement, was cigarettes! Soon, however, they were plied with food –including white bread that they hadn't tasted for a many a month. Among the thirteen on board there were two families, the Molnes with two sons and the Roalds with one son. One of the boys was the same age as Douglas, the other two a bit younger so, in their curiosity, they soon became friendly. The parents spoke good English, and in no time at all Douglas was a welcome guest on board. The fishing boat was a grand adventure playground. Over the next month, after school and at weekends, Douglas would often visit his new friends, until the time came for them to leave. They were going up to Buckie to join other expatriate Norwegian fishermen living there. Sadly, he went to say goodbye, and in the awkwardness of a teenage parting his friends gave him the Norwegian flag that had been proudly displayed at the stern of *Elieser*. Douglas kept this as a treasured souvenir and the happy memories continued well into his old age, when he eventually presented the flag to the local Signal Tower Museum at Arbroath. The discovery of this flag led me to track Douglas down and find his childhood story.

If Douglas Allan had been waiting in anticipation of a Norwegian boat arriving at Arbroath it was like buses – a second turned up soon afterwards, and it was actually the only other one to do so during the war. It arrived on 19 September, as was amusingly described in the *Dundee Courier* of 20 September and the *Arbroath Herald* of 26 September. Thirteen young men and one woman, a nurse, arrived on a motorboat after a six day crossing. Off the coast they had encountered a coastal patrol boat that guided it towards the harbour where it anchored offshore until the tide was right to go in through the lock gates – with their Norwegian flag proudly flying. They motored in to a warm welcome from a crowd that had gathered on the quayside.

'When the crew jumped ashore – the young woman was the first to land – they were as happy as a band of schoolchildren. All the party appeared to be in their teens,' observed the reporter, who went on to gush, 'The nurse, a brunette in the land of fair haired women, was… attired in a grey costume with blue blouse, and had on a tan shade of stockings. She carried a handbag.'

Well, she clearly wanted to look her best for the good people of Arbroath who surged forward. Soon the boat had to be roped off, with guards posted to keep the visitors segregated until the police arrived. They had been living on diminishing supplies of black bread and water for the last three days, so they were delighted at the tasty offerings of food brought down to the harbour by kindly folk. It would be surprising if they were not presented with a taste of the local delicacy, the Arbroath smokie. The next day they were on the London train and on their way to a new life.

Just up the coast at Montrose the small fishing boat *Viola* arrived safely on 15 September, the one and only escape boat to arrive there. Although the crossing was straightforward, there were some remarkable young men amongst the thirteen on board with some exceptional achievements and stories. A simple measure of this is that six of the thirteen died over the course of the war. On board were two close friends, Gabriel Salvesen, aged 22, and Tor Hugo van der Hagen, 25, from Farsund. Salvesen was the elder son of a wealthy shipping family and was training at the Maritime College. Van der Hagen had gone to the north to join the fighting during the invasion, and both of them were restless to cross to Britain to join the Allies. They heard that *Viola* was leaving Flekkford on 13 September1941 and asked to be picked up. To avoid being spotted, they and a group of half a dozen similarly minded young men hid behind a large rock on the island of Langøy, just outside Farsund waiting to be picked up. In the darkness they heard the familiar 'tonk-tonk' engine noise of the fishing boat on to which they happily climbed. As they got under way, Gabriel Salvesen went to the wheelhouse to ask the skipper, Olav Skarpnes, if he could have a favour. Would he pick up a further passenger who was waiting at an agreed point further out in the fjord? This was Ingrid Pedersen, his fiancée, the 'prettiest girl in Farsund', his 'perfect match'; she was determined to be at his side. But Skarpnes would not entertain the idea at all, saying that a woman on board would bring bad luck. He was adamant, and he would not be persuaded; Salvesen was crestfallen but was consoled by van der Hagen who reasoned that Ingrid could follow in another boat later.

Nearing their journey's end, *Viola* encountered a British warship which gave their position as being 40 miles east of the Bell Rock lighthouse, and pointed them in the direction of Montrose, where she landed. She didn't stay long at Montrose being directed onwards to Dundee, 30 miles down the coast, where they were immediately among friends. There was a sizeable Norwegian presence at Dundee – two submarines and four minesweepers of No 71 Minesweeper group with their remarkable ships' mascot, Bamse (teddy bear), a fourteen stone St Bernard dog. Bamse subsequently became mascot of the whole Norwegian Navy and later of all free Norwegian forces.

Van der Hagen and two others were old friends of the charismatic Odd Starheim (who had arrived on *Viking* in August 1940) and were recruited by him straight into Kompani Linge. Only van der Hagen survived, a true hero much decorated including a Military Medal from the British. The owner and skipper of *Viola*, Olav Skarpnes, and his brother Ingvald remained on their boat fishing until spring 1942, when they were both induced to join the navy and to use their boat in special operations. They worked out of Peterhead, as a secret satellite operation of the Shetland Bus, and both of them were killed on a mission in 1943 when their boat struck a mine. The morose Gabriel Salvesen was feeling bruised by the separation from his fiancée and did not follow the others into special operations, instead joining the merchant marine. He ended up on a fruit transport ship, and after some months he had a change of heart, realising he did not escape in order to 'transport bananas' for the war effort. Regaining his determination to fight, he returned to Scotland to join his friends in Kompani Linge. After several dangerous missions, he found himself as part of Operation Martin on the Shetland Bus boat *Brattholm I* on the island of Rebbenesøya (near Tromsø) on 29 March 1943 (See Chapter 5). In that dreadful incident Salvesen was amongst those captured, tortured and executed.

The escape of *Viola* had severe consequences for the Salvesen family, whose houses, estates and assets were seized by the Nazis in retribution. They found themselves literally on the street, in need of shelter and support for the rest of the war, willingly given by the people of Farsund. But they never resented the actions of Gabriel in leaving to fight for Norway, supporting his commitment as he expressed it in one of the letters he sent home (received much later). In it he wrote, 'Fight for everything you hold dear, die if it matters'.

For van der Hagen, Salvesen's closest friend, there was to be a touching denouement when he returned to Farsund two years later. He sought out Ingrid Pedersen, to bring his condolences. Sympathy turned into something deeper, they married, raised a family and enjoyed over forty years together.

Forty years after the Farsund men hid behind the rock on the island of Langøy waiting for *Viola*, the survivors and relatives assembled at the same place to commemorate the six men who did not come back. Tor and Ingrid van der Hagen were amongst those who fixed a bronze plaque with the names to the rock in September 1981. The banner of the plaque reads *'Alt for Norge'* (All for Norway). It is remarkable how *Viola* and other small boats like her carried so many outstandingly brave men.

Another boat in that September 1941 that had bad luck was *Sjølyst* from Austevoll, well laden with around twenty-five people. It ran into bad weather and engine problems and had to turn and run with the storm homewards. On the way, a huge wave washed Henrik Karsen (of Fitjar, Austevoll) overboard. With great seamanship he was recovered, but he had drowned, and his remains were returned to the priest at home. Returning his body to Austevoll was risky as there was high alert on the island and all the passengers had to scatter around the district and make themselves scarce. There was no turning back for these people – they were marked by the Gestapo and desperate to get away. After a further abortive attempt, seventeen of them later got on board *Sjølivet* (a similar name but a different boat) which left Austevoll on 21 September. After being buzzed by a German plane, they were enveloped by a thick fog and made their escape. The remainder had another chance a month later when the original *Sjølyst* was mobilised for a second attempt, this time with fourteen men and two women on board. It left the tiny island of Møkster (near Austevoll) on 30 October and, being much better prepared this time, had a straight run over to Lerwick.

On board was 23-year-old Sverre Ludvig Borgund Hamre, a young man of great promise. From school he had gone into the army and had fought during the invasion. After this he laid low until he had a chance to cross to Britain on *Sjølyst* to rejoin the free Norwegian Army based in Scotland. He was commissioned into the Norwegian Brigade in Scotland shortly after arrival and progressed steadily with his promotions. As with many in the army, Hamre became bored with defence duties in Scotland, and applied for a more active role, becoming one of only sixteen Norwegian officers selected to have command within a British infantry regiment, the 4th Battalion, The Welsh Regiment. He was a company second in command and then company commander. The battalion took part in the Normandy landing in June 1944 and was involved in some of the fiercest of the fighting at Caen, the Falaise Pocket and 's-Hertogenbosch in the Netherlands, where he was severely wounded. He earned himself a St Olav's Medal with Oak Leaf, and the British Military Cross. From this outstanding war record, Hamre went steadily to the very top, becoming a full General and Chief of Defence for Norway for five years, 1977–1982.

Young Sverre Hamre typified the best of the young Norwegian Vikings who escaped to join the Allied forces. True to their nature they contributed much to the final overthrow of the Nazi regime.

Chapter 9

Sieving for Spies
(September 1941)

Britain was alert to the point of obsession with the possibility that there were spies about. Dozens of different public posters proclaimed the spy was 'Enemy No 1', that 'Careless Talk Costs Lives', 'She's not so Dumb' and similar caveats. So it was hardly surprising that the arrival of large numbers of foreign nationals on British shores posed an enormous threat to national security that was taken very seriously. The Abwehr thought that escaping Norwegians presented a convenient way to send agents into Britain, using 'soft underbelly' arrival places in Scotland, the Faroe Islands and Iceland. This was why all arrivals anywhere on Allied soil were arrested and questioned on landing, being kept under close guard by the police or military until they had been cleared at the 'London Reception Centre'. There were few exceptions to the drawn-out process, which could take several weeks. There were two aims to the system, probably of equal importance – to gather intelligence from the occupied countries and to weed out spies.

At the port of arrival, a designated intelligence officer (usually from one of the services or could be directly from MI5) would do an initial screening. In isolated landings, such as Stonehaven, the initial questioning might be done by the local police. The most important task was to gather current information of German activity, construction projects, gun emplacements, coastal convoy movements and similar information. Many Norwegians brought diagrams, maps and photographs with them as useful offerings. These could have immediate, sometimes even urgent, relevance to operations happening or in planning.

'London Reception Centre' was the nom de guerre for the Royal Victoria Patriotic School for Girls, an enormous Victorian Gothic building at Wandsworth in south west London. It had been built in 1859 by public subscription to house girls orphaned in the Crimean War. In the First World War it became a hospital, afterwards reverting to being a school. From March 1941, its gargantuan space was taken over by MI9 as a central screening centre for all civilian refugee arrivals from all Allied occupied countries; in the early days, these were mostly from Norway. After arrival at London Centre a more detailed de-briefing would take place, which in some cases amounted to an interrogation. Norway had such a small population that it was fairly straightforward to cross-check individuals and accounts. The famous 'spycatcher' Lieutenant Colonel Oreste Pinto was involved in isolating the more difficult cases from the 30,000 refugees (from all countries) that passed through. After their experiences, some Norwegians, always fond of nicknames, called the Centre 'Sing-Sing', after the famous American penitentiary of that name, but also reflecting that some had to sing for their supper, whilst some had to sing for their lives.

Travelling to London Centre from distant arrival points was always done under police or sometimes military guard to stop abscondments. In some cases, the guard was not what he seemed to be, as described by Arne Melevik ('Nipen') who had crossed in *Ingeborg*. On the way to London, his group had a uniformed British policeman with them who feigned not to have a word of Norwegian. As the train rattled along, the chattering escapers suspected he was having a good listen in to the conversation and tried to trick him into revealing his intent. He maintained his stony-faced detachment until a dirty joke caused an explosion of laughter – he was unmasked. This was just one of the ways that the new arrivals were sieved for potential spies.

After arrival in London, the refugees were held at the Reception Centre and as processing went along they were 'boarded out' to hotels which had a contract with the Norwegian government. These hotels included the County, the Douglas and the Bailey; living there

gave them their first taste of freedom in the metropolis. In spite of
the bomb damage, the air raids and the blackouts there remained a
tremendous *joie de vivre* in the capital which was infectious. Many of the
Norwegians arriving were fishermen formerly living in remote island
communities who had little experience of city life. Some had never
seen a bus before, let alone ridden in one. The London Underground
was a total amazement – you could go round and round on the Circle
line, going nowhere in particular, just for the ride and the price of a
one-stop ticket. As they explored, it was usual for escapees to link up
with one or two fellow Norwegians who would show them the ropes,
buy them a drink or two – and ask 'too many questions'. Kåre Iversen
(of *Villa II*) described how he was targeted in this way several times
in one evening, being followed right up to the doors of his hotel. His
boat had, after all, conveyed the dodgy Swedish spy so he was probably
under enhanced surveillance. This was all part of the grand scheme of
counter intelligence screening. It is not known how many spies were
caught in the sieve of the Royal Victoria Patriotic School, as many of
the relevant MI6 files are still, even today, closed. Spies were probably
more likely to be caught in the act of crossing or landing – as a result
of local intelligence from Norway or intercepts from Bletchley Park, as
the next story illustrates.

At first sight, the escape of *Hornfjell* to Iceland looked innocent
enough, but British radio intercepts indicated otherwise. Owner and
skipper Martin Steffensen and his crew of three left Bø in Westerålen
(north west of Lofoten), picking up four passengers somewhere before
leaving Norway on 23 August. Where had they been and where was
the pick-up point? The intercepts indicated that this was an attempt
by the Abwehr to get into Britain via the back door, but it was not clear
as to who was implicated in the plan. Was it a lone agent or all four
of the passengers and were the sailors complicit? The unravelling of
this required that all eight on board *Hornfjell* were arrested on arrival
at Reykjavik, where they were held and questioned under armed
guard for two weeks. They were all transferred to Glasgow, also under

armed escort. By the time they arrived in the city, suspicion had fallen on one of the four passengers, Olav Sætran. He was advised of his rights and urged to make a written statement. What a statement; that night he Sætran responded by hanging himself with his scarf from a water pipe, thereby confirming his complicity. But were the others in the conspiracy? There must have been a presumption of this as the remaining seven men were transferred to the London Reception Centre and grilled over a further period of two months. There was obviously a high index of suspicion. The outcome of all of this is still secret – the files are still closed. In spite of this debacle the Abwehr continued to regard Iceland as an easy option to get agents into Britain, and over a dozen German agents were sent there during the war. To the chagrin of their masters, most of them turned themselves in on arrival, as in doing so they would avoid a possible death sentence if unmasked. Three of them were 'turned' and used as double agents.

The *Arvind* arrived at Tórshavn on the Faroe Islands on 27 September 1941 after an uneventful four-day crossing from Ålesund. At first inspection this looked like a routine escape, like so many from that area (although most boats from Ålesund usually went to Shetland). However, the 'escape' had been organised by the Abwehr, with all eight men on board being agents. The preparations had not gone unnoticed by local Ålesund folk, suspicions had been confirmed and a message had been transmitted by Milorg to London. On arrival at Tórshavn, they were immediately arrested and the rest of the story is hidden in some secret vault.

At a remote whitewashed cottage by the sea at Crovie Bay, some 30 miles to the east of Buckie in the north east of Scotland, the war arrived on the doorstep of Francis Reid in the very early hours of 7 April 1941. A hammering at the door brought him to confront two strangers dressed in matching blue ski suits, wearing rubber boots and propping up two bicycles. In almost faultless English, one of them explained they had come from Norway, which came as no surprise in view of other local reports of Norwegian refugee arrivals. He then went on to reveal a startling twist – that they had been deposited offshore by a German flying boat from Stavanger and that they had paddled ashore in a rubber dinghy laden with the two cycles and other baggage, which they had left on the beach. This was a strikingly similar *modus operandi* to that of Vera Schalburg and the two other Abwehr agents who had landed not far away at Port Gordon just seven months earlier. But the similarities ended at the door of Francis Reid. The strangers actually asked to be directed to the local police – that would be reasonable enough for refugees to request. Much puzzled by the information he had been given, Reid kept his head, cleverly giving the strangers directions to nearby Gardenstown – but by a long circuitous route. Thanking him and handing over a £1 note as a tip, the two set off on their bikes. Reid (who had no phone) then took a short cut along the coastal path and raised the alarm at Gardenstown police station. Reinforcements were rallied and positioned in anticipation of trouble when the strangers arrived. In due course, the two cycled into the small town, where they were quickly surrounded, disarmed (they had pistols) and arrested. Thus arrived in Scotland two of the most important Abwehr 'spies' of the war. The two were in due course to be used as double agents to significant effect later in the war.

They were 22-year-old John Herbert Neal Moe, the fluent English speaker, and 25-year-old Tor Glad. They willingly surrendered themselves to the police at Gardenstown and were soon spirited south to the attention of Major Robert Stephens of MI5. Their Abwehr mission was twofold – to penetrate the establishment gathering intelligence and then to blow things up when they identified suitable targets. From the outset Moe said he had followed a plan to join the Abwehr in a ruse to get to Britain to join the Allies. He also thought that his Abwehr training and inside knowledge would be of value to the British secret services. He was, in fact, a British citizen – his mother was an English opera singer and he had been born in London. All of this could be checked out easily. The status of Glad was less clear in that, although a former sergeant in the Norwegian army, he had worked willingly for the Germans from the beginning of the occupation. He seemed to be somewhat ambivalent about the drawbacks of fascism. He had recruited John Moe to the Abwehr because of the asset value of his faultless English. It was a possibility that he had gone along with Moe's surrender on their arrival as a deeper deceit to penetrate MI5, effectively using Moe as his cover – in upshot he would be a triple spy. He had little option, however, but to cooperate with Stephens for the time being or he would be tried as a spy; that could cost him his life. He would have to be closely watched.

MI5 then set up one of the more successful double agent operations of the war, based on a well bugged and well watched house in Hendon, where the two Norwegians installed the radio transmitter they had been sent with. In a typically MI5 tradition of humorous nicknames, Stephens christened them 'Mutt and Jeff' from a popular American comic strip of the day. The names remained even after Glad was removed and spirited away to internment on the Isle of Man in the autumn of 1941 for the rest of the war. Perhaps he encountered the beautiful Vera Schalburg while he was there. Glad had fulfilled Stephen's suspicions by being thoroughly unreliable, prone to heavy drinking and garrulous in company. He was seamlessly replaced by an MI5 understudy. Moe, however, remained steadfast, intelligent and useful. In this way, the Mutt and Jeff operation continued successfully until late 1944.

Elaborate measures were made to validate the Abwehr agents' successful establishment in Britain and their access to secret information. Where proof of sabotage activity was required, this was carefully staged with real but harmless explosions backed by outraged newspaper reports of the damage and loss of life. Among these pieces of theatre Operation Bunbury in August 1943 stands out. They requested a parachute drop of explosives and equipment which were of great interest to MI5 in themselves. These supplies were then supposed to be used in an attack on an electricity generating plant in East Anglia. There was indeed a choreographed explosion (of no consequence) which was trumpeted by the Nazis as a triumph of sabotage by their agents, destroying a major power installation. The German airwaves crackled with the news that 'over 150 workmen were killed and more than double that number wounded'.

Where a narrative of their activities was needed, the deceits continued. When Glad was imprisoned on the Isle of Man, a message was sent to the effect that he had joined the Norwegian Army and had been sent to Iceland for training. When he 'returned' to Britain in late 1942, it was the understudy Jeff who (together with Moe) resumed the transmissions. In January 1942, Moe messaged Germany that he had been able to join the British Army on account of having an English mother and being born in England. After a suitable interval for his training, he sent further information that he had been selected for the Intelligence Corps and had been posted to Scotland. For the Abwehr this was nothing short of a masterstroke. Moe needed his own radio transmitter in Scotland, as the original one was still at Hendon. He requested that one together with other supplies be dropped by parachute in Scotland. In due course, the Luftwaffe dropped a radio complete with code books and sabotage equipment in field on the north east coast of Scotland somewhere near Peterhead, where it was collected by the police and gleefully examined by MI5.

It was in Scotland in 1943 that the apotheosis of the Mutt and Jeff operation was played out as part of Operation Fortitude North. This was the northern component of a huge deception to shift attention away from the Normandy beaches as the target for the Allied invasion of Europe. Since mid-1941 there had been a series of stratagems (including the commando raids) indicating that the Allies were planning an invasion of northern Norway. This became more pertinent after Russia had become an ally with the prospect of the opening up of a significant northern front. Hitler never ceased to fret about this possibility, pouring men and materiel into his *Festung Norwegen* (Norwegian Fortress). These previous ploys were now rolled forward into Fortitude North with the 'formation' of a completely new but entirely fictitious British Fourth

Army Group, with headquarters in Edinburgh Castle. The command structure and all the component units of this army were delineated and named meticulously, including five non-existent US divisions.

John Moe was ideally positioned to report all of this to the Abwehr, especially now he had his own radio transmitter in Scotland. At no stage over three years of his career as a double agent did his German masters doubt his reliability or veracity. A carefully scripted stream of transmissions reported the arrival of troops, the locations of headquarters, building of camps and arduous training exercises for a seaborne invasion. The radio deceptions were reinforced by carefully coordinated false newspaper snippets such as fictitious football results between non-existent regiments or marriage engagements between soldiers of bogus formations and local women. The Abwehr was taken in comprehensively, and there can be little doubt that the threat of the British Fourth Army worried Hitler into keeping up to 400,000 troops in Norway, troops that were far away from the beaches of Normandy.

John Moe had confirmed himself to be a true Norwegian patriot. He may not have taken up arms to fight hand-to-hand the occupiers of his country, but he made a significant contribution to the decoy success of Operation Fortitude, which saved many thousands of lives. The full extent of this success was not released from the secret files until 2002. As a result, Moe received scant applause for his work, even in Norway which bestowed no honour on him – a substantial deficiency. Dicing with the Abwehr was not without personal risk. He can now be re-assessed as being something of a major player in the great game of military deception.

There were virtually no Norwegian fishing boats that were not made of wood. Norway was a country that embraced traditional wooden ship building in parallel with its seagoing culture. Almost every coastal community had a boatyard and skilled shipwrights. It may seem to be obvious, but it should be observed that there is no place on a wooden boat that is safe from machine gun bullets. High velocity projectiles can easily pass through marine planking; in the case of smaller boats they could pass through from one side of the vessel and out of the far side. There really was no place to hide except perhaps behind the bulk of the engine.

Three men escaping from Haugesund found this out in the most terrifying of circumstances. They left the adjacent island of Karmøy on 9 September 1941 in the small coastal fisher, *Ottar*. The engine completely packed up on the second day, so they drifted for the next three day in heavy seas, unable to set sail. When the storm settled, they again headed westwards, this time under sail. On 18 September, having been at sea for nine days, they were well within British waters not far from land when a German plane appeared and decided to strike. Relentlessly it pressed its attack, coming round six times to rake the little boat with machine gun fire. The pilot must have thought he had finished the job or had run out of ammunition as he finally departed. Miraculously Erling Ellingsen survived unscathed. Magne Østensjø was dead, and Herluf Brå was severely wounded with a bullet through a lung and another having shattered an arm. For the rest of that day and night Ellingsen battled to keep the boat afloat, bailing water out and plugging holes at the waterline, whilst trying to keep his injured friend as comfortable as possible. He also had to try to keep sailing onwards to safety and help. The following day, a 14ft boat with six refugees from Holland came across the stricken *Ottar* and was able to render some assistance. Later that day the two tiny craft were picked up by a British minesweeper and delivered to Great Yarmouth in Norfolk. That was almost 600 miles south west of Karmoy – three times as far as they had anticipated when they set out. The injured Herluf Brå survived but had to have his arm amputated so he was no longer fit to fight his assailants. The dead man, Magne Øostenjø, was buried in Caister Old Cemetery, where his grave is cared for by the War Graves Commission.

Most of the boats escaping from the south coast were small inshore open or half open boats because it was an in-shore fishery. The narrow passage of sea between Norway and Denmark, the Skagerrak, did not require larger fishing vessels. It was a dangerous stretch of water because it was the 'bottle neck' of the Baltic Sea which at that time was mostly controlled by the Reich. It was teeming with Nazi shipping, military and civilian. The small boats setting out on an escape adopted a modus operandi of moving westwards staying close to the shore, as if fishing or having a holiday, until they got to a point at which they must 'jump off', heading for open sea. Most of the boats left the coast in the region between Mandal and Farsund at the southwest tip, and over the war about twenty boats left from this southern coast.

In September, two boats left directly from Mandal with different stories to tell. The 21ft open boat *Tassen* left on 6 September and was quite soon driven back to port. Setting out for a second try on 8 September, they again encountered very heavy weather and had to drift with a sea anchor for eighteen hours. After a six-day ordeal they reached land at Amble, about 30 miles north of Newcastle. The second boat was un-named but bore the registration VA 77 HH, and we know far more about its adventures as a result of an account given after the war by Roy Nilsen, one of the escapers. He and three friends, Nils Nilsen, Finn Adriansen and Ernst Engervik were plotting to leave Mandal at the same time as *Tassen*, but such was the secrecy that the two parties did not know about each other. First, they needed a boat, and Nils Nilsen found an open motor boat of about 20ft which they duly obtained by honest purchase for 3,000 kroner and hid it in a small creek. The biggest problem was to get enough fuel, and this was tackled in great style. The Germans had thrown together a small air station just outside the town with a wooden runway, and Engervik, one of the four, had taken a job there as a driver. As he went about his work, he noted that security was surprisingly lax, observing that one local car, whose owner was a collaborator, drove in and out without even being checked by the guards. Moreover, the privileged owner also received free fills of petrol.

With remarkable chutzpah, Engervik and Ariansen 'borrowed' this car from its Quisling owner whilst he was having his dinner in the town. It was only a few minutes' drive to the airfield, where the sentry just waved them through. They drove straight up to the petrol depot, asked for a top-up which they got without question and then drove out again. Having siphoned off the petrol, they quickly returned the car to its starting place, the owner blissfully unaware of its excursion and the deception. Such youthful audacity in the face of the accompanying risks is hard to grasp.

The four young men completed their preparations and set out on 11 September but didn't get far. The boat was leaking faster than they could bail it out. It was far too risky to return to Mandal, so they landed on the uninhabited rocky island of Utvår and considered what to do next. They beached VA 77 HH and tipped it over to inspect the leaky planking. As they had previously demonstrated, they were resourceful young men so over the next couple of days they combed the island for lumps of pitch and tar washed ashore from passing ships. They sacrificed some shirts, cutting them into strips and mixing them with the pitch to push into the gaps in the planks. On re-launch, the caulking worked well and the boat remained dry. On their third day, they set off again as darkness fell.

At 4.00 the following morning, well out to sea, they were alarmed to hear a plane some way off. They had time to execute a simple deception – they cut the engine and draped themselves around the boat as if they were all dead. The Dornier seaplane swooped down low to have a closer look and the ruse worked – it just wheeled around and flew away. The following morning, they spotted a thick layer of coal dust on the surface of the water. Although they couldn't see it, they must be nearing the coast. Sure enough, they later spotted a large shipping buoy and tied up to it to await discovery. In due course a tugboat came, taking them under tow into the coal port of Blyth, about ten miles north of Newcastle. It was 17 September and they had been on their way for six days. At that time Blyth was the largest coal exporting port in Europe, and it was a mucky place where the poor-quality coals and dust (slag or tailings) were simply tipped into the sea. In 1941, the filthy dust was, however, a harbinger of safety for the four men from Mandal.

In Oslo a tiny spark flared into a conflagration of defiance, the largest civil action yet seen against the occupiers, and it did not end well. On 8 September, a severe new milk ration was imposed, including complete prohibitions to serve milk in restaurants or in places of work. From this small inconvenience the effects could not have been foreseen. The national trades union *Landsorganisasjonen* (LO) was infuriated by such a petty measure on top of rafts of other restrictions and regulation. It was the straw that broke the camel's back, and a nationwide strike was called for the next day. As this spread, the Secret Police went around arresting hundreds of shop stewards. For good measure they arrested around 300 academics, newspaper employees and even just random people who were demonstrating any support for the strike. Terboven was incandescent and without further ado he declared a state of emergency, imposing martial law. He famously said, 'This was not unwanted. So far, I have run after the Norwegians in vain. Now I'm going to force them to their knees'. He was as good as his word. All forms of recreation and entertainment were cancelled, and a strict curfew imposed. The following day the retribution started with summary trials (without evidence) of senior LO officers, Rolf Wickstrøm (a lawyer) and Viggo Hansteen (a senior union representative), accused of being the ringleaders and sentenced to death. They were dragged away and within hours they were shot by the SS. Four others were sentenced to life imprisonment, with four more death sentences handed down the following day (later commuted to life imprisonment). All LO offices were shut down and Quislings inserted to take over the unions completely. The substantial funds of the unions were seized.

Overall, there was a major disruption in the status quo of the country. Even the Boy Scout movement was dismantled, with the order to hand in all uniforms. Terboven's whirlwind response had the desired effect – the strike was called off and the protests petered out. The state of emergency was cancelled on 16 September, with a triumphant statement, 'The Norwegian people's will for peace and order has won.' That was, of course, far from the truth. As word of the 'Milk Strike' (as it became known) and the executions spread through the country it only hardened the resolve to either join Milorg, or to take to boats to join the fight from overseas.

In the Stavanger area there were two resistance groups operating, the Oftedahl Group (named after Carl Oftedahl) and the Helland Group (after Georg Helland). The German secret police, Sipo, were closing on both of them during September and it was hoped to get some of the members away in the boat *Drott*. The first attempt had to be postponed because there was so much German activity in the area. Suddenly arrests were being made, it was an emergency situation and they had to throw caution to the wind, heading for the sea. Just fifteen people climbed on board *Drott* on 17 September and they got to Peterhead in two days. Of those left behind, a total of eleven were arrested, including Oftedahl and Helland, and all of them went through the brutal cycle of torture, trial and execution, which took place on 29 December 1941.

Ingvar Andreas Sagan, the owner of the fishing cutter *Odd* would not have been amused when the Germans requisitioned his boat along with him and his two deck hands to do some coastal cargo work. The tasks were carried out near Sunnfjord (the mid region between Bergen and Ålesund). Of course they couldn't trust him, so two armed guards travelled with them. Resentment turned into a plan – they wanted to escape to Shetland, following in the path of so many others. Leaving the mainland on around 20 September they called in at the Island of Bulandet in the outer Skerries to ask for directions at which point the Germans were seen to be on board. What happened next no one knows, as none of them was to be seen again. The assumption subsequently was that the three Norwegians had overpowered the two guards and headed out to sea. They could then have hit a mine or been attacked by an aircraft. Two days later, another boat was on the way to Shetland, the *Sjølivet* from Austevoll, and was out in the open sea. The skipper, Lars Drønen, reported that they had passed the wreckage of a fishing boat, but he had not been able to identify it. Certainly, the timing of this sighting fits with the possibility that this was *Odd* and that it had met its end shortly before – any longer and the debris would have dispersed over a wide area. Just before this discovery they had been buzzed by a German plane but managed to lose it in a dense fog. They wondered at the time if this same plane had attacked the wrecked boat. No other vessel was reported missing and it is generally supposed that this wreckage was indeed that of the unfortunate *Odd*.

No luckier were a bricklayer, a blacksmith and a roadman who, already involved with the resistance, tried to escape in a small boat from Bergen on 22 September. Somewhat older than many of the escapers, Ingvald Iversen (65), Charles Johnsen (30) and Lars Svanevik (36) were caught in the act, thrown into Bergen District Prison, tried under field martial law and all sentenced to death. From Ulven concentration camp they were transferred back to Bergen Prison. After three weeks they were taken the short distance (4 miles) to Gravdal Naval Base on 12 February 1942, where they were executed. It is likely that the task had been given to the Kriegsmarine and not the usual SS or Wehrmacht squads. This may have been because it was the navy that had arrested them in the first place, and the navy was expected to see it through. The bodies were then packed into crates along with dynamite and taken by a naval vessel to Korsfjorden about 30 miles distant, where the sailors lit the fuses and threw them overboard. Why do this? Was it a celebration of a job 'well done'? On the other hand, was it that no one in the Kriegsmarine wanted to be reminded of such a distasteful task?

In any circumstance, the age of 15 is a tender one at which to make a firm decision to defy your parents and run away to sea, let alone during an enemy occupation. This is what Karsten Danielsen decided to do as the youngest of a group of six youngsters at Davanger on the large island of Askøy (just to the west of Bergen). The six ranged in age between Danielsen at 15 years and the oldest at 22 years. They had certainly caught *Englandsfeber*, spending that summer looking for a boat to steal. By then boat owners had begun to remove engine parts to prevent such thieving. They sought the help of an older seaman who pointed them at the 55ft *Gullborg*, a robust boat that had been used for firefighting. A local skipper was recruited, Martin Davanger, and they made the usual preparations gathering fuel, food and equipment for the journey. There was a Saturday night dance on 20 September to which many of the young people of Askøy converged. The six conspirators intended leaving straight after the dance. In the middle of the dancing, Danielsen asked his best friend if he wanted to join them. He agreed at once, and in no time the word spread excitedly around the dance floor. Later, as they were preparing to cast off on *Gullborg*, three young men on bicycles raced up to the quayside and climbed aboard, together with someone's girlfriend who had appeared. By prior arrangement, *Gullborg* made two more passenger pick-ups, the second being at Fjell where the number of passengers has risen to twenty-six. As planned, they headed into the open sea just after midnight on Sunday, 21 September. Apart from a passing German plane the next day, which showed no interest, their journey was uneventful and they arrived safely at Baltasound on the island of Unst after two days.

Instead of returning safely home from the dance, Danielsen had left a letter for his parents, who he knew would have prevented him from leaving. It must have been with considerable consternation that they read:

Dear Mum and Dad and everyone else – I leave tonight for England. We have arranged everything in advance so we only need to shove off. If you find this letter tonight you mustn't say anything before tomorrow morning. I have taken some personal things and clothing with me. It won't be long before we return. Some others from Davanger are joining us. Much love, Karsten

Between Mandal and Kristiansand on the south coast lies the small community of Søgne, where Valdemar Lund had gathered four other eager escapers. He had his own 22ft open motor boat *Fri*. Leaving on

26 September 1941, the five of them had one of the more horrendous crossings in the annals of the escapes, being lucky to survive after ten days at sea. Encountering bad weather, they were well out into the North Sea when the engine began to give trouble, as was so often the case with these frail craft in heavy seas. They began to drift southwards, going about 200 miles off course (over several days) until they found themselves over the Dogger Bank, a huge area of shallow waters. Whilst providing good fishing, it is also extremely dangerous for small boats in foul weather. As any mariner could tell you, in bad weather the shallower the water the greater the swells become, ending up in crests and breaking waves. These were the seas that *Fri* drifted into, being tossed around like a cork in a cauldron. Two of the men were washed overboard. They must have been 'roped up' to the boat, as both of them were hauled onboard again, that being in itself a feat of seamanship, avoiding tipping the boat over. By the time they came out of this nightmare, they were running out of food and water, reduced to strict rationing. Even when they got the engine going again, they were confounded by running out of fuel, and when they raised sail there was no wind. They became weaker and more dehydrated by the day.

In the distance – there it was! It was the drone of a plane and it was friendly. It was an aircraft of RAF Coastal Command which on spotting them circled to inspect. A short time later a second plane came in and dropped supplies of water food and fuel. The water would have been the most important gift, literally a life saver, as by then they had completely run out and were severely dehydrated. They recovered themselves enough to continue their journey under their own steam. Eventually they were picked up by a Royal Navy ship where the first task was to feed the starving young men. They were then delivered to the port of Sunderland on the north east English coast. The dramatic circumstance of the RAF rescue caught the attention of the press, reported fully in the *Daily Herald* of 10 October which applauded the RAF and Royal Navy actions, and concluded with saying, 'Finding the Norwegians were without money the sailors passed round the hat and collected several pounds.' You might have thought that their ordeal would have kept them away from the sea, but Waldemar Lund joined the merchant navy (and survived a torpedo sinking). Einar Kristiansen joined the Norwegian Navy in the MTB (Motor Torpedo Boat) service earning a St Olav Medal with Oak Branch as second in command of MTB 688 in daring actions in1944 and 1945.

Eighty years later in 2022 the dramatic escapes that set out from the south coast of Norway were commemorated in a moving project called *Englandsfarere 80* år *etter* (England voyagers 80 years on). Bjørn Tor Rosendahl, Director of the Centre for History of Seafarers at War at Arkivet, Kristiansand, was amongst a group launching the project in 2018. They aimed to reproduce faithfully a small boat escape from Kristiansand based on two successful crossings – *Svane* (Swan) which crossed with four 21-25 September 1940, and *Fri* 26 Sep-6 October 1941 as has just been described. The group planned to use a boat of exactly the same size and build as *Fri*, a 22ft Grimstad skiff, and they planned to set out in 2020 exactly eighty years after *Svane*. That departure was delayed by the Coronavirus pandemic. The intervening years were punctuated by a number of setbacks. During sea trials in their first boat, which they decided to name *Fri II*, and then in its successor *Fri III*, they found that both suffered similar problems to the wartime boats – leaking, structural failures and engine problems. Eventually in December 2019 they found a more modern version (still traditionally built) which sported an almost new Volvo Penta diesel engine; she was to be called *Fri IV.* The group undertook meticulous planning and underwent serious training, of course being able to use the full panoply of modern navigational and communications aids. They were fully equipped using survival gear designed for the North Sea oil industry. In spite of all of this, they still found their adventure to be a harrowing experience and they marvelled at their predecessors who left at very short notice with little time to prepare and no weather forecast at all.

On 13 April 2022, a 'weather window' opened and *Fri IV* with its four crewmen set off – Frode Stokkeland, Jarle Føreland, Willy Pedersen and Tony Teigland. By 1940 standards their crossing was straightforward, and they landed at Buckie on 16 April after a journey of 430 miles. They arrived to a skirl of the pipes and a heroes' welcome by townsfolk (several of whom were descended from wartime Norwegians), dignitaries and an eager press and TV. The adventure received much media coverage on both sides of the North Sea.

En route they had paused and poignantly lowered into the North Sea a wreath of fresh flowers with a Norwegian ribbon attached. It was a memorial to those who had succeeded – and those who had not – with their crossings during those dark war years.

The little *Fri IV* flew at its stern a flag of the Royal Norwegian Postal Service signifying that it was carrying a special postal delivery. This was a letter from the Norwegian Minister for Defence, Odd Roger Enoksen, which was read out to everyone on the quayside. It concluded with this striking paragraph – which says much about this passage of our history,

With this letter I wish to express my gratitude to the people of Buckie for their great hospitality to Norwegians during the Second World War and for their efforts to keep the historic bonds to Norway and the Norwegians alive today. It is my hope that the small wooden boat carrying this letter can serve as a reminder of the decisive rôle (that) Buckie, Scotland and the rest of Britain played in Norway's five year long struggle for freedom. Moreover, may this also serve as an inspiration for a continued special relationship between our nations and our people.

Chapter 10

Equinox
(September–October 1941)

Kristian Elias Stein gave his name and his life to one of the earliest and certainly the largest export and resistance groups in Norway. A postal dispatcher at Bergen central post office, he was easy-going and charming – but he was enraged by the invasion of his country and very early on during the invasion he and the whole of his family started to engage with others of like mind. With his position in the post office, it was ideal for Stein to use the express coastal postal service to travel up and down the coast to establish contacts and recruit volunteers. By the summer of 1941, the Kristian Stein organisation numbered around 1,500 members operating in tightly knit cells and was involved in the export of refugees, the underground press, intelligence gathering and radio transmissions to the Allies, with an armed military sabotage division. This was a great achievement for the Stein family and their friends, but by its size, geographical and operational diversity it had rendered itself vulnerable to penetration by the Gestapo. In September, some of the Stein Group noticed one of their number visiting the main Gestapo headquarters at Veiten in the heart of Bergen. He was none other than Marino Nilsson who just two months earlier, together with the traitor Finn Kass, had betrayed the Nielsen and Torsvik export groups at Ålesund. Nilsson had turned up in Bergen feigning that he was suffering from cancer and that he was wanted by the Gestapo. He used this strategy to inveigle himself into the Stein Group, and now he had been unmasked. It became imperative to get some of the main organisers out, but the first attempt was frustrated by the weather. As the weather temporarily abated, Markus Nese volunteered his 37ft

Hardanger cutter *Arnafjord*, a coastal work boat. The boat was only four years old and very stoutly built, so he was confident it would survive the North Sea. It left Hernar on 27 September with fifteen men and five women on board. They encountered a re-awakened storm, enduring a very rough crossing, but arriving safely in Lerwick two days later. Stein and his family were not on board, gallantly choosing to stay to help others to get away, a decision that had fatal consequences.

It proved to be the last Stein Group escape from Norway. In the fateful night of 2 October 1941, the Gestapo struck, arresting Kristian Stein, his wife Borghild, his 16-year-old daughter Svanhild and a cohort of senior confederates. In the midst the raid, Svanhild managed to take some incriminating lists of names from her father's jacket pocket and get rid of them under the noses of the Germans. The organisation's offices were comprehensively ransacked and names of other members were uncovered. Further information was extracted from the prisoners by the usual unpleasant means at the disposal of their captors. Over several weeks the city of Bergen was turned upside down. In all well over 200 people were arrested with 204 being transferred straight to Germany; Stein and eight others were executed. A further forty-six died in captivity or shortly after liberation. Borghild and Svanhild Stein were held for months, lying 'like professionals' to cover their involvement, and were eventually released. The evil Marino Nilsson had been helped in his work by NS policeman Johan Hilmar Bjørgan. Both of them went on to commit further atrocious betrayals of their own countrymen.

As news of the Stein Group arrests reverberated around Bergen, two brothers knew that they had to get away. Johan and Trygve Sognnæs were involved in underground work and now felt the structure was burning under their feet. On the pretext of a holiday trip to the country they booked a coastal boat through to Lifjorden a popular canoeing destination in the Solund area 100 miles to the north. It was a route already followed by people escaping from Bergen. When they reached the port of Skjerjehamn, German security came on board. They were nearly trapped but managed to slip over the side of the boat and onto the quay without being seen. They then sneaked aboard a smaller local ferry that crossed over the Sognefjord to Hardbakke where they had been told they might find an escape boat. It became a case of out of the frying pan, into the fire as the ferry was intercepted and boarded by a German search party. Petrified, they then had a surprising turn of luck. The German party meticulously examined the brothers' innocent hand baggage so thoroughly that they failed to notice Trygve's small backpack. It contained illegal navigation equipment, maps and other items which would have seen them straight into the hands of the Gestapo.

Somewhat rattled, the two brothers reached Hardbakke and managed to make contact with the Pollen family, who owned several fishing boats. Another three fugitives from the Stein Group in Bergen also turned up at the same door, suggesting that the family had had dealings with the escape business before. Additionally, two local men who had decided that they wanted to reach the free forces asked to join them. The family readily agreed to help with the escape. Sverre Pollen, his brother Severin and another family member offered to take everyone on their old boat, the 63ft fishing cutter *Fremad II*. This was an interesting boat on its own account, because of its history before and after their adventure. The boat had been built as a sailing fisher in England in 1888, where it was named *Boy Jack*. With the advent of steam engines around 400 sailing boats were sold to Norway and *Boy Jack* became *Fremad* in 1905. In 1940, ten days after the Nazi invasion of Norway, whilst on Søfjord (inland from Bergen) the boat had been seized by a company of German soldiers, and the crew of three was ordered to take them to a point behind Norwegian lines. This did not go well as they were spotted by Norwegian forces that opened fire, killing many of the soldiers onboard, along with the boat's young cook. *Fremad II* had been bloodied and damaged. Eighteen months later, and by now fully repaired she could seek atonement in taking ten men to freedom. There could be no delay as the Gestapo was scouring western Norway for remnants of Stein Group. The grand old boat left Hardbakke on 5 November 1941, landing at the far north of the Shetland island of Unst two days later.

The three Pollen boys who took *Fremad II* over the north sea all joined Nortraship – the Norwegian merchant marine. The two Sognnæs boys joined the Norwegian navy. They all survived the war but were probably outlived by the ancient fishing boat. She was taken into Allied service for the rest of the war when she was returned to the Pollen family. She underwent several changes of ownership, alterations and refits and by 2014 when she was taken out of service, she was the oldest working fishing boat in Norway at 126 years old. From 2017 onwards she underwent a massive restoration (£2.2 million) at the Hardanger Ship Conservation Centre. It would be interesting to know if the shipwrights discovered any Norwegian bullets buried deep in the English oak timbers. She had a second launch in August 2020; it was 132 years after her first one on the other side of the North Sea.

Any mariner would tell you that gales accompany an equinox, although modern meteorologists discount the theory and the reality. The equinox fell on 22 September and the 'equinoctial gales' of ancient adage arrived late – around 25 September – and lasted until the end of the month. As well as *Arnafjord*, the weather caught up around a dozen boats desperate to get away, some because of Gestapo activity. These boats were leaving Norway almost blind to the weather, excepting for the relatively unsophisticated interpretations of mercury or aneroid barometers and anemometers. All radio receivers had been removed, so mariners could not eavesdrop on British forecasts. Even these were not brilliant as the Meteorological Office had none of the technological scientific sophistications enjoyed today and relied on coastal weather stations as far away as Iceland, Faroe and Svalbard to give some advance warning of pressure and wind changes. Suffice to say that the archive records described a 'complex low pressure system' sweeping across from Iceland, crossing the British Isles and landing in the North Sea. Two large boats were organised by the Bremnes export group, under urgent pressure to get people away from Bergen, leaving Bomlo together on 27 September. *Utnoring*, an old sailing drifter of 72ft length with twenty-two on board was the largest wooden vessel so far to make a crossing, reaching Lerwick in two days. *Nordlys*, at 50ft length, but crowded with fifty-seven on board (the largest group so far) struggled and went off course reaching Aberdeen in three days. Three other larger boats, *Olav* with seventeen on board, *Feie* with twenty-four and *Fiskaren* with twenty-five all got across to Lerwick, thoroughly shaken and stirred. Of the four smaller boats that set out at this time the *Statt* with eight on board was lucky in making it to the outer Skerries, Shetland, after an anxious journey and *Juno* was nearly lost, having to turn back. The other two, *Valborg* with seven fugitives and *Knut* with twelve were both lost without trace. Various reports in the British press noted that wooden boat wreckage of Norwegian origin had washed up on the east coast of Scotland after this storm which indicated that they had broken up as they neared land. The Gestapo drove their quarry into small boats and the sea finished their dirty work.

The escape of *Nordlys*, which survived the crossing from Bomlo, might have passed without further comment, except that the *Sunday Mirror* of 12 October carried a remarkably detailed account of the extraordinary escape of a woman on board along with her friend. The article used the cover names of 'Olga' and 'Petra' for the two women, with a third character they named as their 'Scarlet Pimpernel'. Olga was a married woman with two children. Her husband had crossed over three months earlier and before leaving they had entered a solemn pact that they would meet up again in London. The article begins, 'There is a girl in London this week who has proudly made one of the greatest sacrifices a wife and mother has made in this war', the sacrifice being that she left her two children behind. Perhaps they were old enough to look after themselves, or, more likely, they were left in the care of grandparents. Irrespective of the merits of leaving the children, the love for her husband propelled her in taking enormous personal risks to escape to join him.

In Bergen at the beginning of September 1941, Olga and Petra decided to travel together and cast about for help in finding a boat, being careful (or so they thought) to ask only trusted friends. One day whilst out walking, a young man fell in step beside them to warn them to leave immediately as the Gestapo were planning to question them. Clearly their plan had been leaked; even friends could not deserve their trust. The man passed over a small piece of paper with an address at a place 100 miles to the south. They fled and a few days later found themselves at a remote cabin at the foot of a mountain where there was no one to be found. There was, however, food, a change of clothes, clean sheets and a comfy bed. What was to happen next? They waited patiently until the next morning when they opened the door and found a note pinned to it; there was no sign of the bearer of the brief note which read, 'The onions are ready. Collect them at ...' – the name of a fishing village some distance away. Puzzled and frankly scared they tramped there settling down to wait again. Where was the next instruction? Was it a trap? This was like a giant treasure hunt, but there was no treasure, only uncertainty. After two days they sat demoralised over a cup of coffee in a café by the harbour, and then asked for the bill. When it came it had the next instruction written on it, 'Be at (name of place) at ten o'clock tonight'.

The girls arrived at the rendezvous to be reunited with the young man who had warned them about the Gestapo and set them off on their long journey. He was their Scarlet Pimpernel – the one who had orchestrated their progress to this point. His final act was to put them on a coastal island ferry with directions for the next steps, wishing them the best of luck. He then retreated into the shadows and the darkness, as would any Pimpernel.

At midnight the pair arrived at the next island stop stepping ashore with five men who were also on the run. Their instructions were to lie low expecting a pick-up at midnight on the following night, 27 September. On cue a boat came in and anchored off the shore; it was *Nordlys*. A man jumped into the sea and swam over to find them. It was just as well they could all swim as that was the only means to get out to the waiting boat. When they climbed aboard, they found that it was already packed with fifty people. Soggy and salty the next stage of their adventure was under way as *Nordlys* headed out into the gathering equinoctial storm.

Their three-day crossing was bad enough, but one last hazard awaited them. Having been blown well off course, *Nordlys* approached an unrecognised coastline and the skipper thought it best to stop to await a guard boat to guide them in. This was just as well as in due course when a British ship approached the captain shouted, 'You're smack in the middle of a minefield! Follow me, and if you like praying, this is just the time to start!' Escorted into Aberdeen harbour (225 miles off course from Lerwick) they were greeted in rapturous welcome by a crew of around thirty Norwegians on a ship that was in port. The Norwegian seamen had witnessed the safe arrival of one of their own little boats from home following the most dreadful storm. No wonder they were overjoyed.

Another week later and Olga and Petra were in London telling their breathless story to the *Sunday Mirror*. The paper even printed a picture of the two of them smiling at each other – but 'Masked – so the Gestapo cannot identify them...'. So not only do we not know their real names but we have missed the chance of seeing what they looked like. It would not have been long before Olga reaped the benefit of her sacrifice and was in the arms of her husband.

In a similar vein and around the same time there is another story of a married woman taking a huge risk to find her husband – but this time taking her five children with her. Two short British newspaper clips outlined the story on 5 November 1941, the *Daily Herald* and the *Belfast News-Letter*. When the two articles are combined it is possible to make some sense of the story. The noms de guerre accorded to the married couple were 'Erik' and 'Gunvor Stend'. Erik was a fisherman who had become isolated in Britain after the invasion of Norway, who had carried on fishing in Scotland for the Allies. Gunvor remained at home running the small family farm on the west coast with the help of her five children. That autumn she heard a report that Erik had drowned whilst at sea; it was dreadful news but she couldn't and wouldn't believe it. He had been born to be a fisherman and in coastal Scottish waters it seemed to be unlikely that he would end his life in this way. Her every instinct told her that he was alive.

One day, Gunvor learned that a boat was leaving their district the next day for Shetland; the skipper offered to take her and the children. Quick to make up her mind she decided to go – she must find out the truth about Erik. Additionally, she was tired of the struggle to keep going on the farm, as the Germans were removing so much produce at source. 'It is a fight to get a meal even in the country,' she said, adding, 'the food situation was like a candle which was burning out.'

In those frantic last 24 hours of preparation 'she gave the cows the biggest feed they had had for a long time, locked up the dog and watered the flowers in the garden'. No doubt she was confident that her neighbours or one of her family would look after the farm and the animals. That night she went down to the beach and rowed the six of them out into the fjord to join the waiting escape boat; it already had nine others on board. They had a very rough four-day crossing, the only other hazard being a floating mine. It was all worth it, as Gunvor was soon able to find that Erik was indeed alive. The report was false, but that was common enough in wartime. From the details given in the two disguised newspaper reports, it is possible to surmise with some confidence that this family was part of the larger Storemark family from the island of Fedje which left en famille on the boat *Feiøy* on 25 September. All the details have an exact fit, except that the number of children is at variance, with three recorded as having been on board – but probably Gunvor's two eldest had been counted as adults.

To continue with this theme of women with their children making a crossing to join up with husbands who had previously escaped, there is one further substantial story in the autumn of 1941 involving a boat that appears not to have been previously recorded. It emerged in two slightly differing newspaper reports, one in the *Sunday Sun* (Newcastle) on 16 November 1941 and one in the *Daily News* (London) on 17 Nov. The subject and her children were given false names as expected – Mrs 'Christina Johanessen' with three sons, 'Alf' (8), 'Leif' (4) and 'Jon' (1). Christina's husband had escaped the previous year and was in America, where he was at that stage of the war probably training to be a pilot. She harboured a secret ambition to join a boat to escape and re-unite the family. Writing regularly to her husband (letters could get through to the still neutral USA), Christina didn't even share this plan with him, as she feared he would forbid an attempt. Her intention must have reached the ears of a well-wisher as one day she was delivered an anonymous message to leave that very night at ten o'clock. In the teeth of a strengthening wind. she and the children left the house creeping on foot down to the nearby agreed point; they were taken aboard the boat and off they set into the darkness. At first all seemed well enough but the following morning she was wrenched from sleep by the 'tic-tac' (her words) sound of gunfire. The little boat was being attacked by three planes which were taking it in turns to swoop in whilst machine-gunning. Not content with that, the planes came in again dropping hand grenades with surprising accuracy. Christina related, 'One of the hand grenades fell down the stove pipe and exploded in the cabin stove only inches (away), but the stove was solid. It did not burst and it saved my life.' The top of the stove was blown off and the cabin was filled with soot. All the passengers turned as black as chimney sweeps. When they had recovered enough to look around at each other they had no option but to burst into laughter.

Less lucky was the man in the wheelhouse who had been hit by a bullet. Christina went on, 'A Norwegian Red Cross nurse, who escaped with us, went up on deck to dress his wounds but the man had been shot in the head and died within half an hour.' The nurse also had to attend to several members of the crew who had been injured by other hand grenades that landed on the deck. The planes withdrew and Christina prayed fervently that they wouldn't return. The next concern was that water was pouring in from several holes at the waterline with water rising above the floor of the cabin and the soot soon turning to ink. Somehow the crew patched the damage and kept the pumps going whilst the gale developed into a raging storm. The passengers had to contend with debilitating sea sickness; only baby Jon was spared, sleeping through it all. They eventually reached the Scottish coast, sooty, inky and soaking. On arrival, Christina was able to cable her husband in America who must have been astounded by the adventure.

The name, date and place of departure of this boat are not known. The true names of Christina and her children are not known. This crossing would have been made about a month or more ahead of the newspaper reports, so the storm described would most likely be the major one that followed the autumn equinox at the end of September and early October. The very specific descriptions given of the attack by the three planes, the use of hand grenades, the wheelhouse man who died of his head wound, and the other crew members injured by the grenades are unique to this account confirming that this boat was previously not recorded. Christina's determination to be re-united with her husband and her vivid account of the crossing in 1941 brought this extraordinary drama to light.

Erling Kristian Marthinsson from Bergen had been arrested in March 1941 for 'radio transmissions to the enemy'. He was tried, sentenced to death and thrown into Ulven concentration camp, to the south of Bergen to await his fate. There he fell in with Carl Willhelm Müller, also under sentence of death so with nothing to lose the two decided to make an escape together which they managed pull off in June. The Germans would have assumed they would head west to find a boat on the coast and would have scoured that area. Wisely, the two headed in the opposite direction, north, past Bergen towards the remote Myredal mountains. They spent nearly three months hiding out there until an arrangement was made to get them away on a boat. In September, Finn Bjelland with his small boat *Kvalen* was sent all the way from Bremnes

(300 miles to the south) to pick them up from the Sognefjord. Something must have gone wrong with the arrangement because Marthinsson and Müller who had been waiting to be collected had moved on. Perhaps they were in danger of discovery. Bjelland was worried for them and set out to try to find them, visiting various other small ports on the Sognefjord. This was in itself risky, to be asking after the fugitives in German controlled ports where he was not known. He had brought five other escapers with him from Bremnes on board *Kvalen* and they shared the possibility of being caught. When he reached the mouth of the fjord at Bulandet on 1 October, he had to make a reluctant decision to abandon the search and head for Lerwick.

So what had happened to the missing Marthinsson and Müller? They attached themselves to fourteen other Bergen refugees who were looking for a boat on the small island of Melvær, well to the west and into the North Sea. A reliable local man contacted Olai Hillersøy, skipper of the boat *Juno*, on 28 September asking him outright to take them all to Shetland, emphasising the urgent plight of the two condemned men. 'Just a moment' replied Hillersøy with a nod. A man of few words he nipped home for his jacket and some food. Then, without further ado or any delay, the sixteen fugitives boarded and they were off. Perhaps Hillersøy should have paused to tap his barometer, as they set out into the same storm that destroyed *Valborg* and *Knut*, and they very nearly suffered the same fate. About half way across at the *Vikingbanken* (a fishing ground of shallower water) they were almost overwhelmed by enormous waves. The hatches sprang open letting water cascade in, but two brave men clambered onto the heaving deck, closed them and nailed them shut. *Juno* was very badly damaged and Hillersøy had no option but to turn around and run back to Melvær. They only just made it as *Juno* was no longer seaworthy. Hillersøy needed another boat, so the cutter *Stølsgut* was volunteered as a loan for the duration. By the time they set out again on 4 October the number of passengers had increased to twenty-one. The storm had passed and they had a blissfully straightforward trip to Lerwick.

Erling Marthinsson was a truly remarkable man. Having thrown off a death sentence by escaping, having been on the run for three months and having escaped death again on *Juno*, he immediately volunteered for Kompani Linge, determined to fulfil his desire to fight back. After he had graduated from the Linge commando academy, he returned in due course to Norway in April 1942 as a radio operator, but his mission was exposed and he was arrested on 31 May. For a second time he was sentenced to death and this time there was no escape; he was executed in October that year.

With the weather worsening in the autumn of 1941, you might have thought that enthusiasm to brave a crossing would have abated. There was enough going on in Norway, however, to continue to fuel the continuation of *Englandsfeber* in the population. The Germans having made people hungry by clearing their larders of food now wanted the shirts from their backs. Starting in September and continuing into early October, Terboven issued a series of edicts relating to the confiscation of personal possessions. With the exception of allowing one set of essential items to be retained per individual, orders were made for the handing in of all overcoats, furs, anoraks, other outdoor clothing (winter hats and gloves), boots, rucksacks, sleeping bags, blankets, tents, skis ... and bicycles. Depots for taking in the goods were set up with the better items being siphoned off for the German military, and the rest bundled up to send to Germany. At the extreme of this madness there was an edict for everyone to hand in their carpets. What was the point of that, except to make life less comfortable? There were the usual threats to promote compliance and the worst of these was to menace people's food rationing coupons. These measures were both impracticable and unenforceable on a nationwide scale; people simply hid things away. But they were designed to make Norwegians even more uneasy, and they rendered as vulnerable anyone who crossed swords with the occupiers or the NS; your home could be raided and stripped. The greatest effect was psychological, resulting in more suppression, anger and desire to get away.

Continuing *Englandsfeber* was also sustained by the alarming rumours that swirled around Norway that autumn, to the effect that Norway could be dragged by Hitler into a war in support of its traditional ally, Finland. The Finns were fighting the Russians, trying to recover territory they had lost to Russia in the Winter War of 1939; they didn't much care who would support them and naturally Hitler was pleased to fill the role. But Russia was now formally allied to Britain and thereby to the Norwegian government-in-exile. If Norway was forced to join in, they would be fighting against their new allies the Russians. There would have to be wholesale conscription and Norwegians would find themselves fighting alongside their immediate hated enemy, the Nazis. Politically complex, such was the stuff of rumours. It was an impossible prospect. It would be far better to go to Britain and fight the Germans head-on.

What's in a name? Erling Mæland was cautious and thought it was important. He refused point blank to have his name added to a list. His brother Magnus thought less of it and signed up. Being brothers, they might probably have argued the point, but Erling stuck to his guns. In the eventuality Erling's refusal saved his life, whereas Magnus paid a terrible price.

The brothers were part of a group of nineteen young men at Jæren (to the south of Stavanger) who were organising themselves to make the crossing to join the Allies in early October 1941. They clubbed together to buy a small boat, *Lykken* (Luck), lying in the small harbour at Obrestad; it was bought in the name of a teenager of just seventeen. Unfortunately, its name was the antithesis of its nature and destiny. They needed fuel, navigation instruments, other equipment and stores to make their escape. Someone tidily and efficiently thought to keep a list of who had paid for what. It was this list to which Erling Mæland refused to have his name attached. Jæren was a quiet area with no strong German presence, but the inhabitants underestimated what the Nazis were capable of. The boys were excited about their purchase of *Lykken*, but disappointed when they tried it out, as the engine was stubbornly unreliable, with the result that their departure had to be postponed, with dreadful consequences. The delay became disappointment and this in turn became tittle-tattle around the harbour, which was picked up by one of the German garrison who spoke Norwegian. On 17 October, the Gestapo arrived in force, raiding the house of one of the group, the one who had made the list. From there on it was a walk in the park for the Gestapo, who in no time at all rounded up all eighteen who were on the list. After more information had been extracted by the usual means there was a further round-up of eleven more men said to be involved, including Erling Mæland. Several, including Erling, endured torture without revealing any more names.

The trial came up on 5 May 1942. Of the eighteen on the list, fifteen were sentenced to death, and they were quickly executed on 21 May 1942 at Trandumskogen tank firing ranges, north of Oslo. The two youngest, who were teenagers, were spared that fate but were sent to a concentration camp. The total so far was seventeen from the list, leaving one not accounted for. He was not charged or imprisoned, he just disappeared from view. The inference was that he was in some way complicit in the betrayal, but, such was the shock in Jæren that no one talked about it and the subject remained shrouded in silence for years afterwards. Erling Mæland was not on the list and survived with a long sentence, whereas his brother Magnus was among the executed. What a dreadful burden for Erling to carry for the rest of his life.

The visual arts, literature, music and dancing form the cultural backbone of a nation. In Norway with its ancient sagas, lore and colourful history these enlightenments were deeply intrinsic to its national identity, and as such formed a focus for resistance to the occupying power. The Germans were quick to recognise this and they sought to suppress Nordic culture at all levels, replacing it with their own Nazi ideology. Newspapers and publishing had been subsumed under their control from early in the occupation. Art galleries were stripped of 'degenerate art' and re-hung to suit Nazi tastes. Orchestras and bands had their conductors or leaders removed to be replaced with NS appointees; performances were vetted and nationalistic music was proscribed. Radios had been confiscated so there was no broadcast music at all. That only left dance, and of course this did not escape attention. At the beginning of October 1941, Terboven issued an edict banning dancing in public places, restaurants, cafés, clubs and so forth. It may seem just petty now, but then it caused confusion and then anger. As so often with Nazi intentions, the regulation had the opposite effect to that intended, it did not lead to subservience but to resistance.

The ban on dancing had not yet reached the small island of Toft lying in the archipelago to the west of Bergen, or more probably they just ignored it. The young folk from Toft and adjacent islands had got together for a dance on 5 October, the sort that would be called a ceilidh in Scotland or a barn dance in the new world. To the sound of fiddles and accordions and aided by alcohol the youngster whirled and whooped as they let their hair down. As well as the girls and the dancing, Jakob Nilsen the 21-year-old skipper of the family fishing boat *Skjærgard,* had an eye on the weather, as he and some other boys were keen to cross to Shetland. That night the sea was calm and flat, with a sea fog rolling in. To Nilsen this was a 'friendly fog' as it would cover an escape until a boat was well out to sea; he knew his way out of the fjord like the back of his hand. After a brief discussion with his friends, Nilsen rushed home to retrieve a map of the North Sea. His parents guessed what he was up to but did not try to stop him. He then brought *Skjærgard* into the quayside. Returning to the dance hall, he interrupted the revellers with the announcement that this was the ideal night to escape to the Allies and that his boat would soon be ready for boarding. With that the whole assembly decanted to the harbour where, fortified by drink, they contemplated the sudden opportunity of leaving everything they knew and just stepping aboard without any possessions or luggage. The boys were encouraged that several of the girls wanted to come too, including Nilsen's girlfriend and his two sisters. However, because of the risks involved, and the old seafarer's superstitions he made a difficult but firm decision not to take the girls. Some emotional farewells took place by the side of the boat, without any of them knowing it would be another three and a half years before there would be any emotional reunions. In the end, ten boys went with Nilsen; the parting was difficult but the crossing to Lerwick was straightforward.

The impulsive Jakob Nilsen was just the right sort to be recruited by Kompani Linge, going through the gruelling training right to the unwelcome approach of a dreaded first parachute jump. He found that he could avoid this prospect by volunteering for transfer to the *Shetlandsgjengen*. He was after all a fisherman, much happier at sea than floating in the air. He became one of the most consistent and reliable members of the *gjengen*, going on fifty-six missions (the highest number), which was four more than the famous Leif Larsen. He was awarded the War Cross and the St Olav's Cross with Oak Branch. After the war Nilsen (who changed his surname to Strandheim) was re-united with his sweetheart Mary Johansen; they married and he subsequently followed a successful career in the family fishing business. Clear-headed and quietly spoken, he became an ambassador for the Shetland Bus, well known in Shetland and Norway. He was presented to HM Queen Elizabeth II at Buckingham Palace in 2005. He always marvelled modestly at his luck in surviving whereas others more deserving of life had died. He was amongst a party of nine surviving veterans who returned to Scotland on a commemorative visit in 2015, when I had an opportunity to meet and interview him. An optimist to the end, he always looked on the positive aspects of the contribution of free Norwegians to the war effort. When he died in 2021 at the age of 101, he was the last surviving member out of the 300 Norwegians who served on the Shetland Bus.

His Majesty King Haakon VII attended a film première in London on 6 November 1941 with his entourage and the whole Norwegian Cabinet. It was an important occasion as the film called *Men of Norway* (another edition was called *Norway in Revolt*) for the first time brought the reality of the situation in Norway to the huge audiences that flocked to the cinema in those days. The twenty-minute film was part of an American series made by The March of Time, a newsreel company. In this episode, the shortage of genuine footage was substantially reinforced by graphically reconstructed footage involving free Norwegians acting the parts. Nowadays we would describe this as 'docudrama'. It was a high quality production, hard hitting in its propaganda message, earning an Academy Award nomination. Its box-office success had significance in demonstrating the state of affairs in Norway, and the contribution by that small country to the war effort. It was a forerunner of a series of successful films on the same lines which followed in 1943 and 1944.

About a third of *Men of Norway* is devoted to the flight of Norwegians across the North Sea, and most of this was re-enactment of escapes aggregated into a generic form. Preparations such as stealing fuel from Quisling cars, stealing food, loading a small boat, leaving in pitch darkness, dodging searchlights, mines, patrol boats and aircraft were all dramatically portrayed. At one point, a true incident was portrayed where a menacing submarine pops up alongside a sailboat. This was the escaping *Trilby* (July 1940). When the identity of the submarine is revealed to be British (the Union Jack is broken out from the mast head) a crescendo rendition of *Hearts of Oak* heightens the drama. The film's 'blurb' says, 'The sighting of a surfacing submarine provides a genuine moment of nail-biting tension.' The focussed message of these escapes couldn't be clearer – defiant heroic Norwegians are risking everything to join their free forces, determined to drive the Nazis out of their country.

No doubt King Haakon and his party at the cinema felt pride and satisfaction at the success *of Men of Norway*. More importantly, the film was released on 26 September in the United States and was a considerable hit. This was a time when Haakon's daughter-in-law Crown Princess Märtha (who had escaped to America with her children in 1940, with the aid of the President) was trying to charm Franklin D Roosevelt into giving more aid to her country. *Men of Norway* would undoubtedly have helped her cause.

Chapter 11

Cutters and Hurricanes
(October–November 1941)

It may come as a surprise to learn that the generic kutter design for the larger west and north coast wooden fishing boats in Norway came from the east coast of Britain in the mid-nineteenth century. These boats had common fishing grounds – the North Sea. The British developed narrow, deep, fast sailers for trawling and drift netting. As the British embraced steam power in the second half of the century, many of their sailing boats were sold to Norway. The Norwegians began to adapt and then develop their own versions of the hulls and rigs. The boats were anywhere between 30ft and 75ft in length.

On the west coast of Norway, two main types of cutter evolved, the Hardanger and the Møre. Both had a straight vertical 'cutting' bow and an overhanging elliptical stern, with the rudder tucked away underneath. Both had a rear deck house, with a small mizzen mast behind it and a foremast to carry a variety of riggings. The Hardanger cutter was narrower, deeper in draught, and faster. Its stern was narrower and elegantly projecting. The Møre cutter was wider, sturdier with less draught and slower. The stern was less overhanging, and more rounded; it was, in effect, more 'tubby'. Early assessments by the Shetland Bus pioneers were that the Møre cutters were better suited to North Sea operations.

Further north, the *nordlander* boats were of more traditional Viking shape (raised and pointed at both ends) with the rudder on the stern post and a single square sail. Along the south coast the smaller lighter boats of about 25ft to 50ft were called *skøyte*. They were fully-decked, usually with two masts. With all of these boats, as the indigenous

Norwegian 'tonk–tonk' semi-diesel engines became fitted, the rigging became smaller. Right up to the Second World War, sail power was still used by the fishing fleet, most often as the primary source.

An example of one the largest boats was *Haugen*, a cutter of 76ft length based at Ålesund. Such a boat had capacity, so there was certainly a demand for it by worried refugees, many of whom were on wanted lists, converging from all over Norway. A married couple, Thoralf and Lilly Walle, had started up a new export group from September 1941 to replace those that had been betrayed earlier that summer. Thoralf was a policeman at Ålesund and in this enterprise Lilly was fully committed to help him. They were very wary of betrayal and practised strict security. They only helped people who satisfied them that they were genuinely on a wanted list or otherwise could prove their need. The Walles organised this trip with *Haugen*, and were lucky to get away with it, as there was a spy on board – or to look at it another way, perhaps they got away with it *because* there was a spy on board, who needed to proceed unmolested.

Haugen set out on 24 October 1941 with thirty-eight people on board, but only after a bad start as the designated skipper failed to turn up. Apparently, his father refused to let him go, but was that the real reason? Not deterred, Jacob Roald a local man from Ålesund and a group of local Ålesund friends pooled their expertise to fill the role, which they did with competence. Roald had only one misgiving; he took a dislike to a former army lieutenant who was amongst the refugees. He had observed the ex-army man staying at the Scandinavie Hotel, right next to the police station. It was a haunt of Germans and Quislings, so you wouldn't expect a 'good' Norwegian to stay there before an escape. Louis Rasmussen who was on the run from Oslo was also suspicious of the young woman travelling with the lieutenant who oddly asked to be put ashore not long after setting out – why would that be? These were puzzles that turned into worries that they would be intercepted, but thankfully this did not happen.

The ad-hoc collective skippers coped admirably well even when they ran into a severe gale, violent enough to sweep away the deck house. It took them three days to find themselves off Bressay, Shetland, and thence to Lerwick. At Lerwick all the arrivals were kept in their Nissen huts for an unusually extended seven days whilst they were endlessly questioned and re-questioned. Something was amiss, but Jacob Roald wasn't to find out what until after the war, when further Norwegian investigations unmasked the lieutenant as an Abwehr agent. He had remained undetected throughout the rest of the war, but now at last he faced Norwegian justice, and was sentenced to ten years imprisonment.

How very annoying it was, when you found a suitable escape boat, to find that the owner had removed important engine parts to prevent it from being stolen. Alfred Sperrevik and some friends had travelled to the Solund area (about 100 miles north of Bergen) where a local had offered a crossing to Shetland. When they got there, the man had reneged on the agreement and disappeared and the nine would-be escapers were left high and dry. So they looked around for a boat to 'borrow', becoming increasingly frustrated as they moved from boat to boat trying to find one not disabled by the removal of engine parts. We know about what happened because Sperrevik kept a diary, which he updated after he had succeeded in escaping. The friends had started to acquire some supplies, taking a risk with the owner of the local store who was a known NS Quisling. They worried that he might become suspicious about the amount of food the boys were buying. With some temerity, the young men approached the owner of the only fishing cutter in the district, the 38ft *Thelma*, Lorenz Ødejord. The older man thought long and hard about the request; at last he pronounced, 'It's my livelihood, guys, but you can have it … take the boat tomorrow evening.'. So this was to be an agreed 'borrowing' of the boat in the guise of a robbery; in this way the owner could decry the theft to all and sundry, and hope to avoid reprisal.

The nine young men were committed now so they gathered their belongings and supplies together. Two extra men from Utvær lighthouse appeared, bringing their number up to eleven. The following evening, 27 October, the party duly 'stole' the boat and chugged away into the darkness. The next autumn gale was on their heels, so they had a dreadful crossing. The following day they were spotted by a German plane, but the weather was so bad that it just circled and flew away. The second night a huge wave swamped the vessel, throwing those who were not on watch out of their bunks into a flooded cabin; nothing on board remained dry. Someone had the presence of mind to smash a hole in the bottom of the door to let the water drain out towards the stern where the bilge pump kept on going. They tried putting out a sea anchor which brought no meaningful respite from the pounding of waves. The following evening, they saw British planes; they waved frantically but without effect as night closed in on them. They spent all that night struggling to get the failing engine going. By dawn they had succeeded and Sperrevik steered towards a red light. *Thelma* finally completed her journey when she ran aground about 200 yards offshore. Some of the young men were so keen to get off the boat that they plunged into the freezing sea swimming the last lap while the rest waited for a rowing boat to come. They had arrived at the northern Orkney island of Sanday.

The bedraggled Norwegians were gathered together by some British soldiers and taken back to their barracks. There they found a table laid up for eleven with 'White and brown loaf, milk, tea, coffee, eggs and bacon – and it tasted good,' Sperrevik wrote, continuing, 'Many packs of cigarettes were on the table, but the icing on the cake was ... a bottle of Aqua White (a Norwegian spirit) ... from the ship, now being passed around.' Sleep would surely follow and be well deserved for these young adventurers.

The Holy Island of Lindisfarne, a tidal island lying off the coast of Northumberland, had little for which to thank the original Vikings. Founded as a monastery by St Aidan in 635, it became the power house of Christianity in northern England. It was renowned throughout Europe for its beautifully illuminated manuscripts. In one of the earlier raids, the Vikings visited in 793 on 8 June. It was a devastating desecration, causing shockwaves throughout the Christian world. The raid was graphically described a century later by the chronicler Symeon of Durham:

> They miserably ravaged and pillaged everything. They trod the holy things under their polluted feet; they dug down the altars, and plundered all the treasures of the church. Some of the brethren they slew, some they carried off with them in chains, the greater number they stripped naked, insulted, and cast out of doors, and some they drowned in the sea.

Over 1,000 years later the circumstance of another Viking arrival on 5 November 1941 could not have been more different. Five utterly exhausted young Norwegians were plucked from a rough sea by local fishermen and landed on the Holy Isle. It all began on the small island of Flekkerøy (just off Kristiansand on the south coast) on 1 November 1941, when the five young students from Kristiansand University set out in a 20ft open boat, belonging to the father of one of them. The boat had no protection from the elements except a low glass–panelled screen wrapped around the bow end. Such a boat is sometimes called a 'day boat', used for pleasure and certainly not designed for open seas. It had in common with most of the boats from that area a 4.5hp Marna engine. They left in cold darkness with some fuel stolen from the nearby German air base at Tveit, enough food for four days, a compass and youthful optimism. Three of the five were soon prostrate with seasickness, leaving the other two to cope with a rough voyage, encounters with floating mines and avoiding an unidentifiable ship's lights in the dark. At least the little engine kept going until, as dawn broke after the fourth night, they were drifting in the breakers on a strange shore. If they had been praying, then these prayers had guided them to this holy place.

A few days later, a radio broadcast from London innocently announced that 'Five boxes of cranberries had arrived in Britain'. It was the agreed coded message to confirm their safe arrival. It would have been happy news in Flekkerøy and Kristiansand, but it must have perplexed the Abwehr eavesdroppers.

Events such as these remain in the recollection not only of those who participated, but also of their descendants and others involved. Nearly seventy years later, on 31 August 2010, a small group of Norwegians organised by Flekkerøy history group gathered on Holy Island to dedicate a wooden bench in commemoration of the five young Vikings from Kristiansand. Among the group was one of the five original refugees, 91-year-old Kai Thorsen, determined to make the trip although confined to a wheelchair, in the care of his daughter Gunnlaug Eriksen one of the organisers of the trip.

The 2010 memorial bench carried an engraved plate with the inscription:

> In great gratitude for the good welcome our brave freedom fighters, Tormod Abrahamsen, Nils Havre, Sven Moe, Jan Stumpf and Kai Thorsen, received here on Holy Island on 5th November 1941, after crossing the North Sea in a small boat. Presented on behalf of families and friends in Norway, 31 August 2010.

Of the five men Abrahamsen, Havre and Moe trained to be pilots in Canada, and all died before the end of the war. Stumpf was brave and he was also more fortunate. He returned to Norway as an SOE agent operating under the codename 'Orion' and was arrested in June 1943. Held in multiple prisons, he somehow came out alive, dying in 2012 (he was not present on the 2010 visit). Kai Thorsen was witness to the ceremony. Also present were two local Lindisfarne couples, the Grays and the Croziers, who had preserved the quaint Marna engine and arranged for it to be sent back to Flekkerøy museum, where it stands as a further reminder of that memorable November crossing.

Severin Roald was master of his 5-year-old 56ft Møre cutter *Heland*, and he was master of his destiny, a strong-willed man who had no difficulty in making up his mind. He was the obvious man for the local Milorg in Ålesund to approach with a request to evacuate two Kompani Linge agents (working for SOE) who needed to get back to Scotland. Karl Johan Aarsæther and Åsmond Wisløff were both themselves former escapers earlier that year who had returned in the summer to help set up and train the Ålesund Milorg unit. Now they had to return for a much-needed radio transmitter, a radio operator, arms and explosives. The reason was clear-cut, and additionally there were two other fugitives desperate to escape. Roald agreed at once. Painting over the name *Heland* with the fictitious name *'Per'* they set off on 4 November 1941, unknowingly into a nascent storm.

Apart from atrocious weather this voyage was different in one respect from most previous crossings. Severin Roald had undertaken the task on condition he was allowed to return home, because he wanted to keep his fishing business going. Hitherto the British had insisted that the flight boats were one way only. The boats were either designated to continue fishing in Scotland or requisitioned by the War Department for naval use. Roald wanted neither of these options. On arrival in Lerwick he had some bargaining to do, and it was agreed that he could return but on condition he took with him stores, fuel, ordnance and agents. This was in effect a 'reverse Shetland Bus' procedure. It was not entirely without precedent as several earlier boat arrivals had been asked to turn around to take operatives back to Norway. Under this agreement, Roald returned to Ålesund on 5 December taking back Karl Aarsæther, his older brother Knut and a radio operator, Fredrik Aaros. Additionally, *Heland* was suitably laden with explosive Christmas presents for the eager local resistance. He went on to do two more 'freelance' runs to Lerwick in *Heland* in 1942, after which he and his boat went formally to the Shetland Bus fleet.

Heland had run into bad weather after leaving on 4 November, and this was but a foretaste of what was to come over the next two weeks. The North Sea was preparing to do its worst, and an ominous picture emerges on the archive weather forecasts. From 6 November, a low pressure system started moving down the Norwegian coast from the Arctic with gale warnings, whilst from Greenland, via Iceland two low pressure systems were moving towards the British Isles. On Saturday 8th the two systems collided directly over Britain, with a dramatic pattern of parallel vertical tight isobars overlaying the country, looking as if the country was 'behind prison bars'. This pattern held for the next four to five days and was accompanied by unremitting gale warnings, with snow and ice in the north.

David Howarth in his classic book *The Shetland Bus* described this very storm as seen from dry land at Lunna House on Shetland:

> By the morning of the 11th it had reached hurricane force...wind velocity well over a hundred miles an hour. At Lunna the salt water snatched from the wave crests...streamed over the isthmus and over the house to a height of a hundred and fifty feet.... The shrieking of the wind was unlike any natural sound – insane, hysterical, demoniac. To go out of the house for a few minutes... was as exhausting as running a race. One returned breathless, with face and hands stinging with salt and the scouring of sand and small stones flung up by the wind.

Into this unforeseeable peril, the *Anna B* left the island village of Televåg (to the west of Bergen) on 10 November, with thirteen men on board. We don't know the timing of events but some way out the engine packed up terminally and they started drifting at the mercy of the sea. Ragnar Ulstein stated that the boat completely capsized, to the extent that the ballast (this would have been lumps of rock) lying at the keel crashed through the floor of the cabin and then out through the roof. If there were men in the cabin (which there must have been), they somehow survived this rocky avalanche. What happened next was not described, but the boat must have rolled back to lie on its side and thereafter righted itself as, when it was later recued, it was capable of being towed. From another point of view, you can't envisage anyone surviving under an upturned hull. But survive they did, drifting for nine days. Only one non-verbatim description survives from one of the men, Jan Helen, who said that they had clung to the upturned hull. This can't have been factually true, rather an embellishment of the actuality as there was snow, ice and a dreadful sea in which a man cannot survive for more that around ten minutes at best. No one man could have lived through that, let alone all thirteen. Nonetheless, it's hard to imagine the conditions which they endured, without power, heat, light, soaked to the skin, with their food contaminated by sea water. On the tenth day they were rescued by a fishing boat and taken with *Anna B* under tow to Fosnavåg – 160 miles north of where they had set out nine days before. Later there was an attempt to tow *Anna B* south to Bergen for salvage or repair, but she had had enough; she broke up and yielded to the depths.

The thirteen fugitives melted into the hinterland of Fosnavåg. You would have thought that after their overwhelming experience not one of them would want to put to sea again. In fact, seven of them were undeterred, lying low for nearly three months until another opportunity arose to have a try at escaping, this time on the boat *Rupee* in February the next year.

It is a sad truth that these events, the escapes, the betrayals, the losses and their consequences have largely faded in the memory and consciousness of twenty-first century Norwegians. But if only one story remains poignantly remembered today it is that of the 55ft boat *Blia*. The *Blia* was built as a well-boat (it had a tank for transporting live fish, to keep them fresh), and as a general-purpose fishing boat. Crucially, it had been built at Farsund (on the south coast) to a lighter 'southern' specification than the tougher west and north coast boats. On 15 March 1941 she had made an uneventful crossing to Lerwick with twenty on board. The boat was deemed to be unsuitable for service in the Shetland Bus, and it remained under ownership of its skipper, 21-year-old Ingvald Lerøy and his brother Arne, who at the time voiced some concerns about the lightness and strength of the boat being unsuitable for the North Sea. In the meantime, they did a little 'fishing for the Allies'. The Shetland Bus people did keep an eye on it as a 'reserve' vessel and helped with some alterations. It was in this capacity that the Lerøy brothers were asked to return to Norway to pick up two SIS agents, Bernhard Håvardsholm and Billy Forthum from the island of Bømlo, with a moral inducement that they could also bring back refugees fleeing from Gestapo attentions. It was a request, not an order as the brothers were civilians and they were not enrolled into the *Shetlandsgjengen*. Wanting to do the right thing, they overcame their doubts about the boat and agreed. In effect this was to be a hybrid operation between an official Bus assignment and a refugee escape mission.

Perhaps security at Bømlo was not as good as it should have been because word was out that *Blia* was coming to do a pick-up and dozens of anxious candidates for inclusion started to arrive in the district. When *Blia* docked at Øklandsvågen on 10 November, people flocked to the little harbour and when boarding started on 11 November there was an unseemly rush of people to get on the boat. Soon she was grossly overloaded and causing concern to the Lerøys. The SIS man Håvardsholm took control of the situation by drawing his revolver, standing at the top of the gangway. All women and children were ordered off the boat and of these all complied except for three who would not budge. The boat was then loaded in a more orderly fashion, but it still ended up far too full, with a final complement of forty-three crowding into the crew accommodation, every other available space and finally into the deep and smelly fish tank.

In 1984 a boat hatch bearing the name *'Blia'* was found at Gulen, about 150 miles north of Øklandsvågen. *Blia* had headed out into the teeth of the hurricane on 11 November 1941, and that was the last that anyone knew of her. Until the 1984 discovery, nothing had ever been found. The speculation that she had broken up because of her unsuitability and because of the overloading swirled around for some years. It was the largest single loss of life among the many North Sea crossings. The average age of the dead was twenty-six. There is a full memorial in the churchyard at Bremnes. The particular circumstances and the size of the *Blia* tragedy has retained an awareness in Norway whereas other stories have faded with the years.

As *Blia* pulled away from Øklandsvågen the three dozen or so who were left standing on the quay must have felt shattered. They had been stopped on the gangway at gunpoint by Håvardsholm. Most of them had travelled hundreds of miles to be there and had already been hiding out for days waiting for *Blia* to come. Amongst them were fourteen women with their children, including one very new baby. It was freezing cold, it was dark and there was an incipient storm. It was also a headache for the organisers of the local resistance, Håkon Særsten and Sigurd Hus. They once again had to find hidey-holes for all these people, providing them with food and necessary supplies. They were the shepherds of a flock of people in desperate need of shelter.

There was a further problem, of course, because the departure of *Blia* had reached the ears of the Gestapo in Bergen, where most of the fugitives were from. They soon arrived in their own boat known as the *Gestaposkøyta*. which they anchored on the east coast of Bømlo. This was no pleasure cruiser but an armed vessel equipped for the capture, interrogation and detention of the Gestapo's suspects. Its appearance along the coast or among the islands struck fear among the inhabitants whether or not they had anything to hide. They were particularly keen to catch Særsten, but he got a tip-off that they were watching his home and the post offices (always the nerve centre of a community). In a sad sub-plot to the tense situation, young Alfred Offerdal, already a marked man in Bergen for 'illegal activities' was hiding in an uncomfortable stone outhouse. He grew restive deciding to stretch his legs to the local post office. There he walked straight into the arms of the Gestapo and after the usual preliminaries paid for this with his life the following January.

As the island general practitioner, Dr Sigurd Hus had a car and a ration of petrol. This was useful not only for visiting his patients but also for moving fugitives from house to house. One evening he drove into a German roadblock at which there was much shouting and stamping, which in itself alerted a group of refugees nearby who were able to melt into the night. As the Germans shone flashlights into the car, Hus, who spoke fluent German, was able convince them of his medical purpose. He was convincing enough that they didn't open the boot, wherein lay two young escapers. If that was a close shave, Særsten got closer. At a night-time meeting with a contact at a crossroads they were surprised by the torchlights of a group of approaching Germans. With seconds to spare, the contact pitched one way and Særsten dived into a gap in a wall, dropping down to the level of a gulley into which he tried to wriggle. He got firmly stuck half way in, and just lay still. The German torches probed the darkness looking for the source of the voices they had heard, but somehow they missed the terrified man at ankle level.

As soon as they could, Hus and Særsten needed to organise another boat and this they managed in the second week. On Friday, 21 November a timber carrier came and anchored off the west coast of the island. The fugitives had to be moved there under cover of darkness, and then had to be rowed over to the boat to climb aboard. As they lay at anchor waiting to leave, an ominous wind was arising, enough to damage the boat. It was decided to call off the attempt; everyone was put back in the rowboats and returned to the shore. Morale must have been at rock bottom at this setback, but it was raised by the intervention of the local priest who stepped in, organising a redistribution of the passengers around different hiding places on the west of the island including his rectory, stables outhouses and cabins in the nearby forest.

These people were in despair and nearing the end of their tethers. To return to their homes was an impossibility as their absence would be tantamount to admission of their 'intent to try to escape to the enemy' and the terrible consequences of that. Hus and Særsten tried to reassure them that they were doing everything they could to get them away but patience was wearing thin, with one poor woman having a complete hysterical breakdown requiring the medical attentions of the doctor. They would have to endure another six days of hardship and exposure before they eventually got away.

Over the coming days, a boat was found and an offer was made to purchase it for cash but this was turned down flat by the owner. Then, with the next boat, the owner agreed but after a day the crew refused. These failures were unprecedented. As the week went on a saviour stepped forward – Captain Thomas Boge, the owner and operator of the 80ft coastal passenger cutter *Haugland I*, which plied the routes between the islands. Hearing of the dreadful situation on Bømlo, he without hesitation offered the boat to evacuate the fugitives. Realising there was no way of avoiding the attentions of the Germans when the boat disappeared, he decided to take his wife Kristiane (38 weeks pregnant) and three children with him. On Wednesday, 26 November everyone was moved to an agreed point on the west of Bømlo where after dark everyone boarded the comparative luxury of a passenger ferry. There was a total of forty-three, including the women and children who had been turfed off *Blia*. Among them was Håkon Særsten who had decided his days were numbered if he remained. Dr Sigurd Hus kept on doing his good work on Bømlo until he was arrested in 1943, suffering 'inhumane torture'. He had earlier saved a German airman who had crashed into the sea and for this act he escaped a death sentence, but he was imprisoned for the rest of the war.

After up to a month of living under cover (in some cases actually without any cover at all) it must have been paradise to be on *Haugland I*, with a galley, hot food, hot and cold running water and toilets. As they set out on 27 November, they found their joy to be short-lived, as they ran into another of the hurricane-force gales of that autumn. A huge depression over Iceland was pushing the isobars together into a deep trough over the North Sea. *Haugland I* was a coastal vessel, not built as a North Sea Ferry and it nearly didn't make it, as headwaves crashed over the entire length of the boat, damaging the bridge. After sixty-four dreadful hours they finally arrived in Lerwick – the relief must have been palpable.

Exceptions to the rule are often welcome, as we find with the 73ft fishing boat *Erkna*; she was the only boat not to be wooden. A rarity, she was built in 1907 of steel plates traditionally joined together with hot iron rivets. After the capitulation, the Germans took a fancy to her and she was requisitioned by the Kriegsmarine. So it was an act of resistance to liberate her from the enemy with the intention of using her for an escape. The Kriegsmarine would normally have had her under strict guard, but she was actually at the Hatlø shipyard in Ulsteinvik, and it is likely that the watch had been stood down whilst she was in dock. The emancipation of *Erkna* was planned and executed by the local Milorg, but the details are not recorded. In the middle of the night of 17 November 1941, sixty people (mostly men) crept aboard. An older man (actually a radio telegrapher), Petrus Gjørtz, acted as skipper, but the boat's own engineer declined to leave his family and refused to go. Aircraft mechanic Knut Olsen stepped forward, figuring he could deal with the engine, which was new. Olsen (21) had cycled all the way from Oslo to Ålesund (around 350 miles) with his friend Knut Asbjørnsen (also 21), and the pair had moved from house to house whilst waiting for an escape opportunity. Local teenager Peter Sperre (17) was greatly relieved to get on board as that same day he had a received an urgent warning that the Gestapo were on to him. Working as a baker's assistant by day, he had been distributing underground newspapers by night. Peter made himself useful in the galley.

As *Erkna* slipped away from the boatyard and crept away from the coast they were stopped by a German *schnellboote*. It recognised *Erkna* as a Kriegmarine vessel and was satisfied by the skipper's papers. Everyone else on board must have squeezed out of sight and held their breath. They were at least blessed by good weather – a gap between two storms. In the engine room the aircraft engineer, Olsen, who was not accustomed to boats, was faced by the overpowering smell of fish and seal meat, which soon translated to severe sea sickness. Young Peter Sperre tried to comfort him with bread and coffee. The only other danger they faced was near their journey's end on 19 November.

As *Erkna* approached the Outer Skerries of Shetland, the local passenger ferry the *Earl of Zetland* steamed to greet her. As they drew near, the lookouts on the *Earl* spotted a rogue floating mine dead ahead of *Erkna*. It was duly disposed of by rifle fire from the Scottish boat, which then towed the Norwegians into the shelter of Symbister on the island of Whalsay. There was a Norwegian intelligence officer on board the *Earl* and he went aboard the refugee boat to start his first screening of the arrivals as they were towed to Lerwick. He had never encountered so many people on board a single vessel – this was indeed the largest consignment of Norwegians that made the crossing.

Peter Sperre joined the Norwegian Army and then volunteered for the Norwegian Parachute Company (part of 1st Airborne Division) and saw action back in Norway. Knut Olsen went into the air force and resumed his engineering career. He firstly worked on Catalina flying boats at Woodhaven on the River Tay, and then on Spitfires in Holland following D-day. The two did not meet again until September 2015, when they were two out of a party of nine surviving veterans that travelled to Scotland, where I was able to meet them and learn about their escape experiences on *Erkna*. Recognising each other, they shared an understanding best expressed by Peter in his own words. 'We travelled to England to fight the Germans. We sacrificed a lot, but most Norwegians never got this chance.'

Erkna was taken into the Shetland Bus service for a while and went on three missions. After the war she was saved from the scrap yard and was fully restored. Built two years before the *Titanic*, she will outlive all those she saved in 1941.

At the tail end of that terrible month of storms on 30 November 1941, a boat set out from Aukra on the island of Gossa (between Ålesund and Kristiansund). Gossa was not much involved in the escape business. In fact, only one other boat went from there and we would know very little, if anything, of this story except for one extraordinary outcome. On 23 February 1942, a bottle containing a message was taken from the sea in Finnmark – at least 1,000 miles north of Aukra, carried there by the Gulf Stream. It had been consigned to the sea as the last act of one of the two men on board, Gerhard Sundby, the other man being Kristian Hægdahl. It was addressed to his mother who lived in Haugesund several hundred miles south of Aukra. Only a tiny percentage of messages-in-bottles are ever recovered, so it was a 'million-to-one' chance that this one having travelled so far and after only six weeks had been found then sent successfully onwards to Mrs Sundby.

From the few details known and from the content of the brief message a picture emerges. Sundby was working in Molde, the 'county town' of Møre og Romsdal, 20 miles away. A sizeable town it had a resistance organisation and an underground press. Sundby is known to have been involved, and he must have had a tip-off to get away. He was able to identify a boat at Aukra belonging to a Nazi sympathiser, so it did not trouble him to steal it. It was a fishing boat called *Grei*. What was very odd was that he took with him just one other man, Kristian Hægdahl, who was unwell – he had just had surgery on an ear. That sounds minor, but in those days complications from ear infections often needed major surgery. Before the antibiotic age, ear infections not uncommonly spread to invade the bone around the ear, occasionally going rogue and fatally worming their way into the brain. Surgery to clear out the diseased bone (mastoidectomy) was a substantial procedure which on occasion failed to prevent progression to brain involvement. So why on earth would Hægdahl want to get into a boat and face the North Sea at the end of November after having had such an operation? It's probable that he too was on the Gestapo wish list at the same time as Sundby and he would be at risk of arrest if he had to go back to hospital. A hospital in Shetland would be a better option.

Unsurprisingly the two ran into bad weather, the engine packed up and they were just drifting. Hægdahl was dying and by the tenth day he was near his end. There was only one day's food left; with no miracle in sight, Sundby wrote his farewell message; it was 10 December. Six weeks later in Haugesund, Mrs Sundby would at least have had some explanation for the disappearance of her son, and so would be better equipped to deal with the grief that submerged so many mothers in that war.

It is possible that there was a cat among the pigeons in the resistance at Molde, as just two weeks later in the depths of December, five more young men needed to get away. They decided to take and sail a *regattabåt* (racing yacht) called *Viking*, which unusually had a steel hull which they considered to be sturdy enough to take on the North Sea. Asbjørn Elgenes and Asbjørn Rasmussen were experienced sailors, but the other three had little experience; it was a tall order. They provisioned themselves for five days, got hold of a hand-held compass, set sail and off they went. In spite of very rough weather, they kept going and on the fourth day they were nearing Shetland, actually catching sight of land. An RAF plane passed overhead – had it seen them? Suddenly there was a surge in the storm, and Asbjørn Elgenes and another lad, Lars Hoel were 'knocked overboard', presumably by the boom suddenly crashing across in a jibe. Retrieving a 'man-overboard' is a tricky exercise even on a flat calm sea. Rasmussen, who was a skilled sailor, located the two but the storm was so violent that they could not be brought back on board, being repeatedly swept away. They were soon reclaimed by the waves. After some hours the rescue had to be abandoned. The remaining three young men were devastated and exhausted; they decided to turn around and head back to Norway and home.

There is a post-script to this tragedy that almost defies comprehension, let alone belief. Asbjørn Elgenes did not immediately perish after being swept overboard and survived long enough to drift towards a life raft on which were some survivors from a ship that had been torpedoed some time before. Those men were also utterly exhausted and nearing their end, and they were physically unable to haul Elgenes onto the raft. His soaking winter sailing gear would have been a dead weight. Clinging on, he gave them his name, his family address on the island of Finnoy (not far from Molde), and a simple message 'Greetings to them there at home'. Then he told them to let him go.

To their amazement those on that life raft were rescued. The RAF plane that the five Norwegians had seen earlier must have marked them and called for help. This corresponds with a report in the *Nottingham Journal* (31 December 1941) that a cargo ship had been torpedoed just before Christmas 'somewhere in the North Sea, and ... the officers and crew spent sixteen hours on a raft before being picked up by a destroyer and taken into an east coast port'. One of those survivors later honourably carried out his solemn mariner's duty to report to the Elgenes family at Finnoy the tragic end and the last words of young Asbjørn. What a burden that family had to carry as a result of the German occupation. Asbjørn's twin brother Severin had already been lost at sea the year before, and their remaining son, Kåre Angel, was involved in an attempted escape on the boat *Viggo* in February the next year (Chapter 12). If anything, his fate was even worse than either of his brothers.

The Norwegian Fighting Man
(December 1941–January 1942)

I f you were to be among the thousands of visitors to Forest Lodge, headquarters of the RSPB (Royal Society for the Protection of Birds) at Abernethy Forest in the beautiful Cairngorms National Park, you would scarcely notice a set of abandoned kennels behind the lodge. If you were to creep in, you would be surprised to find the walls covered in Norwegian graffiti, indicating the incarceration of soldiers serving their time for some long-forgotten misdemeanour. This was a detention block for tough soldiers of Kompani Linge, none too pleasant, especially in winter. Although there are flashes of humour, sketches of gaunt faces bemoan their situation and calendar days are crossed off in anticipation of release. The prisoners were hard men, being further toughened up. They were in the middle of their rigorous special forces training in Norway's famous Kompani Linge.

The primary aim of those who risked so much to escape to Britain from April 1940 onwards was to join the Allied forces as free Norwegians and to wage war against the occupiers of their country. There were of course all sorts of ancillary reasons for hazarding the crossings, such as flight from the Gestapo or the Sipo, Quislings and their like, reprisals, betrayals, Jewish persecution, enforced labour, displacement from their homes, hunger … and occasionally love. On the whole, everyone really wanted to contribute to the war effort. These were people self-selected by their courage in crossing by sea, and almost all gave significant support to the Norwegian government in exile.

None more so than the men who were recruited into Kompani Linge and the Shetland Bus. In the earliest days following the Nazi invasion there were some spontaneous initiatives to return people back to Norway for intelligence and sabotage work. Even before the capitulation, James Chaworth-Musters and Percy Boughton-Leigh had hazardously launched missions back to Norway, acting possibly on their own initiative but more probably under the auspices of the SIS. After Churchill launched the SOE in July 1940, the formation of Kompani Linge and the Shetland Bus began to materialise during that autumn. Two enterprising British Officers, Major Leslie Mitchell and Lieutenant David Howarth RNVR, were appointed to form the Shetland Bus operation. Much has been written about the Bus, but much less is known in Britain about Kompani Linge.

Lieutenant Martin Jensen Linge, a former reserve officer in the Royal Norwegian Army, was a successful stage and screen actor in the 1930s. He immediately re-enlisted and threw himself into the fighting when the Germans came. He then became a liaison office to the British when they arrived at Åndalsnes. He was injured in a bombing raid and he was evacuated by the British, being the first injured Norwegian to arrive in Scotland. After he recovered from his injuries, he fumed about what had happened to his country, and burned to get back into action. His assertion that 'Our land is perfect for secret resistance and guerrilla warfare' caught the attention of the Norwegian government, and then the Scandinavian section of the newly formed SOE. Appointed as 'Liaison Officer', he was far more than that, restless to drive his agenda forward; he seems have been given a remarkably free rein.

Linge was one of those extraordinary characters that were thrown up by the war. Aged 46, he was a married man with two children, who might well have taken a much easier path. He was a natural leader, using his considerable acting and linguistic talents to charm politicians, senior military officers and the lowest ranks alike. He was as much at home in the bottom of a ditch as he was in a London club. He soon fell in with Chaworth-Musters and Boughton-Leigh, and the unlikely threesome set about organising an ad-hoc Norwegian SOE unit and recruiting some warlike candidates. There was plenty of choice amongst those who, in effect, had already passed a rigorous selection test during their daring escapes.

They found candidates amongst the earliest arrivals as they were being inducted into the Norwegian forces. They listened out for interesting arrivals and, in the instance of Odd Starheim (Chapter 3), Martin Linge himself travelled all the way to Aberdeen to recruit him and his companions while they were still in jail – a catch fresh from the sea, so to speak. As soon as the London Reception Centre was up and running, they had a constant supply of likely lads who showed courage and initiative. Linge was so magnetic that it was rare for anyone to refuse his invitation to join his little *gjengen*. They were, to a man, volunteers and enthusiastic students. These early recruits received basic army induction and training over the autumn of 1940. Skills such as drill, skill-at-arms, signals procedures and field craft were upgraded by visits to Meoble Lodge in the west Highlands for winter warfare training, to No 1 Parachute Training School at Ringway, and to what was called 'finishing school' at Beaulieu in Hampshire, where the secret skills of SOE operations were taught. The Norwegians were based at Fawley Court at Henley-on-Thames and Stodham Park, Liss, Hampshire. Their training was rather spread about and not best suited to what Linge wanted to do in Norway. They needed a bigger adventure playground to hone their skills.

The wonderfully named Irregular Warfare School had been established by Military Intelligence at Lochailort (to the west of Fort William in the Scottish Highlands) as early as May 1940. It became a repository for an interesting range of volunteer eccentrics desperate to see some action, for example the famous former Shanghai Police officers, Dan Fairbairn and Bill Sykes (the 'Angelic Twins') who instructed thoroughly ungentlemanly and wholly brutal methods of gutter fighting and assassination, armed and unarmed. The aristocratic

Simon, Lord Lovatt, brought his own private army of Highlanders to the party to teach field craft, and living off the land. Where there was a party there was to be found David Niven, the famous film star (he was actually one of the 30 per cent who dropped out). There were dubious characters who had acquired skills that had necessitated a stay in one of His Majesty's prisons. This diverse assembly loved to shoot at things and blow things up. They didn't believe in blank ammunition where live firing kept the men on their toes. Every man was a volunteer, and they were all at that time in army uniform, The Royal Marines were not invited to join the party until February 1942, and the green berets were adopted later still. The initial groupings were called Independent Companies, later to be superseded by the enduring term 'Commandos'. But the Norwegians were never really Commandos – they were Linge men, they kept to their designation Norwegian Independent Company 1 (NORIC.1), later to be renamed plain Kompani Linge.

Soon the whole of the central and western Highlands was turned into a vast 'theme park' for special operations training. In due course, the Norwegians were allotted their own school, STS 26 (Special Training School 26) spread over Dumintoul Lodge (the headquarters), Glenmore Lodge and Forest Lodge with their estates. These covered much of the entire Rothiemurchus and Abernethy forests, including tens of thousands of acres of wild Highland uplands and mountains (to the east and north east of Aviemore). The area was similar to central Norway, and it was an ideal training ground. The Norwegians relished the environment; 530 men went through the school, of whom 57 were subsequently killed in action. The numbers may seem to be small, but Norway was a small country. Moreover, Kompani Linge punched well above its weight in terms of successes. Some of the most conspicuous commando operations in the Second World War were at their hands, including the highly significant raid on the heavy water plant at Vemork in Telemark. Those men confined to the kennels at Forest Lodge made a huge contribution to the Allied cause.

All the enterprise and energy generated in Scotland during 1941 matured to deliver a seasonal gift for Adolf Hitler that year, 1941. On Boxing Day at 06.00hrs, a force of 300 commandos, including Norwegians, landed unopposed on the northern island of Moskenesøya at the southern tip of the Lofoten Islands, well within the Arctic Circle; this was Operation Anklet. The sleepy hung-over Germans were overwhelmed and captured, Quislings were arrested, radio stations were destroyed, German ships sunk, and 200 islanders were 'recruited' to return with the task force to join the free forces. As a bonus, an Enigma code machine complete with its vital rotors was captured; this was to be sent to Bletchley Park. After two days mopping up, it was time to return to Scotland. There were no Allied casualties and, if ever justification was needed for the commando concept, this was it.

Anklet was actually a raid diversionary to the larger Operation Archery that went ashore on 27 December, much further south on the islands of Vågsøy and Måløy (between Bergen and Ålesund). The landings should have been simultaneous with those in the north but were delayed by bad weather. The delay meant that the Germans were alerted by the news of the Lofoten raid. Following a highly accurate naval bombardment, a force of 570 commandos stormed ashore, including a small detachment of Norwegians, selected for local knowledge. One of the landing craft deployed a secret weapon – the skirl of bagpipes being played by Major 'Crazy Jack' Churchill leading with *The March of the Cameron Men*. However this proved to be no Boxing Day jaunt. These Germans were awake and, unknown to intelligence, a small group of battle hardened *Gebirgsjäger* (mountain troops) were on Christmas leave from the eastern front. The invaders met stiff resistance with sniping, house-to house and hand-to-hand combat. This actually tied the Germans down whilst the rest of the commandos rapidly went about their destructive business. They blew up all the fish-oil factories (important for the manufacture of high explosive), two radio stations, a power station, coastal defences and a lighthouse. Additionally, 10 German ships were sunk, 120 Germans were killed, 98 taken prisoner,

Quislings were arrested, and 70 Norwegian refugees (including women and children) were evacuated. The bonus of this raid was a complete copy of the German Enigma Naval Code. The whole force was away by last light the same day. In military terms it was a considerable success, but this was far surpassed by the worldwide propaganda triumph that followed. Mr Churchill had been seen to 'set Europe ablaze' and he was delighted.

Hitler was furious, becoming convinced that the Allies were planning to invade northern Norway to join up with the Russians in Finnmark thereby creating a new northern front. He ordered a further strengthening of his Norwegian *Festung Norwegen* (Fortress Norway, part of his Atlantic Wall). The German army was reinforced with 30,000 extra troops. He ordered a build-up of coastal defences, air bases and aircraft. At its height the Germans had built 221 coastal gun batteries, 340 anti-aircraft emplacements, 50 airfields and 90 radar stations. He diverted his beloved great battleship *Tirpitz* to the north. All of this was to deter a perceived Allied invasion, and it diverted huge amounts money, men and materiel away from other fronts. At a *Führer-Konferentz* on 20 January 1942, Hitler significantly declared that 'Norway is now the area of destiny in this war'.

Amongst the twenty-two killed that day lay Captain Martin Jensen Linge who fell leading a charge on the German headquarters; at that moment, he was the embodiment of the Norwegian fighting man. For the men of his unit, it was a devastating intimate blow affecting every single one of them. There were recriminations. The Norwegians protested vociferously that they had not been sufficiently consulted by Combined Operations (who had planned and executed the raids) and that their local knowledge of the targets had been undervalued. Crucially, the local Milorg groups had been neither consulted nor warned. In the ranks of NORIC.1 there was disquiet in what they saw as gratuitous death and destruction in their beloved country. Not a few asked to be transferred to other arms of the free forces. There was such disquiet at ST 26 in Scotland that for a few weeks the men were placed in 'quarantine' at Forest Lodge to cool off. Reality prevailed and the Linge men arose in tribute to their founder, renaming their unit Kompani Linge, more determined than ever to give the Nazis a bloody nose. In Norway today Martin Linge is remembered in many ways – statues, street and place names – even a North Sea oilfield.

In Scotland his creation, Kompani Linge, is remembered in a memorial at Glenmore which reads:

This stone was erected by the people of Badenoch in honour of the gallant company of Norwegian patriots who lived among them & trained in these mountains 1941-1945 to prepare for operations in occupied Norway. By skilful & daring raids on military & industrial targets they harassed the enemy & denied them vital supplies. These dangerous missions were not carried out without losses. 57 brave men of Kompani Linge gave their lives in our common cause.

The raiders of Operations Anklet and Archery with their spoils of war were back at their bases in Scotland by the last days of December 1941, in most cases elated but in the Norwegian camp deflated. From both points of view, a few wee drams of the national drink would have helped them to negotiate a Scottish Hogmanay. Britain awoke to triumphant news; it was the first major Combined Operations strike of the war. It was at last a good news message to usher in the New Year of 1942.

Shortly after midnight on the very first day of January 1942, the first boat of the year set out to cross a forbidding North Sea. On New Year's Eve, from all over Norway, a party of twelve gathered on the island of Vigra at Ålesund, but this was no celebration, it was desperation. They had been convened for an escape by Frederik Aaros, the Kompani Linge radio operator who had been taken across by *Heland* in December. He needed to return to Scotland, along with Knut Egil Almquist a secret agent probably of the SIS. Among the other fugitives was a local man Reidulf Hagen, formerly a member of the Torsvik Group who had been arrested in July and suffered the indignities of the Gestapo. In December, when Hagen was lined up for an ominous transfer to Oslo for further questioning, he feigned illness to be admitted to hospital, under guard. Approaching midnight on 16 December, he was 'sprung' from the hospital by local men. A rumour was put about that he had committed suicide, and this took the heat off the search for him. A van was waiting outside which drove him to a boat which then whisked him to Vigra where he had been hidden, patiently waiting for his onward escape.

With the help of the Walle Group in Ålesund they had got hold of the boat *Trygve*, with Fredrik Aaros designated to be the skipper. It was actually his second escape as he had first been on the tiny boat *Lady Nancy* in May 1940 (Chapter 2) so he knew the ropes. In the early hours of the New Year, the twelve men left the island and on this occasion had a more straightforward crossing than Aaros had had in 1940, arriving safely in Lerwick. Aaros was a Linge man and that meant going back to Norway again; he defied danger. On 12 August 1943, he and Tor van der Hagen (who had escaped on *Viola* in September 1941) were transmitting from an isolated mountain hut when they were ambushed by the Germans. Van der Hagen managed to escape, but Aaros was taken. Rather than reveal under torture his extensive knowledge of the local resistance and fellow agents, he gallantly took his own life, using his commando knife. It was an entirely selfless act. In 2020, a memorial bronze plaque was unveiled at Søgne to this very brave and highly decorated Linge man.

As a result of the Lofoten and Måløy raids, the Germans completely shut down all coastal traffic. It wasn't really a logical move, but it gave 22–year old Reidar Pedersen with a group of six friends a few days to assess the possibility of making an escape from Leirvik on the island of Stord. Pedersen wrote a little account of the tale, giving some insights (*As I See It*, private publication 2001). I was also able to glean details from him in interviews in Scotland 2004–07. The seven had their eye on a strongly built cutter adapted as a coastal cargo boat used for carrying rocks, lime and occasionally timber; she was called *Eli*. Hearing that the ban was to be lifted, the following day, Sunday, 4 January, the boys, as if innocents, offered to help load and fuel the vessel, with the ulterior motive of borrowing the boat for their venture. Sunday came and the young men put on their Sunday best so as to look as if they were more interested in attending church than climbing aboard a cargo boat. Sauntering towards the rendezvous point, a farming family, realising their intent, drew them into their house and emptied their larder into the boys' knapsacks. They found an old rowing boat to row out to *Eli*, pulled the boat up on deck and were soon under way. The boat was fully laden with rocks so they would not lack for ballast. As they reached open sea, they ran straight into bad weather and made a wise decision to shelter in a quiet harbour. They used the interlude to 'batten down the hatches' of the large hold and to cover the deck with fishing gear to divert the attentions of several planes that passed by. The pilots were not very observant, as *Eli* wasn't showing a fishing boat registration as strictly required.

On the second day, the wind got behind them, they raised sail, revved the engine and shot off, making good speed and reaching landfall after 29 hours, late on the 7 January. Seeing some lights on the shore, they simply dropped anchor and went to bed; they were, after all, exhausted. The next morning, they rowed ashore in the little rowing boat, to find that the lights had come from a military barracks where they were welcomed with a feast of a breakfast by kindly soldiers. They discovered that they were at the north of Unst in Shetland – any further north and they would have passed by and into the Atlantic. A pilot came to guide them southwards; on the way he admired their small rowing boat and by the time they got to Lerwick he had done a deal to buy it. Each Norwegian stepped ashore with thirty shillings in his pocket (about £90 in today's money). No one breathed a word that they had just sold stolen goods.

The previous November, Severin Roald and his stout boat *Heland* had undertaken a 'reverse' east-west bus trip from Ålesund to Lerwick, taking the Linge agent Karl Aarsæther. In December, he returned to Norway with Aarsæther, his older brother Knut, the radio operator Frederik Aaros and a boat laden with arms and explosives. Roald had returned to fishing in January 1942, but when the Aarsæther brothers asked him for another shuttle back to Scotland he didn't hesitate in agreeing to do it, despite the risks. By this time, he would have been well aware of what they were up to – and what they were up to was interesting; they were setting up their own 'private army'.

The war gave those with personality, initiative and drive opportunities they would never get in peacetime. So it was with the Aarsæther brothers – Karl aged 22 and Knut 26. In spite of the generally acknowledged observation that siblings make difficult pairings, the brothers had a remarkable and enduring partnership throughout the war. Both were commissioned officers in Kompani Linge and with the connivance of SOE were conducting their own side show in the Ålesund area; the code-name was 'Antrum', and the brothers went on to form, train and arm a secret fighting force of 1,000 men. A novel feature is that they alternated command between them. They were a highly self-reliant pair because they stayed independent of the main Milorg organisation until 1945. Their little army was highly effective, particularly with shipping intelligence, but they also managed refugee traffic, liaised with the Shetland Bus and supported SOE incursions. From time to time they indulged themselves by blowing things up. The effectiveness of Antrum can be measured by the decorations that were awarded to Karl and Knut.

The two Kompani Linge brothers were duly picked up by Roald on *Heland* around 20 January. The weather was appalling that January; just the week before the boat *Viking II* leaving from Masfjorden (north of Bergen) with ten men was lost without trace. Roald decided to head south, keeping to the coast before striking out to sea. At Florø a German boat put a shot across his bows and ordered him in to the port.

His fishing papers were in order but he was told not to leave until the morning, which he did in company of the local fishing fleet. Continuing south, he had to hide away at Utvær until a change in the wind the next day. When it came, they set out under sail in heavy snow, which at least would stop any discovery from the air.

Back at Lerwick, whilst the Aarsæther brothers sorted out their requirements with SOE, Severin Roald was prescient enough to do some Shetland island fishing, making an excellent catch. When he got back home to Vigra, he quickly put the brothers and their highly explosive cargo ashore. He was then able to check in at the port office at Ålesund and could demonstrate he had been away fishing legitimately. No one would be able to tell the difference between Scottish and Norwegian herring and the ruse worked.

After playing with him like a cat with a mouse for a year and ten months, Josef Terboven and his superiors in Berlin finally gave Vidkun Quisling what he had craved for so long. On 1 February 1942, the State Act was passed, installing Quisling as Minister President of Norway, head of a new National Government. The man who had attempted a coup d'état by seizing the microphone at NRK on the first day of the German invasion had finally got his way. But it was not as he entirely wished, as Terboven was retained as overlord above him and for this Quisling was secretly furious. There were banquets, concerts, parades and rallies in celebration. His image appeared on postage stamps and in public buildings. He quickly moved his family into the Royal Palace in Oslo. Nonetheless he now had sweeping new powers, and he was like a schoolboy in a sweetie shop, although the effect was more like a bull in a china shop and in a matter of weeks he issued a raft of new edicts like confetti. Among these, those of the greatest consequence were measures to restrict Jews, directives to the clergy to comply with Nazi ideology, directives to the teachers to comply with a Nazi curriculum, and the imposition of compulsory membership of children in the NS youth organisation (the equivalent of *Hitler Jugend*). By these unsophisticated measures Quisling hoped to cleanse Norwegian society of anti-Nazi conviction, and to direct it toward his vision of a highly controlled fascist utopia. Quisling flew to Berlin on 13 February, and there was much clicking of heels and flashing of cameras. Sardonically Joseph Goebbels recorded that their guest was 'Naïve...unlikely to ever make a great statesman.'

At ground level, Quisling informers and collaborators were to have rather more success at infiltrating the resistance groups. One such group gathered together waiting for a boat at Bremnes in early February consisted of twenty-five men and five women who were all involved with the resistance, accompanied by eight of their children. Astonishingly, several of them had been through the previous failed attempt with *Anna B* three months before when that boat had capsized, and they had drifted for nine days. Since then, they had been hiding in the mountains. It is a measure of their desperation that they were prepared to risk it again. Noteworthy among the group was Lars Gjendemsjø, a teacher who was arrested on 2 October 1941 when the Stein Group in Bergen was broken up. He was so severely tortured by the Gestapo that he had to be taken to hospital, from where he escaped with assistance of colleagues on 18 November. He had been in hiding ever since. Also among the passengers was Bjørn Mowinckel Nilsen with his wife Helen. Nilsen later wrote a detailed account in *Shetland Life Magazine* ('The *Rupee*'s trip to freedom' September 1996) which illustrates the complex and dangerous odyssey they had to make.

Leaving Bergen, the Nilsens were given these instructions, 'Go by night steamer southbound for Stavanger.... Buy through tickets to Haugesund ... leave the ship at the first port Lervik under cover of darkness. Report to the local inn and ask for room only.' The codeword to be given was 'cast iron'. Joined by others at the inn, the next day they took a local ferry to a remote village where they were installed in a potato shed, hardly tolerable as there was a howling wind with three to four feet of snow on the ground. They shuttled to and from the local inn for food and warmth. After dark that night they were instructed to leave in small groups, trudging with their belongings for two hours to reach a large boathouse. A boat was supposed to pick them up from there at first light, but for some reason failed to appear. The next instruction was to leave their entire luggage and walk for another two hours to a tiny quay. There, at last, lying offshore lay their escape boat the *Rupee,* a strongly built cutter used for cargo, with her skipper Ingolf Andersen, his Glaswegian wife Elizabeth and their 17-year-old son Norman acting as his crew.

The fugitives were ferried out to her in a small motor boat, but it was soon discovered that the engine was playing up, delaying them for nearly two more worrying days. Eventually a local man, an engineer, hearing of their predicament answered the call to help. 'Give me a few seconds. I need my jacket,' he said. Bringing the number on board up to forty-one, he promptly sorted the engine out and kept it going during the voyage. Five long days after leaving Bergen, the Nilsens and their companions were on their way. Without lights and veiled in falling snow, *Rupee* chugged past a German shore battery without being seen; she was well out into open sea by dawn. It almost goes without saying that there was a storm, bad enough to smash the glass in the wheelhouse swamping the boat with water. But they made it, reaching land at Fetlar, Shetland, where they dropped anchor just off the beach at Houbie just as the fuel ran out. The bedraggled men and women with children in their arms staggered out of the freezing surf and into a blizzard. They were soon dried, thawed and fed by welcoming local families. The women and children stayed with the families and the men laid their heads down at the local shooting lodge, under the watchful but compassionate eyes of the Fetlar Home Guard. They were all utterly exhausted and sleep descended rapidly.

The foul weather delayed the pilot boat coming to collect them and they were able to enjoy the rest and the hospitality of the Fetlar folk for two more days before they were shepherded onwards to Lerwick. A coded message transmitted to Bergen confirmed the late but safe arrival of *Rupee* and her passengers.

Twice before export organisations at Ålesund had been destroyed after infiltration by Sipo and the Gestapo. On 26 May 1941, the Torsvik Group had been broken up after penetration by Finn Kaas, working for Sipo, and on 2 July 1941 the Nielsen Group had been betrayed by Marino Nilsson, working for the Gestapo. In September that year another export group had started up to fill the vacuum – the Walle Group. It took the name of Thoralf Walle, a brave man indeed as he was a local policeman who was also working for the resistance. It was a very difficult balancing act between deceiving his NS employers and working underground. He was fully supported by his young wife Lilly, her close friend Gerd Gjørtz, (only 21 and using a cover name 'Heidi') with a small group of friends.

The Walle Group was no match for the infamous *Rinnanbanden* (Rinnan's band), started by the Norwegian informer Henry Rinnan, unquestionably second only to Quisling as the greatest traitor of the occupation. From early 1942 onwards he created the most extensive and feared anti-resistance movement of the occupation. Recruited by Sipo in Trondheim he was funded and given autonomy to operate his own department, given the designation *Sonderabteilung Lola* (Special Department Lola). Over the next three years Rinnan expanded his operation to around seventy agents. They brought about the arrests of hundreds of members of the resistance, many of whom died at their hands. An undoubted psychopath, Rinnan exhibited personal depravity of the worst kind, much enjoying the torture of his own countrymen and women. It was astonishing that he managed to keep his operation going right through until the end of the war, as will be seen.

So it was that 'Heidi' was approached in the autumn of 1941 by Jan Eriksen from Oslo, sent by Rinnan, who asked for help with organising for the escape of some important people. She was taken in by the stranger who thereby insinuated himself into the group. He started sending information about the new Walle group to Rinnan's headquarters in Trondheim, with a young woman acting as courier. In January and early February 1942, Rinnan's Lola group planned an operation against Walle and his associates. Two Quisling agents from Oslo, Bjarne Jenshus and Ingvar Ålberg, were sent from Olso posing as fugitives on the run, and they were duly added to the waiting list for a boat. That boat was the fated 40ft *Viggo*, a name that became forever associated with what followed. The Gestapo knew the date, 21 February, but not the point of departure. They were tracking some of the organisers, hoping they would lead them to the embarkation point. Naval units were on standby to pounce. By chance, the Gestapo surveillance car ended in a ditch and they lost the trail, allowing the passengers (including the Rinnan agents) to board without being seen. They might have got away with their escape, but *Viggo* ran aground and took some time to refloat, returning to hide up for a night in a remote bay. The two agents feigned some pressing need to go ashore, where they promptly telephoned Henry Rinnan who was comfortably ensconced in the Hotel Scandinavie in Ålesund. They gave the new location and the trap was re-set.

The following morning, 23 February, the little *Viggo* was wakened to a burst of machine gun fire and was quickly surrounded by German boats. Rinnan and a Sipo officer were among the spectators who boarded in triumph as all thirty on board were arrested. Simultaneously the Gestapo and Sipo picked up another fifty-two local people associated with the escapes. All eighty-two were lined up outside the town hall, a public humiliation from which the resistance in Ålesund never fully recovered. Of those on board *Viggo*, eighteen were executed and one died at the hands of Rinnan's people. Among them was Karl Angel Elgenes, whose brother Asbjørn had drowned during the failed escape attempt of *Viking* just before Christmas. Two women, a Swedish citizen and a famous author, Sigurd Evensmo, escaped the death penalty but they received long sentences in a concentration camp.

Sigurd Evensmo owed his release in 1943 to the beautiful, mystifying and controversial Anne Marie Breien, who is worthy of note in the context of saving at least sixty Norwegians from Grini concentration camp. When her own father Roal Breien was arrested in January 1942, Anne Marie had the temerity to approach the Oslo Gestapo chief Siegfried Fehmer to plead for his life – with success. After this and with the encouragement of Milorg she kept up a friendship with Fehmer during which she both fed information back to the resistance and also secured the release or early release of the prisoners. She placed herself in a perilous position but was not thanked at the end of the war because of what was perceived to be her improper relationship with the detested Gestapo chief (who she testified against). Instead, she was arrested and held for a year, and although released without charge she received no official recognition, no medals. Efforts by Sigurd Evensmo and others to rehabilitate her reputation were only partially successful. In 1981 she was awarded a war pension, but she remained tainted by Fehmer for the rest of her days, even far away in America where she sought sanctuary and anonymity.

On 23 February 1942 terror set in to Ålesund as the Germans went about their work. Much of what we know about these events (and more besides) was recorded by the Shetland author James W. Irvine, who visited the Walles in 1987 researching for his impressive book *The Waves are Free* (Shetland Publishing 1988). Thoraf and Lilly Walle both got separate tip-offs and went to ground. Lilly went to her friend Gerd Gjørtz's house and hid herself wrapped in a blanket on a shelf in a tiny kitchen store as Gerd answered a hammering at the door. There stood some Gestapo men who were looking for a man on their list. They failed to realise that the name on their list – Gerd, a female Scandinavian name – was not the same as the German male name Gert; they were definitely looking for a man called Gert. Having satisfied themselves that there was no man in the house and failing to find Lilly they moved on. Gerd had missed being arrested by a single letter in her first name.

Later, Lilly moved on dressed as a man and spent a day hiding in a potato store. The next day she was back in woman's clothing and pushing an empty pram. Eventually she was re-united with Thoralf, who had had the luck of falling in with Tor Stenersen, a Lieutenant in Kompani Linge, a man armed and trained in escape and evasion. Over the next month

Stenersen guided and looked after the young couple as they struck out on foot inland and to the south, circling back to the coast near Åheim. The distance was about 200 miles, and the winter was so bad that they had to be taken in for long periods by *Jossings* (good Norwegians). At last (it must have been at the end of March) they were picked up by a boat sent from Shetland to pick up Stenersen and offload arms; it was the fully equipped and armed Shetland Bus boat *Olaf,* skippered by the renowned Per Blystad. Toralf and Lilly Walle were safe at last and returned to Ålesund after the war, but their saviours, Stenersen and Blystad, were less fortunate, both losing their lives later on.

In the aftermath of the arrests at Ålesund, terrified people were ducking and weaving to avoid capture as the manhunt went on. A signaller in the Antrum resistance group managed to transmit an SOS to Shetland (via London) outlining the predicament. This message was quickly processed, with a request being forwarded to the redoubtable Severin Roald asking for help. Although he was not a member of the *Shetlandsgjengen,* he had been given a radio to keep in touch, and he had been asked to be on standby in case something urgent cropped up. When the Germans had surged into Ålesund on 23 February, Severin had put to sea and was hiding out with *Heland* at the nearby uninhabited island of Erkna; he was now well placed to evacuate those on the run. A plan was put in place for him to do a recue from the island of Vigra, adjacent to Ålesund.

We can find out what happened next through the eyes of Arild Rypdal as a 7-year-old. The story was told many years later when he was an award-winning author. It was recounted in the informative book *Englandsfeber* by Trygve Sørvaag (Eide Forlag 2002). Arild was the son of Trygve Rypdal, a businessman who was head of the local division of the Antrum resistance. Even as a youngster, Arild knew there were strange goings on in the district about which he could not talk. He vividly remembered the situation in his home town. 'The German occupation lay like a blanket of darkness over everything. People whispered, food was scarce, travel and radios were forbidden. In the schools we now learned German instead of English.'

One day he found a radio transmitter in a box buried in the snow in their garden, which his mother dismissed as a device for scaring mice but he wasn't fooled. 'For a small boy it was a time of thrills and frights... Questions were as dangerous as answers,' he said.

One memorable day his mother Sylvi came to the school and removed him in the middle of class telling the teacher that they were 'going fishing' – some chance, as the weather was atrocious. The teacher knew exactly what was going on. Sylvi dressed Arild and his younger brother Trygve, aged 3, in multiple layers of clothing packing just one suitcase for them all. As they moved to a rendezvous with his father Arild described how 'Ålesund was in a state of siege. The Germans had cordoned off everything, and patrols were everywhere'. His father had arranged for a boatman with a tiny boat to take them across to Vigra in daylight. All four of them had to huddle out of sight in the small cuddy at the bow end so that it appeared that only the boatman was on board. Somehow he slipped through the barrage of German boats and they were landed on Vigra. They then had a 5-mile trudge through deep snow and a blizzard to find that their destination village was in the middle of a Gestapo raid. Eventually they were taken in by a friendly family who had already been searched. During the second night, the children were roused from sleep and the family went to stand with others on a small jetty in freezing windy conditions, patiently waiting. It was just two days after the arrests had started. At 04.00 out of the darkness came the familiar 'tonk-tonk' engine noise of a fishing boat and with uncanny accuracy Severin Roald and his brother Jon brought *Heland* alongside. Describing the departure Arild said:

Everything happened in a matter of seconds. People swarmed out from their hiding places: from under the jetty, from behind the boathouse, from snowdrifts. I was stiff from fear thinking it was a German ambush, but then I understood. People were piling over the gunwhale and disappearing below deck ... the skipper reversed the propeller. The boat had been at the jetty for a scant 30 seconds, then it slid back into the darkness.

At a similar pick up jetty Roald stayed longer. Jumping ashore he called out, 'I'll be right back,' returning after a few minutes with his wife Inga. This time he knew he would not be returning, his luck could not hold out beyond this; this was a one way trip. Among the twenty-three on board were several Roald brothers and cousins, and others who were all involved in resistance in one way or another. One notable man was Harald Peter Ratvik who was later captured and executed in the infamous Brattholm betrayal incident of 1943 (Operation Martin).

For Arild, the excitement turned to torment as *Heland* hit a severe storm with a blinding blizzard, accompanied by 'violent' seasickness for most on board. On the third morning, Severin Roald, with unerring precision, brought *Heland* to anchor at Lunna Voe, the headquarters and home of the Shetland Bus. Both skipper and boat were to stay with the Bus service with Roald becoming chief shipwright of the unit.

Several commentators have somewhat glibly observed that North Sea Traffic ceased to take place after the capture of *Viggo* on 23 February 1942. It is true to say that the rate of escapes fell away substantially, the numbers of people on board each boat dropped and the boats became smaller. It may be that those writers thought that the Shetland Bus had taken over all responsibility for subsequent evacuations of refugees. The Bus did indeed pick up around 350 people in the course of its operations (these are not included in this book), but its primary purpose was to take the war to Norway. Life after *Viggo* undoubtedly changed as the story spread across the country, but spontaneous (sometimes organised) civilian escapes continued until the very end of the war. Around forty more groups of desperate people (twelve percent of the total) were still prepared to climb into small boats to risk the North Sea.

The seeds of the next great disquiet in Norway were sown in the same month as the betrayal of *Viggo*. After his investment as Minister President the newly enthusiastic Quisling had enacted that the clergy must cease to be anti-Nazi, and that teachers must adhere to a Nazi curriculum. As Terboven already knew and as Goebbels had commented, Quisling was simply, almost desperately, naïve. When resistance followed, Quisling did not take kindly to it; priests and teachers alike would have to be taught their sermons and their lessons the hard way.

Chapter 13

Turbulent Preachers and Teachers
(February–April 1942)

Vikund Quisling, residing with his family in some style in the Royal Palace in Oslo, seemed to think that he could bring about his new Norwegian promised land by subordinating its spiritual and educational beings to his agenda. He sought to do this not only by edict, but also, very crudely, by contract. The salaries of the clergy and of teachers were both direct responsibilities of the state, and he now controlled the purse strings; he would starve them into submission.

On the very day of his elevation to Minister President on Sunday, 1 February 1942 Quisling wanted to have the event celebrated in cathedrals and churches across the nation. As far as the clergy was concerned, this was no cause for celebration. The Dean of Nidaros Cathedral at Trondheim, Arne Fjellbu, was already a marked man for his opposition to the regime and that day, in a pre-emptive strike, a gang of Quislings entered and occupied the cathedral, draping hated NS banners and emblems around the building. When he arrived to conduct Sunday worship, his way was blocked by police, and he was turned away. The congregation remained outside with a crowd swelling to some thousands singing hymns in protest. Fjellbu went on to hold a service elsewhere.

News of the 'Nidaros Incident' spread rapidly and attention shifted to Eivind Berggrave, the Primate of the Church of Norway, already a man conspicuous for his anti-Quisling views. Over the next fortnight he guided his seven bishops to produce a declaration of non-compliance, a missive called *Kirkens Grunn* (The Church's Foundation). It was accompanied by the resignation of all the bishops on 24 February. Their salaries were stopped, of course, and Quisling wanted arrests, but Terboven resisted as he rightly thought that the bishops would become martyrs, focal to the growing anger. Allowing himself one petty act of spite, Quisling ordered the arrest of Fjellbu's son who was thrown into a concentration camp without charge. Alarmed, the rest of the clergy kept a low profile until Easter.

Meanwhile, on 20 February, the teachers who were required to join the new NS Teachers' Union delivered their document of non-compliance. In just a fortnight they had amassed an impressive 12,000 signatories out of 14,000 on the pay roll. At a stroke, those who had signed lost their salaries but continued to work without pay, supported by their communities. So the next step for Quisling was to order the closure of schools for a month. Where it was possible, schooling continued in people's homes and public halls. It was a huge shock to parents and children, and it was accompanied by the parallel order that the older children must enlist in the NS youth movement. A nationwide petition against this, signed by hundreds of thousands of parents, was delivered to Oslo as soon as 3 March. Quisling was not doing well with his new order, and he wanted vengeance. This time there were no religious qualms to hold him back, and he proposed an exemplary mass arrest of teachers. In a bidding war, Terboven suggested 1,000 arrests, but Quisling wanted more and pushed the figure up to 1,200. As with the ritual punishment of a Roman legion, he wanted a decimation of the recalcitrant teachers. The first arrests started on 13 March with mass arrests a week later. The fate of the teachers was soon revealed. Thrown into a military camp at Jørstadmoen in central Norway, about half of them were 'selected' for slave labour in the frozen far north. The rest were sent to Grini concentration camp. For those heading north, transport was by way of being crammed into cattle trucks, standing room only. At every opportunity on the journey, locals turned out to demonstrate their solidarity by passing over food and clothing whilst singing national songs. Things were no better when at Trondheim they were packed into the small coastal steamer *Skjerstad* including into the hold, under heavy SS guard. Their treatment at the hands of the guards and the conditions were horrendous, with the journey to Kirkenes lasting over two weeks. At every stopover, the local population converged on the port to demonstrate solidarity for the poor wretches on board. Arriving at Kirkenes on 29 April they were put to hard labour alongside Russian prisoners, considered by the Nazis to be virtually sub-human. Those sent to Grini didn't fare much better, as a brutal regime of interrogation, forced labour and exercise outside in the snow was instituted, designed to make life as unpleasant as possible.

On 20 April, Quisling issued an ultimatum to the insubordinate teachers to sign up to the NS union by 10 May or they would be banned from teaching and from all public employment for life. When that deadline was steadfastly ignored, Quisling, in a final flutter of pique, ordered that a further 160 teachers would be sent to Kirkenes, in conditions just as dreadful as those meted upon the first tranche. The dreadful treatment of these teachers and their progress to the far north was meant as a lesson for all. Nazi thinking was, as usual, far off the mark.

As had happened before, such brutal measures were an abject failure for the Quisling government. The resolve of the Norwegian people was strengthened by the courage shown by the clergy and the teachers. The final act of defiance came on Easter Sunday, 5 April 1942 when in almost every church in the land the priest in charge read out a prepared statement based on *Kirkenes Grunn* and announced his resignation. In total, 1,139 ministers resigned and only 39 agreed to conform to the NS gospel. Quisling, cloaked in hubris, was staggered at the defiance. Terboven again advised against mass arrests and Quisling instead ordered the arrest of the Primate, Eivind Berggrave. Berggrave was known and respected not only throughout Norway but also on an international stage, particularly in America. Tempted as he might be, Quisling had to be careful with his disposal. He was initially held in

Grini concentration camp and then he was banished to house arrest under guard at a remote cabin for the rest of the war. With only thirty-nine NS priests and very few NS lay volunteers allowed to take services, concessions were eventually made whereby parish priests could return to their congregations without salary. Their communities raised funds to support them, and in this way, churches remained open until the end of the war.

In similar fashion, the unsalaried teachers continued to teach where possible until the NS gradually re-opened the schools, sensing that the argument was being lost. Quisling's great experiment in social engineering ended in enduring failure, which was disguised by a fudge. Teachers had to sign a non-committal non-binding watered down pledge to work in the 'public interest'. Politics were removed from education. Over the summer, those imprisoned began to trickle home, but it was not until 4 November that the last prisoner was released. The courageous action of those Norwegian teachers has since been held as a paradigm for peaceful resistance in the context of many of the conflicts that have followed in the years after the Second World War.

Not many teachers or clergymen tried to escape from Norway, and one can surmise that their sense of vocation, amplified by the adverse circumstances of the occupation, morally bound them to stay with their pupils and their congregations. Nonetheless there are some examples where there was no choice but to flee. Jan Hermann Hermansen and his wife Klara Selge were both teachers on the small island of Espevær, lying about ten minutes across the water from the large island complex of Bomlo. From the outset of the occupation, they voiced their opposition, sailing close to the wind with the Gestapo on several occasions. Much later, Klara wrote an account of their escape ('The *Kapp I*'s journey to freedom' in *Shetland Life*, February 1996). As early as May 1940 they had been offered an escape boat but flatly refused to leave the community. As their involvement with 'illegal activities' continued, they received several visits from the Gestapo, including when Jan and two associates were seized for a trip on the *Gestaposkøyta*. This was not a good experience but on this occasion the men were put ashore without giving anything away.

Naturally, neither of them signed up to join the NS Teachers' Union in February, and their school was closed with both losing their salaries. Towards the end of March, the Gestapo paid them another visit, issuing them with an unambiguous warning that they were being watched. Any attempt to flee to Scotland would result in their children Solveig (13) and Jan Ottar (3) being seized and taken away. This had the opposite effect, making them all the more determined to get themselves and the children away. Their close family friend Toralf Eiken offered his boat *Kapp I* and they laid plans for it to be 'stolen' for their escape. He prepared the boat, provisioned it, fuelled it and moored it very conveniently at a jetty. Hermansen was very concerned for his friend the local priest Peter Robberstad, who he knew was also being closely watched. Robberstad was deeply involved in the local Bomlo-Bremes escape export business, alongside his brother Nils. He was one of the signatories of the *Kirkens Grunn* declaration, so Hermansen went to try to persuade him to go with them. It was Easter week and the pastor felt he could not abandon his congregation at such a time. Besides, Easter Day was the day designated by the church to read out the prepared statement signifying the mass resignation of the clergy. Robberstad declined the offer, paying a price later when he was arrested, ending up in the infamous Dachau concentration camp in southern Germany. The Hermansen family was joined on *Kapp I* by five others who came across from Bomlo – a married couple, a woman hoping to join her husband who was already in England, and two students, making nine for the trip. Unfortunately, the Hermansens were the only ones on board with any sea-going experience, and that was restricted to recreational holiday boating; but they had great mutual confidence in each other and shared an undiminished determination to escape the persecution.

Kapp I pulled away from Espevær at 22.30pm on Easter Saturday, 4 April 1942. Within half an hour, as they left the shelter of the coast, a huge wave broke over the stern, swamping the engine room causing the engine to misfire. They were able to splutter onwards at reduced speed knowing that they must clear the coast by daybreak. At least the wind was howling behind them from east to west, which helped to push them away from the coast. At midday on Easter day the saltwater-soaked engine breathed its last, and they were at the mercy of the sea, raising the foresail when it was possible to do so. In this way they zig-zagged across the North Sea over the next three days until on the morning of 9 April the wind vanished and they were motionless. From the mast-head Hermansen spied land about thirty miles away, but they had no way of getting there. To add anxiety to the frustration, a Luftwaffe plane coming from west spotted them and dropped low to circle around three times having a good look at them. It didn't attack, probably because it was returning from a mission and had expended its payload before turning back to Norway. But would it alert other planes, or even a U-boat?

Faced with this dilemma, Hermansen looked to the small lifeboat lashed to the deck which had been damaged by the storm. They all set to repair it, forcing thick grease into the cracks coating the whole bottom with it. They assembled a jury rig in case the wind got up and slid the greasy sea-slug into the water. It floated well enough, so the Hermansens climbed down into it. The five others simply refused to get into the tiny boat, preferring to trust their luck to staying on board the larger boat to wait for rescue. Hermansen was the only one capable of rowing or sailing the 30 miles to land where he could summon help for the stricken *Kapp I*. In effect the decision was made for him – the skipper would have to abandon his ship and his passengers in order to save them. The windless conditions continued as they pulled away from the larger boat as Hermansen set himself to the oars. Eventually the wind did pick up, the sail filled and the lifeboat bowled along, but it still took around eight hours to arrive in darkness (at around 22.00) in a bay where they could make out a radar mast. They fired off some distress rockets in its direction but there was no response. Sailing on, they reached a beach at the end of the bay and ran up onto the sand.

They fired off more rockets, but again there was no response. It was dark, there were no lights – where to go now? Suddenly they saw the sidelights of a lorry moving along a road parallel to the coast. They climbed up to this and followed it to the nearest house. Rousing the occupants from their beds they received a warm welcome and they were able to find out where they were – they had landed at Norwick Bay on the Shetland Island of Unst. Hermansen's immediate priority was the safety of the hapless people drifting on *Kapp I* so, without any delay, the family pressed onwards to the RAF radar station at Skaw, only about half a mile away.

Imagine the RAF contingent's surprise at being roused at midnight by the bedraggled Hermansen family on foot with young Jan Ottar in the arms of his mother. The sleepy airmen who hadn't seen their distress rockets quickly promised to send a rescue boat for *Kapp I* at first light. Local store-keeper Duncan Mouat then arrived with his van (the one they had seen earlier) and offered refuge for the Hermansens at his parents' home. Over the next two days, David and Joan Mouat fussed over the Hermansens, striking up a friendship that was to last for sixty years.

The rescue boat was not required, as *Kapp I* blew along the same path as the little lifeboat and arrived in Norwick bay early in the morning. The five inexperienced people on board were unable operate and drop the anchor and the boat benignly grounded on the soft sand of the beach on its own account. The five jumped ashore to be re-united with the Hermansens and welcomed by the Mouats and other locals. Over five stormy days, without power, with little sail assistance but with good fortune, *Kapp I* had delivered her nine passengers to safety at Unst. In due course, Hermansen went into government service in London and his wife went to teach at the Norwegian boarding school at Drumtochty. The couple always remembered the Mouat family and they corresponded for years, culminating with a visit by Duncan Mouat's daughter Minnie to Klara and Jan Ottar in Norway in 1999. I was fortunate to catch up with Minnie on Unst in 2015, when she was able to fill in parts of her parents' accounts.

That spring, probably in April (the date isn't known) a remarkable crossing succeeded against all odds. It was by two young men in a sealskin-covered Eskimo kayak just 16ft long. Four other known attempts by kayak had ended in failure and tragedy. The tiny craft was measured at just 16in wide. Although this escape has not been previously recorded, we have it on good authority, contained in a speech of 17 May 1942 (*The Scotsman,* 18 May 1942), delivered by the First Lord of the Admiralty, Albert Victor Alexander (later Lord Alexander of Hillsborough). The occasion was a rally at the London Coliseum in front of 2,500 people to mark Norwegian Constitution Day. Following a stirring speech by King Haakon, Alexander used this story to illustrate the dedication of young Norwegians to join in the struggle to free their country. Describing the escape with some drama, it seems that the young men could fit very little food or water into the boat. They paddled quietly past Nazi guards under cover of darkness and struck out into the North Sea 'determined to make Britain – or be drowned in the attempt'. They were tossed about by the sea endlessly and couldn't rest for a moment, eventually becoming almost totally exhausted. In this nearly terminal state, they were spotted by the lookout of a British destroyer and plucked to safety.

'Whereas the Vikings of Old came to conquer here by force of arms, the modern Vikings win our hearts by their courage, their steadfast faith and their burning love of freedom. These men are brave, but also are those they have left behind,' were the closing words of the First Lord of the Admiralty.

Following the capture of *Viggo* at Ålesund, the break-up of the Walle Group and the rescue of the rest of the fugitives by Severin Roald with *Heland* in February, Terboven decided to take a look for himself at this troublesome region, known as 'Little London'. The Ålesund area had been by far the busiest in the export of refugees and had been intransigent in the face of German efforts to shut it down. The success of Henry Rinnan and his NS agents was surely proof that the occupiers were gaining the upper hand. The population was on the back foot; eighty-two had been arrested and publicly humiliated. Eighteen of these were now on death row. The Reichskommisar wanted to make the most of his visit to underline the recent successes. On 31 March, he arrived in a well-publicised visit accompanied by an entourage of senior Gestapo, Sipo and NS Police officers. Not only were they there to demonstrate their superiority, but they also wanted to examine the reliability of the local enforcement agencies. It didn't take long to realise that the Ålesund police department was a leaky vessel in terms of loyalty to the Nazis. After all, Thoralf Walle, leader of the group, was himself a police officer and was now at large and on the run. During the visit several policemen were dismissed, and various operational procedures were tightened up. The measures proved to be effective as no more boats were to leave from the Ålesund area for the rest of 1942. To round things off and to loose off some parting shots, Terboven imposed some petty but annoying orders – a total ban on the sale or distribution of alcohol and tobacco. He also shut down the only cinema.

As we have seen, many of the people wanting or needing to get away to Britain came from Bergen. The city lies well protected from the North Sea by a linear archipelago of islands running parallel to the coast from Fedje in the north to Sotra in the south. Naturally this string of islands offered ideal places to assemble, to hide, and to launch an escape. One busy village was Telavåg on the south west of the island of Sotra which had seen around a dozen escapes depart from there and adjacent villages, the last being *Anna* in January 1942. The escapes had been organised by Laurits and Martha Telle, three of whose sons had already escaped to Scotland. Their elder son Lars was at home helping with the organisation, assisted by a small group of six others. Somehow the village of Telavåg escaped the attentions of Quislings, the Gestapo and other informers and all was quiet there. No incidents or suspicions had been logged in the police or Gestapo files up to that point. Perhaps it was this very quietness that led to the Shetland Bus team at Scalloway to identify the small village as a place to land some of their agents. So it was that on 21 April the boat *Olaf* (on the second of two runs) landed the two Linge SOE agents Arne Meldal Værum and Emil Gustav Hvaal along with a cargo of ten tons of arms and explosives which was stowed in the Telle boathouse. The village was at once extremely vulnerable.

By unfortunate circumstance, the NS Statspolitiet officer, Johan Bjørgan who six months earlier had helped to wrap up the Stein Group appeared on the scene, entirely by chance. He had decided to combine a fly-fishing holiday on Sotra with a few low-key enquires, which included a malicious accusation that Laurits Telle hadn't handed in his radio receiver. In holiday mode, he arrived on a bicycle in civilian clothes with a rucksack on his back and a fishing rod tied to the crossbar. With disastrous mischance, the fly fisherman was taken to be a refugee looking out for an escape boat. With such an introduction he soon learned more about the village's involvement in the escape business, and eventually learned about the two men who were, incautiously, staying at Telle's house. This was a scoop. He forgot about the fly fishing, got on his bicycle and returned to the police chief at Fjell. He had already made his catch.

As soon as Gestapo headquarters at Bergen received the news, the Germans reacted with surprising speed and efficiency. The same evening a fast boat with NS police and Gestapo agents was on the way to Fjell, where they planned their raid on Telavåg overnight at the police chief's residence. Their boat raced into the village at 07.00; it was 26 April. A German minesweeper with armed men hovered offshore. Nine Gestapo men and three NS policemen men disembarked, stalking towards the Telles' house. Elizabeth, the Telles' daughter, was out and about early; spotting the intruders she cried out a warning. The men pulled out their weapons and broke into a run; smashing through the front door, four of the Gestapo men ran upstairs to the attic surprising the SOE men in their beds. The highly trained Linge men launched themselves bodily at the intruders, grabbing two pistols, shooting dead two and injuring the third. But Vaerum was himself killed and Hvaal was severely wounded, being hit nine times. The dead Germans were both senior officers in the Gestapo, Behrens and Bertram, as was the wounded man, Klötscher. Incredibly, out from this carnage stepped 14-year-old Åge Telle, the youngest member of the family, who had been sleeping in the same room; he was untouched.

By the end of that day, German reinforcements had turned the village upside down. They soon discovered the incriminating arms cache and arrested the extended Telle family (including the traumatised Åge) and the other principal suspects. All of them along with the wounded Hvaal were transferred back to Gestapo headquarters in Bergen. For Terboven the death of the two Gestapo men was deeply felt Nazi business, and it was personal as Behrens was a friend of his. He brushed aside Quisling, travelling to Bergen with senior German officers to take command of the situation. It presented an opportunity for him to demonstrate once and for all who was in charge, and it was an occasion for him to mete out exemplary punishment for this outrage against the Reich.

In the days that followed, the village of Telvåg held its breath wondering if anything more would follow, and it didn't have to wait long. On 30 April an elaborate funeral with full military honours was held for the deceased Gestapo men in Bergen. In attendance were most of the higher echelons of the Nazi machine and there was saturation publicity. Meanwhile, in contrast, the body of Værum was disposed of at sea to avoid him being celebrated later as a hero. Later the same day, Terboven and his entourage arrived at Telavåg to initiate the retribution. The senior Nazis climbed a small hillock to get a grandstand view of a carefully planned operation. Cameras clicked and whirred as German troops displaced all the villagers from their homes and made them stand and watch as every building, storehouse and shed, was burned down or blown up. When this was well under way, the villagers were separated and marched in long files down to the quay to be taken away. Around 300 men were taken to one school building in Bergen with around 260 women, children and the elderly to another.

Following Terboven's very specific orders, the clearance of Telavåg continued for some weeks, in the hands of a company of military engineers. Every vestige of life there was removed – even the stone foundations of the wooden buildings were transported away. Wells were filled in and the jetties and quays were demolished. Boats were either sunk or seized, and the livestock was slaughtered or removed. The whole of that quarter of the island of Sotra was designated as a prohibited zone. Notices were posted declaring that anyone attempting to enter the zone would be shot. As could be anticipated, the human cost for the inhabitants was even more painful.

At exactly the same hour as the Gestapo funeral was being held, eighteen men imprisoned at Grini concentration camp were taken out and shot. They had nothing whatsoever to do with Telavåg, they were the ones who had been captured at the betrayal of *Viggo*. The group of twelve 'ringleader' villagers who were arrested on the first day endured a brutal time at Gestapo headquarters in Bergen. Of these, Lars Telle and the Linge man Emil Hvaal were executed, whilst the others were sent to Ulven concentration camp, including the 14-year-old Åge Telle. Of the 300 men arrested, one was executed at Grini, and seventy-two were sent to concentration camps in Germany where thirty of them died. It was said that the death toll amongst these men would have been far higher had the Red Cross not succeeded in being allowed to deliver their celebrated food parcels to the camps towards the end of the war.

The women, children and the elderly fared better but not happily. Moved from pillar to post there was a constant threat of the group being divided or of the children being split from mothers to be exported to Germany. This was avoided by spooking the Germans that they were infected firstly with scarlet fever and then with diphtheria. The biggest drain on them was the regular arrival of news of the deaths of their menfolk. On 17 May 1944 they were all released on the conditions that they could not go anywhere near Telavåg and they could not talk to anyone about what they had endured. With no homes, no possessions and no money, they left one purgatory for another scarcely better.

There can be little doubt that Joseph Terboven's jackboot left a profound stamp on Norway. The carefully curated newspaper reports, the dramatic pictures of the destruction, the images of lines of prisoners being shipped out, the coverage of the grand funeral of the Gestapo men, the execution of the *Viggo* prisoners and the dreadful outcomes for the innocent villagers – the smell of all of these things leached out across the small nation. All of these events came on top of Quisling's disastrous moves against the clergy and the teachers, bringing the morale of the people of Norway to a new low. This was particularly so with those involved in the traffic of refugees. They knew well enough the risks posed to themselves, but now the risk to the greater civilian population had been laid bare.

On the day of the razing of Telavåg, the great Nazi propagandist Joseph Goebbels, from his vantage point in Berlin, noted in his diary, 'if the Norwegians cannot learn to love us, they must at least fear us.'

Not at all fearful were three 20-year-old friends from the remote small village of Rosendal (lying on the south coast of the great Hardanger fjord, south of Bergen), who were set on crossing to join the war effort in Britain. Bjarne Skaale already owned a 24ft open motor boat *Fram* and his friends Anders Kirkhus and Jens Linga deemed it suitable for them to attempt the North Sea. Through resistance contacts they were asked to pick up a fourth man from Mælandsvågen on the west side of the island of Bomlo, lying at the mouth of the great fjord. They left Rosendal on 27 April and under cover of darkness motored the fifty miles or so to the pickup village – but the passenger was not there. This was a real worry, as he may have been arrested by the Gestapo, or in some other way the rendezvous could have been compromised. They did not linger and set out westwards without delay.

They cleared land safely but during the following day the engine began to give trouble, finally giving up altogether. Undaunted, they jury-rigged a sail with a spar, some blankets and other available materials and continued with the wind. After five days at sea, they entered the mine-free convoy corridor, which ran the whole length of the east coast of Britain, and it wasn't long before a minesweeper plucked them to safety. They were landed at Scapa Flow at Orkney.

Fram was (as far as is known) the last boat to leave Norway for a whole three months until the end of July. In the pattern of events this was an unprecedented interlude. The reverberations from what became known as the 'Televag Tragedy' were felt all over the country, and held would-be escapers in check. The ever optimistic and unvanquished Norwegians clung to the hopeful expectation of an Allied invasion of north Norway that summer and began to salute each other with a V-sign (particularly in front of German soldiers) accompanied by a new greeting, spoken loudly – 'August!'. If nothing else, it kept the Germans on their toes to expect fireworks that month. But people had taken a real fright about attempting to escape; Telavåg had caused a sea-change.

Chapter 14

Sea Change
(April–December 1942)

O ver that summer of 1942 Norwegians, along with their other European Allies, sensed a sea change in the progress of the war. The wily desert fox, Erwin Rommel, had been halted by the British army at the First Battle of El Alamein in July. America with its almost infinite resources was now behind them, supplying vast amounts of food and war materiel. It was shortly to make its first major military deployment in the European theatre to North Africa. At a further distance, successes at the battles of Midway in June and Guadalcanal in August had also shown that America could gain the upper hand against the Japanese.

Russia was now on their side, and everyone could see that Operation Barbarossa, Hitler's eastwards invasion of Russia, was not the runaway success he initially expected. In the north, Leningrad had not been taken in ten months and was to hold out for a total of 872 ferocious fighting days. In the centre, the massive German assault on Moscow had not only been halted but also, to Hitler's surprise and fury, the Russians had mounted a successful counter attack over the bitterly cold winter of 1941–42. The Führer's only further option lay in the south where he wanted to push for the industrial and transport centre of Stalingrad with the oil field of the Caucasus beyond. This operation was being planned for August 1942 and as is well known, this too turned into a disaster.

Change was in the air. Norwegians may have picked up on rumours about the determination of Churchill to launch an invasion of the north and Finland. The plan was known as Operation Jupiter but it was fiercely opposed by Allied commanders and was abandoned. Not knowing this, Norwegians clung to the hope of an Allied invasion and it was not surprising that they enjoyed promenading in front of their German occupiers saluting each other with V-signs and crying out 'August!' The tides of war were indeed changing.

With this sense of change in the air, the voluntary compulsion of Norwegians to escape to join the Free Norwegian Forces – *Englandsfeber* – abated. There was no point in taking so many personal and family risks when it seemed that the Allies were actually winning the war. They might be of equal or greater use sitting and waiting with Milorg for the August invasion. Moreover, the Germans and their Quisling collaborators had gained the initiative in penetrating and shutting down the export groups and had thus considerably raised the stakes in making escape attempts. Fugitives could no longer make organised long distance journeys to the coast to join a boat, nor could they hide out in boathouses, potato sheds or cattle byres with any safety. Larger cutters used in crossings were harder to source because of increased surveillance by German harbour controls (they often removed engine parts to disable them). All stages of the organised escape routes had become vulnerable.

Already around 90 per cent of the Norwegian 'escape Armada' had made the crossing to Allied territory. The complexion of the escapes of the last 10 per cent now changed. The boats and the numbers of passengers were much smaller, the departures locally organised and spontaneous. Generally, those involved were under direct life-and-death threat of capture by the Gestapo and had no choice but to take the gamble. The crossings continued sporadically through the next two years and into 1945 when the last escape was made in April that year, just one month before the end of the war. That in itself illustrates the desperate situation of the fugitives.

Now that the Shetland Bus had become better established there was a new lifeline for refugees. Although the Bus operation was principally for offensive military purposes, occasionally it responded to a desperate call for help, or undertook an opportunistic evacuation of civilians. Such opportunities picked up in October 1943 when America presented the Bus with three powerful and fast submarine chasers. At this point, the Bus service changed its nature by becoming an official uniformed arm of the Royal Norwegian Navy. These larger warships were capable of taking refugees back to Scotland on their return trips – and did so safely, as none of the new boats was stopped by the Germans. In total, these rescues brought 353 people back to Shetland – but these are not included in the statistics of this book, as the operations were military ones, not civilian.

Additionally, there were now two alternatives to crossing the North Sea. In the far north Norway borders with Russia, 'holding hands' across the top of Sweden. As Russia had emerged on the same side, there was a new escape route as Norwegians could cross directly into Russia either on foot (or on skis), or by boat along the coastline of the Barents Sea. There were then various ways in which they could get back to Britain. It is not known how many took this hazardous option, but it was probably no more than a few hundred people. To the east it now became a little easier for Norwegians to escape to Sweden, as that country began to relax its attitude, its physical and military barriers to admitting refugees. The Swedes had also sensed a change in the direction of the war and they were shifting their stance, wanting to be in with the winners.

Ministerpresident Quisling was oblivious to these subtle changes in the conduct of the war. He was preoccupied with his failure to subordinate the clergy and the teachers. Hardly a sensitive man, he must have nonetheless been aware of the Nazi hierarchy's disdain if not ridicule at his efforts. In May he felt a need to make a demonstration of his absolute authority, and he would conduct this personally, choosing a soft target. A particular thorn in his flesh was Jar Primary School in the affluent area of Bærum just to the west of Oslo, where the teachers refused to sign up to the NS teachers' union and continued to keep the school open, working without pay, and in other ways niggling at the NS educational management. It was something of a cause célèbre among the teachers and university staff in the country. The would-be dictator of Norway was reduced to taking out his spite on a primary school.

Without warning, on 22 May 1942 a convoy of a dozen cars arrived at the handsome three storey building. Out stepped Quisling in his immaculately polished jack boots accompanied by Ragnar Skancke, Minister for Church and Education, and Jonas Lie, Minister for Police. They were accompanied by perhaps thirty armed police officers, who distributed themselves in and around the building. It was a set-piece staged to intimidate everyone in the school, to be recorded by press and photographers. The frightened children were sent home, and their teachers herded into an assembly room at gun point. Skancke took to the floor with a warm-up speech about signing up to the NS contract. When this failed to impress the audience, Quisling took over in an unreasonable rage, stamping and shouting, 'It is you teachers who are to blame for the fact that we have not had a new beginning. It is your fault that Norway today has not become a free and independent kingdom.'

The very idea that Norway would be 'free and independent' under Quisling was preposterous. One by one, the teachers, gripped at each side by armed policemen, were pulled forward to be questioned individually and none denied refusal to join the NS teachers union. Moreover, not one of them in that room agreed to sign up to the NS contract. They were, all of them, solidly and directly defiant in the face of the tyrant. Apoplectic with rage, Quisling ordered their immediate arrest, imprisonment and life-long ban from teaching. There was to be no propaganda here, the story did not reach the Nazi press. Nevertheless, it found its way into the underground press and soon the news spread across the country. The brave teachers were elevated to the status of martyrs with the overall effect being the exact opposite of what Quisling had set out to do.

The continuing oppression of Norwegian people involved with escapes is well illustrated by the treatment of 58-year-old Abelone Larsdatter Møgster, a formidable woman of the tiny island of Møkster. Part of the island community of Austevoll (about 30 miles south of Bergen), Møkster is only about 350 acres in size and at that time was home to perhaps sixty souls. Its prosperity lay in its central position within a crescent of islands from which it could service the fishing community. For over thirty years Møgster had built up on her own account a substantial general store, chandler's shop, fish merchant's and a shipping agency. When younger, as an attractive and successful young woman, she had suffered the loss of one and then a second fiancé to tuberculosis. That was enough; she never married, instead she poured all her energies into her expanding business, becoming absolutely central to the life of her island. She much preferred the male tasks of rowing, mending nets, unloading fish crates, handling stores, carpentry and so on, to cooking and domestic chores. She was mistress of all she surveyed – she could have been entitled *Dronning av Møkster* (Queen of Møkster).

But she had a softer side. She loved to carve figurines, dolls, wooden shoes and useful small implements. These could be gifts for the extended Møgster family, but they were usually destined to be sold for the benefit of the Red Cross, of which she was a great supporter and organiser. In company she would often be seen sitting in a corner with a sharp knife whittling away at a piece of driftwood, chewing on a piece of tobacco humming a favourite tune, *Blåbukken* (Blue Buck). Little did she know that the Red Cross was to save her life later in the war.

For Abelone Møgster was also in the risky business of helping with the North Sea traffic. Being in such a quiet outpost she was well positioned to act as a quartermaster for boats about to make a dash for Shetland from the surrounding islands. These boats were mostly leaving from nearby Austevoll and the larger island of Bomlo to the south, and their passengers mostly comprised people fleeing from Bergen. By the summer of 1942 about thirty-five boats had left these islands. Møgster operated independently but at the behest of an export group located at the town of Rubbestadneset on Bomlo about 20 miles to the south. This group was based on the factory of Wichmann Motorfabrikk (which made renowned marine engines), owned by the Haldorsen family. Ola Olsen the factory manager was the leader of the export group, with Haldor Andreas Haldorsen and his brother Benjamin Magnus both being involved.

It is not possible to say if they were betrayed, but this seems almost certain as the Gestapo had very precise intelligence not only about those at Wichmann but also about Møgster. In a planned operation on 25 June 1942, the Gestapo arrived from the sea in their *Gestaposkøyta*, first swooping on the Wichmann factory where they arrested Olsen with the two Haldorsen brothers. They then moved straight on to Møkster in case anyone raised an alarm there. Abelone Møgster was surprised and was seized, being thrown into the boat where she was taken below decks where she was immediately introduced to the rubber cosh. She was 58 years old, but she was tough and she absolutely defied her inquisitors. She berated the Norwegian Quisling interpreter at the end of her interrogation, her tirade being heard across the harbour. Her brother, Anders, was also taken that day. His offence was to have an illegal radio – someone on the island must have informed about this.

The following day, the unhappy band of prisoners was taken in the boat back to Gestapo headquarters at Veiten in Bergen where they were more comprehensively tortured in the basement over the next weeks. Møgster must have been more trouble than the others, giving nothing away, as she received by far the worst outcomes. She was assigned the special status of 'NN' (*Nacht und Nebel*, night and fog), whereby those designated were sent to imprisonment in Germany and not expected to survive, simply joining the ranks of the 'disappeared'. The others were sent to less severe camps in Norway and survived the war. Møgster, throughout her hard-workingd working life, had always harboured a fantasy about going on a lovely holiday cruise. Now she found herself herded onto the disgusting prison ship *Monte Rosa* and shipped off to Ravensbrück women's camp (north of Berlin) where she arrived in

May 1943. The oldest of about 100 Norwegian and Danish women in the camp, she was the most resilient and inspiring. She tackled every problem with humour and with gusto. In practical terms, she could improvise, fix things, mend clothes, clean, wash, and chop wood with the best of them, whilst in terms of morale she would joke and sing her favourite song, *Blåbukken*, holding everyone together. All around there was indiscriminate terror, filth and death. Not without reason she acquired the title 'The Angel of Ravensbrück'. She was required to defend her status among the Scandinavian women when, for whatever reason, the woman leading the French contingent came to challenge her to a fight. It was a David and Goliath affair, with the tiny Møgster facing the very much larger Frenchwoman. Møgster darted forward at her opponent's knees lifting them upwards, tipping the woman flat on her back. There was no more trouble from that quarter.

Perhaps because of her status in the camp and because of her personal NN designation, she was 'selected' to be among a group of 2,000 women to be sent on a 'death march' to Mauthausen (in Austria 500 miles to the south) in early 1945. As the Allies were closing on Berlin, the Nazis were attempting to disperse the evidence of their concentration camp crimes in a number of these terrible 'death marches'. Of the group of women from Ravensbrük, only 700 arrived at Mauthausen. They expected nothing less than death there, but in March 1945 she and others were rescued by the famous 'white buses' of the Swedish Red Cross, organised by the impressive Swedish humanitarian mediator, Count Folke Bernadotte. Travelling north in the buses, the women went through Denmark and on to Sweden where they were received in a rehabilitation camp. For Møgster, it was just recompense for her unstinting support of the Red Cross earlier in her life.

Abelone Møgster, returned to her island as a heroine on 31 May 1945; she weighed just 38kg (84lb or just under 6 stones). Her extraordinary record in the war accorded her a considerable standing in Norway in her later life. She was awarded the Kings Medal of Merit in Gold. An amazingly strong woman, she was rewarded with a long life, dying in 1975 at the age of 92. As an islander, it was very appropriate that an Antarctic island was named after her – Møgsterbrekka. In 2011, a brand-new fishing boat was launched commemorating her; it was named MS *Abelone Møgster*. In 2023 in a remarkable coincidence I met Møgster's granddaughter, Susanne Møgster Sperrevik, who was on a visit to Aberdeen. She kindly helped to add colour and detail to the story of her remarkable relative.

Not far from where Abelone Møgster's story unfolded lay another tiny island, Moster, at the southern tip of the main island of Bomlo. In August, the surviving remnants of the Bomlo–Bremnes export group arrived there to make a desperate escape. Among them the most wanted man was Birger Larsen from Bergen, the leader of the group which had organised the voyage of *Rupee* in February. In an incident at the end of May he had a very close shave when he was travelling by boat to a remote jetty to pick up two Bergen fugitives and two agents being brought overland land by the local resistance. As he was drawing close, he could see that he had been beaten to it by the *Gestaposkøyta*, and that Gestapo men were in hot pursuit of the surprised outlaws, shots ringing out. There was nothing that Larsen and his boat crew could do, and they made themselves scarce. The incident was followed by arrests locally and in Bergen, with terrible consequences. The Gestapo net was surely closing in on every one of them.

Another of the group on Moster was Nils Robberstad, the brother of the priest Peter Robberstad who that Easter had refused the offer to escape on *Kapp I* in order to stay with his parishioners. Nils Robberstad was a former merchant marine officer deeply involved with Bergen escapes, now with the Gestapo at his heels. He felt that 'the deck was burning beneath his feet'. It was he who purchased a 38ft fishing boat *Smart* for the escape, paying cash. He wanted to take his wife, Ingerd, with him, and they were joined by Birger Tvedt (a policeman) with his girlfriend Astrid, plus one other, Jacob Vik. The six of them left Moster on 10 August 1942, with Nils at the wheel where he stayed for the next

36 hours without a break. All went well enough until they ran into a dense Scottish haar. Sensibly they cut the engine and in the silence they banged on saucepans, oil drums and the like to make as much noise as they could. Their ersatz fog horn worked, with a boat appearing from the gloom to tell them that they were only 20 minutes from Lerwick.

The subsequent career of Nils Robberstad as an agent deserves to be included, as it was unusual. He was commissioned into the Norwegian Navy and after a while he was summoned to London and invited to return to Norway, to which he agreed. But it appears that he has not under the command of Kompani Linge, the Shetland Bus, SOE or SIS. It seems that he acted as a one-man 'freelance' agent under the direct instruction of London. In this role he made six excursions back to Norway on intelligence missions, catching the Bus for his return journeys. On the last trip in 1944 he knew the Gestapo were close behind him and he needed to cross a fjord to get away. A man came with a small rowing boat but on arrival took fright and started to row away. Robberstad pulled out his revolver and 'I told him I would shoot him dead if he didn't come back!' With this encouragement, the boatman got Robberstad away from the jaws of the Gestapo and he went on the run for nine days before being rescued by his navy friend Leif ('Shetland') Larsen with his submarine chaser *Vigra*.

At 70 years of age, King Haakon VII of Norway was, by any contemporary account, an imposing man. Standing ramrod straight at 1.9m (6ft 3in), as thin as a rake and with a somewhat Victorian bearing, he was loved by his people and revered for defying the Nazis who had driven him from his country. He was not only a figurehead for his government-in-exile, he was the rallying point for all free Norwegians fighting for the Allies. He was also much respected by the other great wartime leaders who looked to him as a wise elder statesman, an exemplar of resistance to Hitler.

The great man, in full military attire, towered over the small 7-year-old boy Per Ivar Støylen, bent forward, took him by the hand, smiled and gently asked him to tell his story. The lad excitedly told of his great adventure – how he escaped from Norway on his father's boat. At the conclusion, the king awarded the youngster a bar of chocolate, a rare treat in those days. This exchange actually happened some months after the dramatic adventure of young Per Ivar Støylen, which took place at the end of July 1942.

His story began with the misadventures of his uncle Kristoffer Nore, well known on the island of Maløy as one of Norway's leading gymnasts and speed skaters. As an army reservist he had been in training for the 1940 Olympics when the war changed everything and he joined the fierce fighting in the north. Later, he resumed a place at Oslo University, where he diverted his energies to the underground movement. Whatever he was up to, he graduated to a Gestapo most wanted list and had to run for his life. It is an embedded human instinct to head for home and Nore somehow managed to evade the manhunt to get back to Maløy some 360 miles to the north west. Arriving at his elder sister Inga's home, he clearly needed to get away to Britain, but there was no active export organisation on the island. In the void, Inga's husband Jeremias Støylen volunteered to take him in his small fishing boat *Forsok*. This was a selfless offer as it would be a one-way journey and he would have to leave behind Inga and their four young children. He considered the risk of taking the whole family with them to be too great. No doubt there was some argument between husband and wife, perhaps even raised voices. What they didn't realise was that their older children were listening in, all ears.

The two brothers-in law set off from Måløy on 27 July 1942. With the coast disappearing behind them, you can imagine their surprise and consternation when 7-year old Per Ivar popped out from under a tarpaulin and announced his presence – 'Here I am, Father!' he cried out. At this point they had gone too far to turn *Forsok* back under the eyes of German observers. Støylen made a quick decision – they had to carry on. He could only hope that the other children would have told Inga what Per had been up to, to explain his missing status. As it was, the three of them had an absolutely straightforward crossing, with a flat sea, an engine that didn't break down, and no German intrusions. They arrived at Baltasound in twenty-five hours, one of the fastest of these crossings on record.

Støylen now found himself as a single parent in his adopted country, and the solution was for father and son to settle in Buckie. Per could be looked after by the Norwegian community in the town, whilst his father and *Forsok* could join the Norwegian fishing fleet. Unsurprisingly, the athletic Kristoffer Nore was selected for Kompani Linge, and earned a St Olav Medal with Oak Leaf for his part in the defence of the island of Svalbard in September 1943. On a later behind-the-lines parachute operation, he had a lucky encounter with a bullet that entered his neck and passed through without damaging anything vital.

In the compendium of the wartime escapes, theirs was an altogether unremarkable example, and hardly merits a note. However, across the centuries everyone has delighted in the stories of stowaways on boats – the younger the better. So it was that young Per Ivar Støylen was elevated, albeit briefly, to the status of 'The Seven-year-old Viking'. The Information Office of the Norwegian government in London seized upon the tale as a good piece to use in their programme of propaganda. On 10 October and over the next few days newspapers all over Britain carried the account with banners along the lines of the 'Seven-year-old Viking', 'Seven-year-old with Viking spirit, or 'The Viking Spirit'. The adventure of Per Ivar Støylen somehow caught the imagination of editors and the public as the embodiment of Viking fighting resolve. The piece, released ten weeks after the event, was timed to draw attention to the opening of the new Norwegian boarding school at Drumtochty Castle in north east Scotland, at which young Per was to be one of the first pupils. Just three weeks later, young Per Ivar stood proudly in front of King Haakon, earning his bar of chocolate. Almost all the other children at Drumtochty were also fugitives who had crossed with their parents, and they had tales to tell to their King. The 'lusty-voiced' pupils gave a vigorous rendition of *Auld Lang Syne* and *Danny Boy*, charmingly, it was noted 'with a discernible Scottish lilt.'

The Royal Norwegian government's Information Office in London had carefully curated the enterprise of young Per Ivar Støylen. In doing so it had recognised the propaganda value of exceptional stories of escapes from Norway. During 1942 it used these and the talents of some of the people who had fled to promote their message. The office had the extensive tasks of keeping Norway in the conscience of her wartime allies, raising morale of all free Norwegians and raising money for King Haakon's Relief Fund which helped to support exiled countrymen and their families. In doing so, it functioned in many different ways. It was the national broadcaster, and the central press office. It was a public relations organisation. It was a publisher of all sorts of material in Norwegian and English. It organised events and tours. It promoted Norwegian arts, film and culture. It used every means possible to further the standing of Norway in the war.

The Information Office had a considerable array of talent amongst its personnel, many of whom had by small boat or by other means escaped to London, to offer their services to their exiled government. Toralf Øksnevad, the already renowned broadcaster, became the 'Voice of London' (via the BBC) from the invasion onwards for the duration of the war. A number of leading journalists escaped in small boats early on – for example Knut Vidnes (escaped on *Stjernen* in October 1941, see Chapter 4) – and were taken into service in London. Jonas Schanche Jonasen, the remarkable journalist who had interviewed both Hitler and Mussolini (escaped on *Soløy* in August 1941) became editor of *Norsk Tidende*, the official free Norwegian newspaper. The renowned polymath journalist, writer, poet, playwright and political activist Nordahl Grieg, who had escaped in May 1940, gave much to the work of the department.

The world-famous opera baritone Waldemar Johnsen (escaped on *Nordlys* in September 1941) became an arts impresario. Johnsen teamed up with the internationally known soprano Soffi Shönning to present no less than 625 recitals, concerts and cultural events during the rest of the war. Many of these were produced in cooperation with ENSA (the Entertainments National Service Association). They had a wealth of singers, musicians and dancers to call upon, including the sopranos Hulda Frisk Gran, Florence Weise and Gerda Grieg. From performances at the Albert Hall attended by King Haakon to local WRI (Women's Rural Institute) meetings, the Norwegian Information Office pressed the case for Norway's war.

Norway's top goal-scoring international footballer of all time, Jørgen Juve, who was also a journalist and writer, was focussed on the sporting crowd. A very popular member of the Information Office as an itinerant speaker at events was Alf Adriansen (escaped on *Duen* October 1941) a photographer who delighted audiences with his 'lantern slide' shows and dramatic descriptions of events in Norway. As reported in the *Rochdale Observer* in June 1942, Adriansen recounted an amusing story about escapes from the Germans, worthy of a full mention:

> The Germans did not possess a monopoly of intelligence and sometimes they were outwitted in an amusing manner. One day a small fishing vessel moved slowly down of the fjords and everyone on board seemed happy. An accordion was being played, and, standing on the deck, were a bride and bridegroom. As the boat passed a German fort those on board waved to the guards, who were so surprised to be cordially greeted by Norwegians that they allowed the boat to pass. The 'bridal party' headed straight for the North Sea, and today they are in England.

Lying almost exactly on the Arctic Circle about 40 miles out into the North Sea is an aggregation of small rocky islands at Træna, so small that they are not marked on most maps. From the east they were protected from prying German eyes by difficult shallow waters and myriad Skerries. As such, they attracted the attention of the Shetland Bus as an ideal place to land shipments of munitions and to run Linge agents ashore. The disadvantages of a 1,200-mile round trip were outweighed by the advantages of safe sheltered anchorages and a helpful local population. Foremost among the helpers was Magnus Olsen, a fishing fleet owner and merchant. A reconnoitring trip from Shetland was undertaken in October 1941, and over the next five months four successful trips were made, landing large amounts of small arms and explosives. It was then the job of Olsen and his group to transfer the cargoes across to the mainland in smaller local boats. This was a complex operation because of the need to store, load and unload tons of materiel into small boats without being detected. On arrival on the mainland, the shipments had to be taken across the mountain into the interior of Trøndelag where there was a very active Milorg unit. At this point in the geography of Norway the country is at its narrowest and, in military terms, most vulnerable to being cut in half by insurgent action, a considerable worry to the Germans and a constant niggle for the Führer.

Some of the munitions made their way to the district of Majavatn in Trøndelag where they were stored at an isolated farm at Tangen, where four Linge men were also hiding out. The Gestapo got wind of this and in early September sent two boats with about ten armed agents to investigate. The people at the farm were alerted just in advance of the raid, and the Germans rowed their vessels into an ambush. There was a sustained firefight during which most of the Germans were killed, whilst the Linge men and the locals escaped into the mountains. This was a huge affront to the Nazis, who launched a massive manhunt, directed personally by Terboven.

News of this reached Træna with a direct threat to Magnus Olsen that the Gestapo were on their way. Olsen organised a rapid exit for those on the danger list, also deciding to take his wife, Olga, and their two young children. The boat *Svalen* left on 17 September 1942 with the Olsens, four other island helpers and four Linge men, making it to safety at Scallaway in five days. Back in Nordland all was far from safe – terror reigned.

The outrage at Tangen farm was an opportunity that Terboven had been waiting for. It was a chance to demonstrate once and again to Quisling who held the real power in Norway, and to redeem himself with the Führer. In August he had flown to Berlin for a meeting with Hitler to discuss the situation in Norway. The Führer was angry that Norway was not peaceful and compliant. He was well aware of the chaos that Quisling had created in his fight with the teachers and the clergy. Hitler was worried that resistance to the NS and the Germans was stiffening whilst the threat of an Allied invasion remained high. Terboven was quick to distance himself from Quisling's antics, but not without censure from the great leader. With a flea in his ear, he was sent home with a clear instruction to bring Quisling to heel, and to exert his superiority.

As he had done before at Telavåg, Terboven swept Quisling aside and took personal command of the situation in Trøndelag, using his higher authority to declare a state of emergency. This gave him sweeping powers including those of summary execution. Over the next weeks around 1,500 houses and farms were raided, 3,500 vehicles stopped and searched, 15,000 people were interrogated and hundreds were arrested. As a starter, Terboven had ten randomly selected prominent citizens of Trondheim arrested and had them executed without trial, in reprisal for the dead Gestapo men. Of the hundreds that were arrested, twenty-four were transported to Falstad camp where they too were taken out into the forest and shot on 7 and 8 October. Hundreds of others were sent to concentration camps with long sentences. In the wake of these punishments, Terboven left stringent restrictions for the entire population of Trøndelag.

To spread the message further across Norway, Terboven ordered a large operation across the south of the country which resulted in 6-700 arrests of anyone associated in any way with escapes or with Milorg. He had given Quisling a lesson in how to deal with his difficult countrymen, one in which Hitler would have delighted.

As the terror pervaded in Nordland during that autumn of 1942, the last boat of that year set out on 24 September. This happened far away and to the south of Nordland and seems to have been an entirely random escape attempt. Three young students, Harald Bilberg, Andreas Larvik and Egil Vasstrand from the University of Bergen, travelled to the remote tiny village of Dimmelsvik lying on the south shore of the great Hardanger Fjord. Why they chose this isolated place isn't known, nor why they chose a *seksæring,* (a 'six-ring' rowing boat with three pairs of oars) in which to make their escape. Such a vessel is in the region of only 20ft in length, an inshore general purpose open boat with possibly a small sail but no motor. At the time of the autumn equinoctial gales, the idea of attempting to row across to Shetland seems foolhardy at best – and it proved to be tragic. They disappeared without trace. Whatever danger those young men had encountered at the university, they must have been absolutely determined to escape and to take such an appalling risk.

The true nature of these dangerous escape attempts, with their successes and not infrequent failures, became translated into a sort of popular melodrama in the eyes of the Allied media. This was nurtured by the Royal Norwegian Information Office, furthering its own agenda. Newspapers, broadcasts and film reinforced the message of defiant young Vikings risking all to be able to fight back against the Nazis. The British public was in thrall to stories of escaping Vikings and their fight to reclaim their beloved country.

Less comfortable reading was a significant leading article written by John Gurney, the Stockholm correspondent of the London *News Chronicle* on 28 October 1942, headlined 'Norway Faces Its Worst Winter'. As Norway entered its third winter of occupation, he catalogued some of the hardships being faced. These included the confiscation of nearly all fish landings (all of the herring catch). The entire potato crop was seized that autumn. Consequently, the population faced near starvation level with rations of around 1,000 calories a day (usually 2,500 would be needed for an adult in winter). Gurney went on to describe the severe restriction of energy usage with a limit on household temperature of 10 degrees Celsius, electricity rationing blackouts, and the closure of schools for four months to save fuel. Additionally, he noted the dire shortages of almost all essential clothing, household items and medicines. To round off his comprehensive article, he described in detail the apprehension and summary execution ('within the hour') of several men known to him during the terror in Trondheim at the beginning of that month. Gurney certainly painted a bleak snow and ice-bound picture.

A completely different and more uplifting account arrived in time for Christmas 1942. It was the bestselling Puffin Storybook *We'll Meet in England*, by Kitty Barne (very well known in her day). The slim volume covered every one of the components of an escape from occupied Norway. It included the planned voyage of the young protagonists, the threat of betrayal, the secret preparations, the leaking boat, the German aircraft searching, the terrible storm, the rescue of an airman and the eventual happy landing in Scotland. The saga was animated by the antics of the Husky puppy, Hurry. All of these things were portrayed with surprising accuracy and empathy. There is no doubt that Kitty Barne had used direct first-hand information from some of those who had escaped by boat. The charming little book gave British teenagers an insight into coping with some of the harsh realities of a brutal war. It was an important lesson for them – and their parents.

Chapter 15

Slack Tide
(January–December 1943)

Friday, 1 January 1943 ushered in a New Year with an area of low pressure sitting between Western Norway and the Shetland Islands. The winter of 1942–43 was recorded as being one of the stormiest on record with 116 days of storms out of 120 consecutive days. Early January northerly winds brought sleet and snow showers – not pleasant conditions for North Sea mariners, but good cover for secret operations. That week Karl Lambrecht was nosing around Norwegian coastal waters looking for landing places and anchorages suitable for a commando raid on the island of Stord (south of Bergen) planned for later that month (Operation Cartoon).

Lambrecht was a member of the Norwegian Navy SIS which operated jointly with British SIS from a base at Peterhead, Aberdeenshire, that was so secret that it was not declassified until the 1980s. The unit ran agents to and from Norway involved specifically in surveillance of German navy and other shipping movements. Whereas the Bus was part of SOE offensive operations, Peterhead was part of SIS and regarded itself as being ultra-secret, difficult to figure out even today. It used its own selection of Norwegian fishing boats, crewed by their own navy men (not from the *Shetlandsgjengen*). The boat under Lambrecht's command was *Gullborg,* the sturdy former firefighting boat that had escaped with twenty-six refugees from Fjell in September 1941 (Chapter 9). Lambrecht was himself a previous escaper. As a part owner and skipper of the fishing boat *Fiks* he had organised the escape to Shetland of seventeen people from Solund (near the entrance to the great Sogenfjorden) on 11 October 1941.

On this mission fifteen months later Lambrecht had another secret and private agenda; he intended to 'go rogue', and use the opportunity to collect his wife Petrine and their four younger children left behind when he escaped in 1941. As his actions were not only head-strong but also clearly against orders, this escape is included among this book's flights, as it was clearly not undertaken as a military operation. Seizing his opportunity, Lambrecht made an off-course dash of about 100 miles north to his home community of Solund, from where he had escaped fifteen months before. There would have been no possibility of forewarning Petrine and the family – he would have simply turned up out of the swirling snow showers giving them a huge surprise. There would have been an anxious wait for them to snatch some belongings together as quickly as possible before completing their unexpected departure. Petrine and the children were no doubt delighted to be reunited with the husband and father of their family. After a safe landing they were soon taken in by other members of the family at Buckie, where they became prominent in the expatriate community.

Lambrecht's future was less settled. He cannot have expected to escape reprimand for his reckless act, but of this there is no record. Rather, he seems to have disappeared off the radar, and he was definitely not in command of *Gullborg* when she returned to the island of Stord on 23 January, as part of Operation Cartoon. The boat was acting as a pilot 'beacon' for seven Norwegian MTBs (Motor Torpedo Boats) carrying British and Norwegian commandos. They very efficiently blew up an important pyrites mine, captured some Germans and sank a steamer. Flushed with success, the MTBs turned for Scotland and ran into a bad storm. *Gullborg*, following a day or so later, was not heard of again, presumably lost with all hands in the same storm or sunk by the Germans. A fate that was surely designated for Karl Lambrecht was side-stepped by his own insubordination.

Three exhausted men landed at Lerwick in the small boat *Reidar* on 8 January 1943, after a gruelling two day crossing from Ålesund. It was their third attempt, the previous two boats being useless. On the face of it there was nothing unusual in the arrival, excepting that the three men were from Trondheim – so why had they travelled hundreds of miles to escape from Ålesund, and why in January? This was the first boat from there in fourteen months, since the purges of 1941, and the town was firmly under German control. Any initial suspicion was confirmed by receipt of an intercept by SIS soon after the arrival that there could be an attempt to land an Abwehr agent. Over the next weeks and months an extraordinary and sinister plot by the Germans was revealed, with a tale of perplexing complexity not released by The National Archives until 2006.

The three were quickly spirited away to the attention of MI5 at Camp 020, their secret centre at Latchmere House, south-west London, under the renowned Colonel Robin 'Tin Eye' Stephens (he wore a monocle). Suffice it to say that two of the men, Gunnar Pedersen and Louis Westrum were quickly deemed to be innocent and were released. Arnold Evensen, a 28-year-old baker, was a different kettle of fish. He immediately claimed that he had duped the Abwehr by volunteering as an agent (code name Alex) solely as a way of getting to Britain, and that he really wanted to work as a double agent for the Allies. This approach had been used before – as with Mutt and Jeff, for instance. Evensen presented his credentials – he had brought with him some photographs of military shipping and installations, intending to prove his intent to change sides. The interrogators were, however, suspicious that the pictures were far too professional to have been taken by him. Moreover, his proposals to return to Norway with radio transmitters lacked plausibility. What game was he up to? Was he attempting a triple-cross? The interrogations entered a deeper level and the revelations became stranger and stranger still.

Evensen claimed that the Abwehr (based at Trondheim) had an alarming plan to wage biological warfare on Britain, using a fleet of Norwegian fishing vessels, a sort of reverse Nazi Shetland Bus. They were to cross over with the intention of releasing the biological agents in different locations around the Scottish coast. He said he had been sent to reconnoitre the possibilities and landing places at the receiving end. Nothing really added up, and the more he was disbelieved the more Evensen was in effect pleading for his life. He was a Walter Mitty agent if he was anything. After months of interrogations, one his tormentors, Major Munthe, concluded that Evensen 'gave me a strong impression of being an abnormal potential criminal idiot – almost certainly sent here by the enemy', whilst a Captain Shanks wrote that 'his mental powers are abnormal, his memory hopeless and his mind an inchoate jumble'. Another officer added, 'He is either mentally subnormal or more cunning than he appears to be – possibly both'.

The conclusion of MI5 was that there was no threat from him or from a Nazi biological plot. He got off with his life and, after a period of detention, he was even released on licence in 1944. Arnold Evensen, the baker from Trondheim, got a job as a baker not far from Latchmere House in west London. Did he keep Camp 020 supplied with pastries?

At the beginning of February 1943, news percolated throughout the world that the mighty German armies besieging Stalingrad since August 1942 had not only failed but that the remnants of the 6th Army had surrendered. Hitler's furious exhortations to fight until the last man had been ignored and he expected the army's commander, Field Marshal Friedrich Paulus, to commit suicide. The Field Marshal declined, saying, 'I have no intention of shooting myself for this Bohemian corporal.' The battle consumed around half a million Axis soldiers (German, Italian, Romanian and Hungarian) in death and capture. Probably more importantly in the long term was the loss of colossal amounts of German war materiel, and the failure to gain access to the oil fields of the Caucasus. Whereas losses on the Russian side were more than double, Russia had almost infinite manpower and was now being resupplied by the Allies. In Churchill's words, this was the 'Hinge of Fate', the turning point of the war. It was soon to be followed by success in North Africa, where in May the Axis armies surrendered, with 275,000 prisoners being taken.

All over free world and occupied Europe a realisation dawned that Hitler could not and would not succeed with his great ambitions. Norwegians at last harboured renewed optimism that they would regain their country. Terboven and Quisling unsurprisingly took another view; they wanted to salvage the German war effort, and thereby their own destinies. On 22 February, they issued joint statements and laws to redouble support for Germany by the 'total mobilisation' of all 350,000 able bodied workers of both sexes. They were to be withdrawn from their normal jobs to be forcibly redeployed in Nazi war construction and production.

The 'total mobilisation' soon became a 'total farce' at the hands of the Norwegian people. The labour offices were overwhelmed by spurious false and spoiled registration papers. Variants of 'Adolf Hitler' and 'Vidkun Quisling' appeared to be keen to be registered for work. Milorg saboteurs had a field day bombing and burning labour offices all over the country, successfully destroying most of the valid registrations. So effective was this campaign that in the end perhaps only a third of those eligible were forced to work for the Germans. As well as blowing up labour offices, Milorg units, by now armed and supplied from Scotland, started an incremental programme of sabotage attacks against German military and industrial infrastructure. The resultant arrests and reprisals were a price that Norway's people were prepared to pay.

After Stalingrad, Sweden began to re-appraise its position. It opted in favour of the winning team and its attitude to Norway shifted substantially. Its borders became porous to escapers and the welcome and treatment of refugees became more generous. In London, the Norwegian government at last began to plan for the repossession and governance of its country. Talks opened between the Norwegians and the Swedes about the rebuilding of Norway after the war. An indicator of the new confidence in London was the commissioning of a new

Victory March to be called *Alt for Norge,* to be used for the return to Norway. The London-based composer Harry Ralton wrote the music, with the academic and poet Wilhelm Kielhau later adding the words. The two were summoned to an audience with King Haakon at which it was sung by Waldemar Johnsen. It was a hit with the king, and it was a hit with free Norwegians everywhere; it is still in use today.

The new buoyancy of mood in Norway as the war turned in its favour meant that fewer people now felt compulsion to risk an escape. Boats leaving the coast dwindled to just a few over the summer of 1943, and, besides, it was now easier to cross into Sweden.

On the night of 27/28 February 1943, one of the most celebrated commando raids of the war took place in Telemark, southern Norway. A six-man team of Linge men carried out what is regarded as one of the most precise and effective commando raids of the war. The six penetrated and blew up the heavy water production unit at the hydro plant at Vemork, stalling Hitler's plans to make an atomic bomb. The raid was later immortalised in the film *The Heroes of Telemark.* The six were under the command of the youngest, the remarkable 23-year-old Joachim Rønneberg, who had escaped on *Sigurd* on 13 March 1941. Of the party, five were former small boat escapers, and the sixth had escaped via Sweden. They were still good at escaping as over the next three weeks they evaded a pursuit of 12,000 Germans to make it to the Swedish border, 200 miles away.

You need to look no further than to these six men to understand that those who escaped were an extraordinary cadre of men, self-selected by their decision to risk escaping across the North Sea. We have seen already many examples of outstanding young men who contributed to the war effort. They became the backbone of the Shetland Bus and Kompani Linge organisations, essential shock troops of Churchill's SOE. They were also contributors to other shadowy groups such as the British SIS, the Norwegian Navy SIS, and the MI5 counter-intelligence service. From the earliest days following the Nazi invasion of their country, there were men willing to go back to Norway to prosecute the war against their antagonists. They certainly added constant irritation to the occupying forces.

Of course, not all of those who escaped across the North Sea were destined for cloak and dagger activities. But all who did come to Allied shores, men and women, did make a direct contribution to the Allied war effort. It is appropriate that we pause to look at the various ways in which these Second World War Vikings helped in the Allied war effort.

Many were fishermen or merchant mariners, and it was natural that they would volunteer for service afloat. There were several options. A small number (usually those who had brought their families) were settled into the Norwegian community at Buckie where they continued to fish to support the food industry, or some helped to repair and maintain the Shetland Bus boats. Those seeking a more active role enlisted in the Royal Norwegian Navy (RNoN). After the capitulation in June 1940, just thirteen surviving navy ships escaped to Scotland. By the end of the war, the RNoN had increased to 58 ships and 7,500 personnel, of whom about half were at sea and half in support. Of those at sea, 930 died, a staggering attrition rate of 25 per cent. The most dazzling exploits were undertaken by the two flotillas of MTBs (as distinct from the Shetland Bus operations) which harried enemy shipping in coastal Norwegian waters. Most of the hard dirty work was done escorting the Atlantic and Arctic convoys, and minesweeping the British coastline. Three submarines specialised in attacking shipping in Norwegian waters and also operated a 'sub-sea' Shetland Bus service taking agents across to remote fjords. One Norwegian destroyer helped to sink the German battleship *Scharnhorst* in the dramatic events of December 1943. Ten ships of the RNoN and a thousand men took part in the Normandy landings. For a tiny nation of 3million people living under occupation, its small navy was punching well above its weight.

As a seafaring nation, probably the majority joined the Norwegian merchant marine. At the start of the war Norway had one of the largest merchant fleets in the world, sometimes referred to as 'Norway's floating empire', with around 1,000 ships and 30,000 seamen. After the invasion, the fleet was placed under a central management called *Nortraship* and offered to the service of the Allied cause. The contribution of this fleet cannot be overestimated as these Norwegian ships kept open vital supply lines across the North Atlantic. In particular, about half of all petroleum fuels were carried on Norwegian ships at considerable risk of death in a flaming inferno. Around 700 ships were lost with 3,600 people who died, an attrition rate of about 12 per cent.

The Nobel peace laureate Philip Noel-Baker later said:

> The first great defeat of Hitler was the Battle of Britain. It was a turning point in history. If we had not had the Norwegian fleet of tankers on our side, we should not have had the aviation spirit to put our Hawker Hurricanes and our Spitfires into the sky. Without the Norwegian merchant fleet Britain and its allies would have lost the war.

For those whose experience of crossing the North Sea was bad enough and who wanted to keep their feet on dry land, there was the Norwegian army. Very few soldiers escaped to Britain at the time of the capitulation, and a new free army had to be created from scratch, rounding up waif and strays from amongst the refugees as well as displaced sailors from whaling and merchant ships. A very motley crew of around 300 were assembled at Dumfries in Scotland to form the new army. The unpromising start was not well supported by the British and failed to achieve good potential, not reaching more than brigade strength of around 2,000 men. Enlistments were often transitory as those who sought more action transferred to other services. In effect the army provided a basic military training and acted as a clearing house. The small numbers meant that their role was self-limiting, being primarily the defence of various locations around northern Scotland, and garrisons at Svalbard, Iceland, Greenland and South Georgia. In time, the *Skottlansbrigaden* found its feet and formed a valuable mountain warfare ski school and an independent parachute company. In late 1943 a force was sent in support of the Russian invasion of Finnmark. The main raison d'être of the brigade was to take part in the invasion of Europe, but this was cruelly denied them as the brigade was kept out of the Normandy landings. The brigade's consolation was to spearhead the re-occupation of Norway and to take control of the surrender of the German forces.

Many of those who went across in small boats looked to the skies. In a sense, their risk-taking was an asset to air warfare. There was no shortage of volunteers and a high proportion of the pilots were escapers. Before the war there was an army and a navy air arm but now they were effectively amalgamated. Aircrew training was undertaken in America and then in Canada (the base in Ontario became known as 'Little Norway'). Crucially the air force placed itself directly under British command, and so enjoyed full integration and support. The two Spitfire fighter squadrons achieved the highest combat success rates amongst all the expatriate formations. They covered the Dieppe Raid and Normandy landings. Flying boats ranged far over the convoys searching for U-boats, and had a second role acting as a 'Shetland Bus-by-air' service for agents. Mosquito fighter bombers (they called themselves 'Viking Mozzies') harried German shipping and coastal defences. Always keen to record their scores, the Norwegian flyers notched up 180 confirmed 'kills', 35 'probables' and 100 damaged but these came at a cost of 71 pilots. For such a small nation, it was a substantial contribution to the Allied air forces.

Amongst the escapers who came to Britain there were not many women (under 10 per cent), but nonetheless they were keen to put on a Norwegian uniform. They were to become known as the *Kvinkorps* (Women's Corps) or *K-soldater* (K-soldiers). Voluntary recruitment was not enough to make get a corps off the ground and conscription of eligible women was introduced in August 1942, raising a contingent of around 660 women, who were trained at Maxwelton House, Dumfriesshire. They were allocated to the three services, with nurses being separate but under the same umbrella. The nurses staffed the Norwegian Hospital in Edinburgh. Other Norwegian women in Britain were employed in reserved occupations in teaching or in support roles within government and defence ministries in London.

The romance and excitement of Viking escapes from Norway was never far from the attention of the public, and the year 1943 brought no fewer than five feature length films to cinemagoers in the English-speaking world. It is hard to comprehend the importance of cinema in those days. It was the cornerstone of keeping people informed and also entertained. It was vital in raising and sustaining morale whilst also being a fairly unsubtle instrument of propaganda. Of a wartime population in Britain of around 48 million, cinema admissions increased from around 20 million a week in 1939 to 30 million in 1945. That means that more than half of the population (men, women and children) was attending a cinema every one to two weeks. With about 4,500 cinemas, the venues were packed for every performance.

In March 1943, the British press announced a Royal Gala Premier of the long-awaited film *Commandos Strike At Dawn*. This was a big budget film shot mostly in Canada, supported by the British, Canadian and American governments. It starred, among others, the famous Norwegian heartthrob actor Paul Muni, Sir Cedric Hardwicke and Lilian Gish. Based on a story by the famous naval novelist C.S. Forester, the plot encompassed every aspect of the by now romantic ideal of a dreadfully wronged Norwegian people courageously escaping to freedom and returning home to drive their oppressors out. It was realistic and brutal enough to depict a Quisling traitor being unceremoniously dumped over the side of the boat that the heroes are escaping in, and it concludes with a dramatic commando raid enacted by real troops in training. The entire proceeds of the premiere went to King Haakon's Fund, a very generous gesture. More importantly, the film was a run-away success, both in America and in Britain, where it continued to run for the rest of the year.

The Norwegian saga as depicted in *Commandos Strike At Dawn* was attractive and easy material for other film makers in those war years. In

1942, there had been the American low budget *They Raid by Night* and the more impressive British *The Day Will Dawn,* written by Terrence Rattigan, starring Ralph Richardson and Deborah Kerr. The year 1943 brought four more Norwegian-themed feature-length films, of which *Commandos Strike At Dawn* was the best of the bunch. Hollywood waded in with an Errol Flynn blockbuster *Edge Of Darkness*, and *The Moon Is Down* based on a novel by John Steinbeck and starring Cedric Hardwicke was well reviewed. Columbia Pictures also contributed the successful *First Comes Courage* starring Merle Oberon and Brian Aherne. A more modest offering to follow in 1944 was the British Ealing Studios *The Return of The Vikings*, a semi documentary-drama produced with the Norwegian government. The plight and fight of Norway was seldom away from of a 'cinema near you' for most of the years 1942 to 1945.

If Norwegians had a need for a reminder that they remained under the Nazi jackboot it became manifest on 28 November 1943. The University of Oslo possessed a fine auditorium which was occasionally used by the Germans for concerts and they had made a booking for that night. Some hot-heads decided to intervene and started a small fire – and then called the fire brigade, intending the damage to be minimal. The fire was a token, only causing the concert to be postponed until the following night. Terboven nonetheless was furious, sure that students were behind the incident. The university had long been a thorn in his flesh, as it had resolutely resisted pressure to become Nazified and there had been several defiant acts before. On 30 November, a force of 300 soldiers (not enough for the job) was sent to surround the campus and arrest all of the students. Acting on a tip-off, at least 2,000 students had already left and melted into the city. As the inadequate cordon closed in, more slipped away, but around 1,200 students, tutors and professors were caught and arrested. Women were allowed to go whilst the men were sent to a concentration camp. The students who had escaped were subject to a protracted manhunt over the next months, but most avoided capture and many of them managed to get to Sweden.

Terboven was so enraged that at first he contemplated the execution of every tenth student, but was dissuaded from this course by officers of Quisling's NS and a direct instruction from Berlin. Eventually, about half of the students were released, and 644 were sent to camps in Germany where 17 died. The university remain closed for the rest of the war. The supposition that it was the students who had started the fire was wrong. It was some rogue members of the resistance who had nothing to do with the university.

As with the persecutions of the labour union, the clergy and the teachers, the violation of Oslo University had consequences beyond the comprehension of Josef Terboven. Universities all over the free world reacted with condemnation and nowhere was this more apparent than in Sweden. Their numbers swelled by students who had escaped from Oslo, tens of thousands of Swedish students and citizens turned out to register their objection. This helped to influence their government to move further towards supporting its immediate neighbour Norway.

The end of November saw an example of an emergency boat escape that was the result of an SOE raid on Bergen that went horribly wrong. The subsequent failure of the boat escape led to further adventures for the unfortunate participants. Midget submarines always invite attention in the annals of wartime sabotage raids, but they very often go awry as in the case of Operation Barbara in November 1943. The plan was to try a newly developed one-man Welman submarine to enter Bergen Harbour and sink the important floating dock. Reservations about the craft expressed by the Royal Navy were over-ridden by SOE, and the raid was launched by Norwegian MTBs from Shetland on 20 November. Two Norwegians and two Britons piloted the four Welmans into Bergen harbour but were unable to penetrate the anti-submarine nets, being forced to come to the surface. They were spotted by a German patrol and one of the Norwegians was captured, together with his Welman; the other three managed to get away. They scuttled their submarines and managed to get to land where they were rescued by local resistance men. The three submariners would have been subjected to an immediate manhunt, and they were spirited north of the city as quickly as possible.

The hunted submariners, Lieutenants C. Johnsen (Norwegian), Basil Marris and Jimmy Holmes (British) were joined up with two Norwegians being hunted by the Gestapo. One of these was 21-year-old fisherman Rolf Nordhus who had been in trouble with the Germans since the invasion started when, as a teenager, he had blasted away at a Dornier bomber with the family shotgun. After this he was continuously involved with the resistance, now he had been betrayed and was on the run. Fortunately, Nordhus later recounted the extraordinary adventures of the little group that followed. The five men scrambled aboard a 62ft boat *Start* and set off westwards on about 23 November. About half-way across, the engine gave up in the throes of a gale, in which they drifted for five days, at which point they had arrived back at the Norwegian coast, passing the Utvær lighthouse. Under sail they managed to find a tiny and secluded cove on the nearby island of Ytre Sula where heavy seas effectively trapped them for fourteen days. A German plane spotted them, and a patrol boat came to the entrance of the cove but was unable to get in. The fugitives decided that dry land was a better option and abandoned ship, just in time, as Germans came overland to grab them the following day. They avoided capture and went to ground for a protracted period, spending Christmas 1943 and New Year 1944 as guests of Milorg.

Radio contact with SOE led to MTB 653 being dispatched to pick them all up in February 1944, over two months after the brave submariners set out on the ill-fated Operation Barbara. Young Rolf Nordhus had demonstrated that he was ideal material for the Shetland Bus, in which he became a regular crewman until the end of the war.

In his Christmas message for 1943, King Haakon had cause to project some hope for the year to come, but he did not underestimate the task of repossessing and rebuilding Norway. He concluded, 'When the war is over, it is my hope that the unity that has been created at home in the midst of these hardships will continue, and that together we will put everything into building the country back up again.'

Chapter 16

Final Surge
(January 1944–May 1945)

In mid-January 1944, weather watchers would have noted that the German News Agency declared a record lowest temperature (minus 53 degrees Celsius) for Norway at Tynset, in the mountains about 60 miles due south of Trondheim. It is hard to imagine the discomfort of that, aggravated by severe fuel, clothing and food rationing. It's the sort of cold where your nostrils become blocked with ice, your eyelashes become caked with crystals, and uncovered flesh becomes welded to metal. Useful life gets frozen to a standstill. Norwegians were better suited to it than German conscripts from the Ruhr and the occupiers must have felt their resolve falling with the thermometer.

Russians also coped better and were turning the winter to their advantage. On 27 January 1944, the 872-day long siege of Leningrad was relieved by advancing Soviet forces. Six weeks later, the bulk of Ukraine was over-run by Russia at the conclusion of a stunning series of victories. To Norwegians, as the news filtered through, there was real hope of an end to their ordeal. Nonetheless some still had reason to want to escape and some were still willing to take to the sea.

Hans-Gunther Lange, captain of U-711 wasn't wasting torpedoes when he came across a fishing boat about 200 miles west of the Lofoten on 13 April 1944, he simply surfaced and came along side to investigate. What he found was a Norwegian boat, *Solvoll*, with five men, a woman and two children on board. The boat had left Tromsø three days before heading for Iceland. In open sea, *Solvoll* had proved to be unstable and they had put into the Vesterålen (Western Islands) to pick up some rocks as ballast. By the time the U-boat came upon them the engine was giving trouble and it possible that they were doomed anyway (the boat was deemed unserviceable by the U-boat engineers and was sunk by the submarine's gun). In an extraordinary gesture 21-year-old Bernhard Nilsen flung himself overboard. It would not have been to avoid capture so far from land. The only thing he could hope to achieve by this was suicide, as he could not have expected to live for more than a few minutes in water temperatures of 5 to 6 degrees Celsius. In ending his life, he possibly hoped to protect his family or perhaps his contacts in the resistance. The submariners fished him out alive anyway, and he and the others spent the rest of war in captivity. The reasons for this escape attempt and the names of the others aren't known. Bernhard Nilsen became prisoner number 17,122 at Grini concentration camp.

For all the approbation accorded to the Norwegian people under Nazi occupation there is one anomaly which defies an easy explanation. This was the enduring success of Henry Rinnan and his *Sonderabteilung Lola* group based in Trondheim. Rinnan, already a consummate traitor, was granted an autonomous status by his Sipo controllers in September 1943. He operated unfettered from then until the end of the occupation. The *Rinnanbanden* made up their own rules as they went along and were given free rein insofar as torture and execution were concerned. The damage visited on the resistance was devastating. Around 1,000 people were arrested, of whom they executed or murdered around eighty. The number of agents was no more than seventy, of which around thirteen were women.

The motives for membership were not always clear, as many were not even members of the NS. Good pay, good 'terms and conditions' were enjoyed in hard times, but naked greed was very prevalent. They simply helped themselves to the property and assets of those they betrayed, sent to concentration camp or murdered. As with spies they enjoyed the great game of deceit and the exercise of abusive power. Internal discipline was carried out in the style of the Mafia and challenge was followed by disappearance. In this way, four of Rinnan's own men were killed off. A year after Marino Nilsson had disappeared his body was found wrapped in a canvas shroud, weighted down at the bottom of Ålesund harbour. It is easy to dismiss the likes of Henry Rinnan as simple pathological thugs, but the fact that he managed to avoid exposure for so long must surely be attributed to an inherent intelligence and cunning.

The *Rinnanbanden* enjoyed a supporting cast of other nebulous informers. Some were knowing and deliberate in their betrayals and they were paid for their efforts. Others were duped into believing they were actually helping the resistance; they were known as 'negative agents' and were later horrified to find out how they had been deceived. The lengths that Rinnan's people would go to recruit a 'negative agent' whilst protecting their cover is illustrated in the following escape story which started in May 1944 on the island of Frøya (offshore from Trondheim).

The island was a transit station for the Shetland Bus, bringing in agents, arms and ammunition. This was highly dangerous work for the local branch of the resistance. There was a tip-off via Stockholm that the Germans were about to raid the island and round up everyone involved. There was an urgent need for them to get away. The Rinnan agent Joralf Borgan (alias 'Per Fosse') had successfully penetrated the locals and decided he didn't want to lose his cover. So he actually helped organise the evacuation of twenty-two refugees on the boat *Gangar* which set out on 14 May 1944. The crossing was easy and a coded message from London confirmed safe arrival. 'Per Fosse' emerged not only undetected but with greatly enhanced credibility. A young woman, Randi Ruø, whose brother Johannes had been amongst the *Gangar* escapers was charmed and completely taken in by him. In gratitude she was induced to move to Trondheim and set up a small resistance group feeding information about it in all innocence to her new friend. This success did not help Joralf Borgan when his turn came to have a fall-out with Henry Rinnan. Like Marino Nilsson he just disappeared.

The encouraging reports from the Soviet fronts were followed by news of Allied successes as they moved up towards northern Italy. The hitherto patient members of Milorg and other groups began to feel the need for more positive action. By now, Milorg was about 50,000 strong, well organised and trained, with weapons and explosives delivered by the Shetland Bus. It says much about their discipline that there were not many 'hot head' attacks up to this point. The very successful campaign of destroying labour office records continued and kept as many as 200,000 people away from forced German labour. There now was a series of planned attacks within factories that were making components for the Nazi war machine and production lines were brought to a standstill.

News of the Normandy landings of 6 June 1944 spread over Norway like wildfire. Everyone's expectations lifted with a realisation that the occupation would be over before too long. The big supplementary questions were – when would there be a Norwegian front? When would the Allies invade Norway? When was the British Fourth Army Group going to sweep across the North Sea? As it became known later, there was no Fourth Army at all, it was an elaborate and successful deception. Although barely recognised in later analysis, it was one of the most important bluffs of the war. The work of the Norwegian double agents 'Mutt and Jeff' (Chapter 9) had helped to establish the plot. Hitler himself had always believed in it, which is why he had poured so many resources into his *Festung Norgwegen*, keeping at least 350,000 Germans in the country at the time of D-day, well away from the beaches of Normandy. The only invasion of Norway came in the autumn from the far north and with devastating consequences. In that heady June, Milorg prepared itself for action in support of Allied forces. Sabotage raids were stepped up, with explicit orders coming from London in July to paralyse the military infrastructure. Bridges, tunnels, rail links and fuel supplies were all fair game, even at the inconvenience of everyone, friend and foe.

That June there were two Norwegians who were not prepared to 'sit-it-out' until the end of the war. Perhaps their situation was too precarious, or possibly they had vital information they needed to get back to Britain. It's not evident as to whether they were resistance men or SIS agents. Erling Lunde and Erling Simonsen had been acting as couriers slipping back and forth between Oslo and Sweden. In May they became effectively trapped by a huge German security clamp-down blocking their return to the Swedish border. Faced with this, they took the train to Bergen hoping to find a boat. They must have had contacts in Bergen who directed them onwards to Os, about 20 miles to the south where they simply stole the 28ft boat *Start*. Even on 13 June, the weather could not be trusted and they immediately ran into a severe storm which washed their food and water overboard on the first day. Over the next days, as they grew weaker, they were blown across the sea realising on the fourth day that they must have passed by the north of Shetland. They managed to turn southwards, passing to the west of Shetland and making Fair Isle (lying between Shetland and Orkney) on the fifth day. Lunde and Simonsen were so weak that they literally crawled to the nearest house to get help. The inhabitants would have known what to do with this unscheduled delivery. Already that tiny speck of an island had played host to eight other Viking boats.

There was still an unfulfilled demand for a reliable escape route from Bergen in late 1944, as so many of those previously involved had been run to ground by the Gestapo. Into this vacuum stepped Hans Helle, who had been involved in the resistance since the early days of the fighting. Meticulous, cool-headed and fearless, he avoided capture throughout the war, though he had several very close shaves. He was one of the few who avoided an arrest. In a desperate situation in August 1944, he spirited a group of seven from the city to his remote family farm Uthella in the Manger area of the Lindas peninsula, to the north. The men remained in hiding for a few days whilst Hans purchased the boat *Snedig* ('Cunning', rather a good name for an escape boat), and a trusted lieutenant, Martinius Grindheim, agreed to skipper it. He then transferred the fugitives to the island of Hernar where *Snedig* was waiting, and the eight men were on their way on 14 August. A considerable risk on this occasion was that one of the seven was an acknowledged Quisling who persuaded Grindheim that he wanted to change sides. The other six would have watched him very closely indeed.

This escape became the blueprint for a series of escapes from Bergen until the end of war. Helle used the coastal steamer *Varden* to run fugitives from the city up to Manger. *Varden* was very old, decrepit and full of useful hiding holes. With the help of a cooperative crew, the old boat didn't yield a single refugee to the German checkpoint inspectors for the duration of the war. Helle claimed to have exported 125 people along this escape line. After the *Snedig* in August, all the pick-ups were by the Shetland Bus, and not by civilian boats.

The much longed-for invasion to liberate Norway came from a different direction than that anticipated, and with consequences far worse that anyone could have possibly foreseen. The theatre for these developments was the very far north, where Russia and Norway share a common border. As Finland (which had been fighting against the Russians) crashed out of the war in early September, it became apparent to German command that the Soviets would sweep into the far north and invade Norway from that direction. In preparation for this, *Operation Nordlicht* (Northern Lights) was launched on 7 October. The plan was to disengage the German army and to withdraw to a line of defence 1,000 miles to the south. Crucially, a scorched earth policy was integral to the plan. On 13 October, General Otto Lothar Rendulic, commander of the northern Wermacht forces, issued a formal order for the evacuation of the entire Norwegian population concomitant with the destruction of every appurtenance of human habitation. This began at once.

The Germans were routed by the Soviets at Kirkenes 22–25 October, and thereafter their army was in a long retreat. The Norwegian command in London sent the Norwegian army Second Mountain Company, under the experienced Colonel Arne Dahl to assist the Russians. One of his officers was Thor Heyerdahl, the famous explorer and adventurer. It was but a token as the force numbered only around 250 men. However, Dahl was energetic and resourceful; he recruited and armed local Milorg people and militias and was joined by Norwegian police battalions that had been training in Sweden. In time, these free Norwegian forces numbered 3,000, proving to be an asset to the Russians, and to their compatriots who were in desperate straits.

The people were being driven south whilst every building was being torched or blown up. It was expected that 50,000 people would be displaced. Quisling hoped that the evacuation would be 'voluntary', and then unhelpfully said, 'Anyone failing to move is an enemy of Germany.' Hard-headed Terboven directed the use of force, and when this wasn't working, Hitler himself intervened with a *Führerbefehel* (a personal directive from the Führer) on 28 October. This fearsome instrument brought with it a 'pain-of-death' threat to any German failing to execute the order. It contained the sinister words, 'Pity for the population is out of place.'

Allied airmen overflying northern Norway reported horizon-to-horizon fires and huge plumes of acrid smoke ascending into the clear Arctic skies. The material cost was staggering as Teutonic efficiency destroyed absolutely everything. The cost in human terms was enormous, as families were turfed out of their homes with no more than they could take with them. What they left was considered fair plunder for the troops, before the evidence of theft was consumed by fire. Yet once more, Quisling, Terboven and their commanders failed to understand the fibre of the Norwegian people. About half of them refused to leave, believing the war to be nearly over. True Vikings, they turned their boats upside down and lived underneath the hulls. They melted into remote areas taking shelter in mountain huts, caves and tunnels, living off what they could catch, steal or scrounge. Blessed with a mild winter, many survived for months to be relieved by Russians arriving with food. Many travelled hundreds of miles to the border crossing into Sweden. Others who had moved to coastal islands did less well, suffering starvation conditions. In February 1945, four Allied destroyers were diverted from Arctic convoy duties to evacuate over 500 poor creatures from the island of Sørøya.

It is a measure of resolute Norwegian fortitude that the death rate attributable to the evacuation was around 340, surprisingly low. But the north of Norway was now an Arctic desert, not even of interest to the Russians who fortunately did not remain in occupation after the war. If they had done so, then modern history would be rather different.

During *Operation Nordlicht* some smaller coastal vessels were sent north to help with Quisling's 'voluntary' evacuations. One of these was the beautiful lifeboat R49 *Frithjof Wiese*, a newish 1935 hybrid of the previous sailing lifeboats and newer motorised boats fitted with powerful diesel engines. She was stationed on the south coast to cover the busy Skaggerak seaway. The status of the Norwegian lifeboat service during the occupation was something of an anomaly. The boats, called *Redningsskøyte* (rescue boats), continued to be manned by Norwegians and in distress situations they would save people irrespective of nationality. To avoid being attacked, they had Maltese crosses painted on the sides. They remained, however, under the control of the occupiers who often used them for coastal errands and patrolling and they operated under very close scrutiny. The previous November, the crew of *Frithof Wiese* had been caught listening to the BBC on the ship's radio, for which terrible crime they were arrested and sent to Grini concentration camp.

The replacement crew of five was even less inclined to be beholden to their masters when in October 1944 they received orders to deploy to Finnmark to assist with the evacuation of civilians. When they had got as far as Møre on the west coast (probably at Ålesund) on 23 October, they were contacted by a group of twelve resistance people being hunted by the Gestapo. Their need was desperate, and the crew needed little persuading to take the fugitives on board, immediately heading west for Shetland.

For the Germans and the Quislings, the reverses of 1944 and the upsurge in resistance activity put them on the back foot; their reactions became more and more irrational. On 6 August, Terboven organised a mass rally at the Colliseum cinema in Olso at which he stressed 'the necessity of the total effort and the final victory'. On 20 September, in desperation he launched one of his by now familiar exemplary punitive raids, under his personal direction. The small town of Hønefoss (an hour north of Oslo) was the target of his ire, being completely surrounded at dawn by hundreds of troops. The air raid sirens were set off and cars drove round the streets with loudspeakers telling the inhabitants to stay inside. Arrests quickly followed and five men were executed on the spot without trial. Grini concentration camp was the destination for 200 people who were selected for arrest.

By this time, the Gestapo and Sipo had become jittery. If the war was being lost, they wanted to settle some old scores. In a new strategy, named with casual euphemism *Blumenpflücken* (flower pickers) these Nazi hard men went 'rogue', and started to pick off the flowers of the resistance. They even missed out on torture in favour of summary execution. Milorg members could not be expected to stand idly by. In scenes reminiscent of Chicago gangsters, they took their tit-for-tat revenge. As the sands of the war were running out, the streets were becoming more dangerous than ever.

Far away on the high seas of the inhospitable North Atlantic the Royal Navy was having success in harrying German military and civilian shipping, aircraft and shore installations along the coast between Narvik and Tromsø. The attacks were launched by air from carriers of the home fleet operating from Scapa Flow, heavily defended by destroyer escorts. And in these wild regions one of the most powerful astonishing escape stories of the war was revealed.

One such carrier foray between 24 and 30 October 1943 was led by the carrier HMS *Implacable*, and among the escorts was the destroyer HMS *Volage*, brand new that spring. A telegraphist who had been on *Volage* since its commissioning was Arthur Carter. The young man was interested in everything that happened on board his ship and he troubled himself to write down the following story, which is so fresh and intense that it needs to be told in his own words:

> Gale force winds and enormous seas are still running. The radar plot showed 'echo bearing Green 90' and it was about the size of a U-boat conning tower. The echo disappeared… each time it went down into the trough of a wave. The night is dark and stormy. The ship slowed down to a few knots which brought most of the crew, not on watch, to the upper deck to find out the cause. A signalman with a 20-inch lamp…directed it onto an object a few hundred yards off the starboard beam. As seen through binoculars on the bridge it appeared to be a small boat with men waving from the stern.

This, then, was the astonishing rescue of the survivors of seven men who had set out from Norway twenty days before – five Norwegians, one Frenchman and one Belgian. There is no record as to why, how or where they went about this. Not far out from the coast they were attacked by a German aircraft. Two of the Norwegians were killed outright and a third was severely wounded. He survived for two days and then he too died. All three were consigned to the deep. A fuel line damaged in the attack was repaired but a lot of fuel had been lost, so that as they were just in sight of Shetland it ran out. They were then at the mercy of the sea as they drifted northwards toward the Atlantic, with their food eventually running out. Perhaps they prayed; it's hard to fathom the odds that were overcome to end up in the path of *Volage*.

Young Arthur recorded laconically, '*Volage* rejoined the fleet.… At least it had been an unusual break in the routine.'

From his vantage point on the bridge, Commander L.G. Durlacher OBE RN was more forthright. In the press he declared, 'it was one of those "once in a lifetime" strokes of luck… If we hadn't made an emergency turn which took us to within 100 yards of their boat, we should never have seen them. It was a pitch black night.' He added details that the survivors had been without food for twelve days and without water for two days. Frankly, any account of this story is destined to fall short of capturing its absolutely miraculous nature.

After the *Volage* rescue, the winter months and the closing phases of the war saw not many escapes emanating from Norwegian waters. Nonetheless, ten boats still made the journey in those last six months. There was one other rather amusing and impulsive escape on 27 October 1943. The brand-new fishing trawler *Dreggen* (The Dregs – not an attractive name in literal translation) had just been built in a Bergen shipyard. The skipper, Hans Laurvik, had taken her out on sea trials with a crew of six on board. Whether an escape had been planned or whether it was a spur-of-the-moment decision, he simply kept on going to Lerwick. Being such a new boat, *Dreggen* was soon pressed into service with *Nortraship*.

The turn of the year 1944 to 1945 was marked by the last throw of the dice for Adolf Hitler and his formidable army and air forces. In great secrecy and almost total surprise he unleashed the Ardennes counter-offensive, later called the Battle of the Bulge. It was a failure in spite of desperate measures by his remaining elite forces, and some appalling brutality by SS units. It had drained the Wermacht and Luftwaffe of almost all their reserves. But if populations across Europe hoped for a quick collapse and surrender, they had failed to appreciate the pathological hold that Nazi ideology exercised over the body, soul and destiny of the German people.

In the new year another unusual escape with a quick turn-around took place on 25 January 1945. Norwegian MTBs were on operations amongst the multiple islands of the archipelago of Bulandet when they surprised and captured a German *vorposten* (a captured boat turned over to German service) – V5305 *Schnepfe*. This had formerly been the Norwegian trawler *Norholmen*, seized by the Kriegsmarine in May 1940. The circumstances of this incident aren't known, but a decision was made to send the boat over to Shetland. An opportunity for islanders to escape to Scotland thereby presented itself, an opportunity they readily and rapidly took, as the boat arrived at Lerwick the following day with twenty-one people on board. The landing in Shetland was recorded in the name of *Norholmen*, an immediate reversion to its Norwegian past. It certainly would not have been flying a German flag on the way over and it seems that someone had been busy with a paint pot changing the name before arrival.

With no real idea as to when the war would end a second lifeboat, *Johan Brusgaard*, went 'absent without leave' from Bremanger on 28 March, with twenty-one on board, most of whom were on the run from the Germans. Two weeks later the last escape took place on 11 April. Six wanted men had appeared at the remote village of Bakkasund in the Austevoll islands and were offered passage on the boat *Heimly* by the skipper John Kleppe. They arrived at Lerwick two days later. Whilst it is now puzzling why they were driven to take this risk as the Nazi occupation was crumbling around them they couldn't have known what lay ahead. There was certainly turbulence all over the country. At one end of the scale hard-line Nazis were getting petulant and trigger happy. At the other end German troops were restive, deserting and drifting into Sweden. As the Allies squeezed Germany from east and west there were observations of troops and materiel being moved across the Skaggerak to Norway. The bulk of the German fleet was sent there, with reports of VI and VII rockets being transferred from Denmark. In crude terms the Nazi rats were leaving a sinking state. In Norway there was widespread worry that fanatical Nazis intended to make the country their last stand, and to continue the Reich in their country. Was there any substance in such a prospect? It is necessary to look back to Nazi ideology behind such an idea.

To do so you have to return to the inception of Hitler's plan to seize Norway in the first place. Hitler had a long harboured particular personal affection for the idea of turning Norway into a semi-antonymous Aryan super state. He was attracted to Viking history and heritage. Quisling had offered him the unachievable prospect of a Norwegian fascist state under his rule, and for a while this found favour in Berlin. In his ascendancy, the Führer had commissioned his great architect Albert Speer to design a completely new fortified city and impregnable naval base to be called *Nordstern* (North Star) as part of his *Festung Norwegen*.

The city for around 300,000 Germans was to be located about 20 miles south of Trondheim. By 1942, plans were drawn, models were made, and all was studied and approved by the great man. In 1943, foundations were started with a prisoner-of-war labour camp being built nearby. Construction ground to a halt by 1944, but it was not until as late as November 1944 that Project *Nordstern* was officially cancelled.

Barely six months later, in the dying days of the war, this idealogical fantasy of a Norwegian Aryan paradise was still in the minds of some elements of the Nazi die-hard elite. If anyone doubts that this improbable idea existed they should be aware that on 6 May, five days after Hitler's suicide and the day before formal surrender, fifty boats full of Nazi zealots were intercepted crossing the Baltic towards Norway.

As it was, the surrender on 7 May was extremely well ordered. The 50,000 members of Milorg emerged and in a remarkably disciplined way took control of the country. They were quickly reinforced by around 12,000 Norwegians who had been training as police in Sweden. There were very few of the revenge actions seen in some other liberated countries, and a round-up of around 30,000 Nazi criminals and Norwegian collaborators took place without fuss. Terboven committed suicide, whilst Quisling, Rinnan and other undesirables were accorded the proper processes of justice that they had denied others. There were in the region of 250,000 German prisoners-of-war, and perhaps 100,000 liberated Russian, Yugoslav and Polish prisoners to look after. Within days, Lief Larsen and his Shetland Bus boats, the Norwegian MTBs and some other Norwegian navy boats made a dash back to their country. Prince Olav, now the Commander-in-Chief of the forces, once again set foot on Norwegian soil on 13 May. On 8 June, the beloved King Haakon, Prince Olav, Princess Märtha and their children sailed up Oslofjorden into Oslo. The welcome was ecstatic. It was exactly five years to the day since the king and the prince had been forced to leave their country.

Among those most deserving the euphoria were those brave Viking patriots who had risked so much in escaping across the North Sea over those five years, to join the fight to free their country. They had very good reason to savour this moment.

In an article in *The Times* in 2023 Sir Max Hastings the famous historian, journalist and commentator, ruffled a few feathers when he ventured to say that the Second World War partisan operations in occupied countries contributed little to the liberation of those countries or to the overall conduct of the war. Although he was writing an article about France, his comments came in a generic form. He said, 'The historic case for Resistance, which perhaps deserves to prevail, is not military but instead moral', adding, 'My own research has reinforced lifelong doubts about the virtues of guerrilla warfare against an enemy as unspeakably ruthless as the Nazis.'

The case for Norway is different. For a tiny nation of barely 3 million people Norway punched well above its weight and proved not only to be a thorn in the flesh of the occupiers, but also a contributor to the Allies of strategic importance. The unions, the clergy, the teachers and the universities were prepared, en masse, to suffer arrest, imprisonment, torture and death to mark their defiance. The nation united behind them, and a well-equipped, organised and trained resistance movement emerged. The German war machine was subverted and sabotaged with increasing effectiveness. The firm resolve of the Norwegian people was widely publicised and held as an example to other occupied countries.

Unique to Norway was the little army of 4,000 Vikings who took to small boats and escaped to Britain to join the free Norwegian forces. These warriors, self-selected by their dangerous escapes, formed the backbone of the hugely successful SOE Shetland Bus and Kompani Linge units. These forces certainly 'set Norway ablaze' and promoted the constant threat of an Allied invasion. Others were important contributors in other arms of the free Norwegian forces, not forgetting their merchant fleet.

Put together, the Norwegian people at home and those in the free forces caused Hitler to divert huge amounts of men, money and materiel into building his Fortress Norway. In January 1942 he declared that 'Norway is now the area of destiny of the war'. At its height, Nazi Germany required a garrison of nearly 400,000 men in Norway – that's one German for every eight Norwegians, man, woman or child. This was of strategic significance as it kept so many Germans away from other theatres, and far from the beaches of Normandy.

Epilogue
A Quiet Corner under the Bow Bells

The revered King Haakon VII of Norway, the figurehead of his country's defiance against the Nazis, died aged 85, in 1957. Into his shoes stepped Crown Prince Olav who, at his father's side throughout the Second World War, had also embodied his country's resistance, becoming Commander-in- Chief of the free Norwegian forces.

King Olav V flew to London in March 1966 to fulfil a small but significant obligation. The Norwegian people wanted to commemorate the friendship and support given to their country by the British people in those dark war years. Britain had welcomed and supported the thousands of Norwegians who formed the free Norwegian forces. Some of the most effective warriors had come to Britain in small boats.

The place chosen was the ancient Church of St Mary-le-Bow at Cheapside in the centre of London, itself a victim of Nazi oppression. The beautiful Wren church received several direct hits in the Blitz of 1941. The Luftwaffe silenced the famous Bow Bells that were part of the fabric of British life. The bells rang out again to national acclaim in 1961 following painstaking restoration of the church. In such ways a nation can hope to expunge the memory of dark days and losses.

In the quiet North Chapel of St Mary's, the King stepped forward to unveil a bronze relief of a very Nordic St George slaying a savage dragon. It is an unpretentious, modest and very Norwegian statement of what was deeply felt. The Bow Bells rang out.

The accompanying tablet records, -

This place in the restored church
of St Mary-le-Bow is sacred to the memory of the Norwegians who died
in the resistance to tyranny of
Nazism in the years 1940–45.
The bronze relief by Ragnhild Butenschon
was given by the People of Norway for whom the
Sound of Bow Bells broadcast throughout Europe
was a symbol of hope during the Nazi occupation.
The sculpture was unveiled by His Majesty
King Olav V of Norway and dedicated by the
Lord Bishop of London on March 25th 1966.

The final balance of Norwegian escape attempts (as at Jan 2024)

BOATS:

Total number of boats attempting escape		**361**
less:	boats lost at sea	20
	boats arrested	12
	boats failed (returned to shore)	<u>13</u>
		<u>45</u>
Total number of boats successfully crossing		**316**

PERSONS:

Total number of persons attempting escape		**4025**
less:	persons perished at sea	146
	persons killed en voyage (enemy action)	5
	persons lost overboard en voyage	3
	persons arrested (by occupying forces)	114
	persons returned to shore (escape failed)	<u>132</u>
		<u>400</u>
Total number of persons succeeding with escape		**3625**

Appendix B

Monthly distribution of boats and people attempting to leave Norway

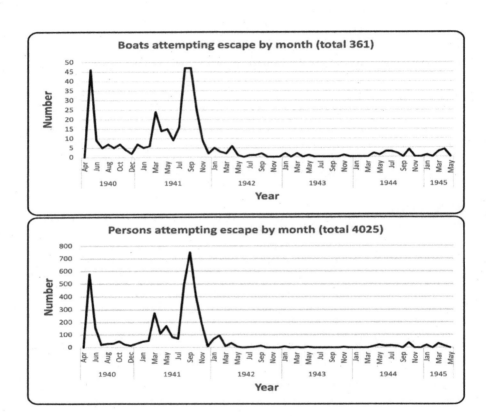

Appendix C

Points of Departure by County & Municipality (an aide to Map 2)

	Escape "Sector"	Municipality	No.	%
NORTHERN DISTRICTS				
Svalbard			1	
Troms & Finmark			7	
Nordland			7	
Trondelag North & South			4	
			19	6%
WESTERN DISTRICTS				
Mør og Romsdal		Ålesund	40	
		Giske	15	
		Herøy	14	
		Ulstein	6	
		Other	18	
			93	28%
Sogn og Fjordane		Vågsøy/Maløy	10	
		Askvoll	10	
		Florø	9	
		Braemanger	7	
		Other	22	
			58	18%
Hordland, incl. Bergen	North Hordland	Fedje	6	
		Austreheim	3	
		Masfjorden	3	
	Øygarden isles	Fjell	12	
		Sund	12	
		Øygarden	10	
	Bergen	City and adjacent	22	
		Askøy	7	
	South Hordland	Bømlo isles	23	
		Austevoll isles	12	
		Stord isles	5	
		Other	9	
			124	38%
Rogaland	North Rogaland	Haugesund & Karmøy	9	
	South Rogaland	Stavanger	3	
		Hå & Egersund	6	
		Other	1	
			19	6%
SOUTHERN DISTRICTS				
Agder Vest & Aust	South coast	Arendal	4	
		Mandal	4	
		Kristiansand	3	
		Other	6	
Oslo		Oslo	1	
			18	5%
ALL NORWAY TOTALS				
Boats leaving known place			331	
Boats leaving unknown place			30	
Total all boats leaving Norway			361	

Points of arrival by location (an aide to Map 3)

Location & place		No
CANADA		
Not Specified		1
N Sydney NS		1
		2
ICELAND		
Not Specified		1
Reykjavik		3
Other		2
		6
FAROE ISLANDS		
Not specified		3
Thórshavn		12
Klaksvik		2
Trongisvágur		1
		18
SHETLAND		
Not Specified		32
Unst	Flugga	1
	Norwick	3
	Baltasound	16
	Haroldswick	2
Yell		2
Fetlar		4
Mainland	Lerwick	131
	Heylor	1
	Scalloway	1
	Sumburgh	1
Outer Skerries		1
Bressay		2
Mousa		2
Fair Isle		9
Burra		1
		209
ORKNEY		
Not specified		4
Sandoy		2
Kirkwall		9
Scapa		5
Deerness		1
		21

Location & place		No	
SCOTLAND			
Unknown, prob. Scotland		5	
Scotland, not specified		11	
Sutherland	Durness	1	
Caithness	Wick	1	
Moray	Lossiemouth	1	
Banff	Buckie	3	
	Crovie	1	
	Portsoy	1	
Aberdeenshire	Fraserburgh	3	
	Peterhead	4	
	Aberdeen	9	
	Portlethen	1	
	Stonehaven	3	
Angus	Montrose	1	
	Arbroath	2	
Lothian	Leith (Edinburgh)	1	
	Dunbar	1	
Berwickshire	Eyemouth	1	
			50
ENGLAND			
Northumberland	Holy Isle	1	
	Amble	1	
	Blyth	1	
	Newcastle	2	
Durham	Sunderland	1	
Lincolnshire	Grimsby	1	
	Skegness	1	
Norfolk	Gt Yarmouth	1	
Essex	Thames Estuary	1	
			10

21 Total of all successful crossings 316

Sources

Core Sources:

Boats in the English traffic, Bergens Sjøfartsmuseet 1995.
British Newspaper Archive: britishnewspaperarchive.co.uk
Norwegian Refugee Arrivals, Lerwick harbour records: Shetland Encyclopaedia.
Norwegian war sailors: Lawson, Siri Holm: warsailors.com
Occupation Live: okkupasjonen.no
Ulstein, Ragnar. (2011 re-issue) *Englandsfarten*. 2 vols: Nova Forlag, Moss.

Museum and Archive Sources:

Arbroath Signal Tower Museum, Scotland
Arkivet Foundation, Kristiansand, Vest-Agder.
Imperial War Museum, London.
Krigsseilerregisteret.no (War sailors register)
Listamuseet, Vest Agder.
Little Norway, Buckie: littlenorway.org.uk
Marinemuseet, Horten, Vestfold.
Meteorological Office Digital Library and Archive.
National Archives, Kew, London.
Nordsjøfartsmuseet, Televåg, Vestland.
Norges Hjemmfrontmuseet, Oslo.
Shetland Archives, Lerwick.
Sjøhistorie.no (Sea history register).

Printed Sources:

Allan, S., *Commando Country*: National Museums of Scotland Enterprises. (2007)
Barclay, G., *If Hitler Comes; Preparing for Invasion*: Birlinn, Edinburgh. (2013)
Berthelsen, O.J., *An Escape, 1941 Norway to Scotland by Open Boat*: private pub. (2013)
Christophersen, E., *Two Places – one destiny Telavåg and Lidice*: Nordsjøfartmuseet. (2012)

Haga, A., *Lang Flukt*: Cappelen Damm, Oslo. (2014)

Hassing, A., *Church Resistance to Nazism in Norway, 1940–1945*: University of Washington Press. (2014)

Hauge, E.O., *Salt Water Thief, The Life of Odd Starheim*: Duckworth, London. (1958)

Hetland, Ø., *In the Shadow of the SS Three Norwegian Police Districts 1940–1945*: University of Oslo Press. (2020)

Hewitt, N., 'How the battle for Norway in 1940 saved Britain': *BBC History Magazine*. (2019)

Holm, J. H., *Smuglere For Norges Frihet*: Private pub. (2021)

Howarth, D., *Escape Alone*: Fontana. (1958)

Howarth, D., *The Shetland Bus*: The Shetland Times Ltd. (1998 ed)

Irvine, J.W., *The Waves are Free*: The Shetland Publishing Co. (1988)

Iversen, K., *Shetland Bus Man*: Shetland Times Press. (2004)

Jones, O.A. (ed.) *Education for Victory, Vol 1.* : U.S. Gov Printing Office. (1944)

Kiszely, J., *Anatomy of a Campaign. The British Fiasco in Norway 1940*: Cambridge University Press. (2017)

Larsen, A., *Åpen Båt*: Eides Forlag. (1961)

Mortimer, G., *The Adventures of Mutt & Jeff*: Historynet.com

Nøvik, O., *På Flukt med Kaare*: Forlaget Rune. (1972)

Parelius, N., *Molde og Romsdal I Krigstiden*: E.K. Hansens. (1970)

Pedersen, R., *As I see It*: Private pub. (2001)

Pettersen, A., *The Hidden Past- the tragedy Norway never understood, forced evacuation and wintering in North Troms and Finnmark*: Restoration Museum for Finnmark and Nord-Troms. (2008)

Reed-Olsen, O., *Two Eggs on my Plate*: George, Allen & Unwin. (1952)

Sælen, Frithjof, *None But the Brave, the story of Shetlands Larsen*: Souvenir Press. (1955)

Sømme, Sven, *Another Man's Shoes*: Polperro Heritage Press. (2011 reissue)

Sorvåg, T., *Englandsfeber (Shetland Bus, Faces and Places)*: Eide Forlag. (2002)

Stratigakos, D., *Hitler's Northern Utopia: Building the New Order in Occupied Norway*: Princeton University Press. (2020)

Svensholt, H.K., *The Norwegian Navy in the Second World War*: Forsvarsnett. (1997)

Tremain, D., *The Beautiful Spy: the Life and Crimes of Vera Eriksen*: History Press. (2019).

Vidnes, K. (trans. Vidnes, J.). *The Escape Journal of Knut Vidnes*: Private pub. (1945)

Whitson, A. & Orr, A., *Sea Dog Bamse WW2 Canine Hero*: Birlinn, Edinburgh. (2008)

Film Sources:

Thunder Afloat: dir. George B. Seitz: MGM films (1939)

They Raid by Night: dir. Spencer Gordon Bennet: PRC Films (1942)

The Day Will Dawn (The Avengers in USA): dir. Harold French, prod. Paul Soskin, script Terrence Rattigan: Paramount (1942)

Commandos Strike At Dawn: dir. John Farrow, writer C.S. Forester: Columbia Pictures (1942)

Edge of Darkness (Norway in Revolt): dir. Lewis Milestone, script Robert Rossen: Warner Brothers (1943)

The Moon Is Down: dir. Irving Picel, writer John Steinbeck: Twentieth Century Fox (1943)

First Comes Courage: dir. Dorothy Arzner, writer Elliott Arnold: Columbia Pictures (1943)

The Return Of The Vikings: written & dir. Charles Frend: Ealing Studios (1944)

The Shetland Gang (Suicide Mission): dir. Michael Forlong, writer David Howarth: North Sea Films/ Columbia (1954)

Online Sources:

Much of the content of this book was gleaned from hundreds of articles and thousands of brief snippets found online. There are too many to list here. I have retained a full list of these sources for consultation if required.

Index